Religion and Nationalism in Global Perspective

It is difficult to imagine forces in the modern world as potent as nationalism and religion. Both provide people with a source of meaning, each has motivated individuals to carry out extraordinary acts of heroism and cruelty, and both serve as the foundation for communal and personal identity. While the subject has received both scholarly and popular attention, this distinctive book is the first comparative study to examine the origins and development of three distinct models: religious nationalism, secular nationalism, and civil-religious nationalism. Using multiple methods, the authors develop a new theoretical framework that can be applied across diverse countries and religious traditions to understand the emergence, development, and stability of different church–state arrangements over time. The work combines public opinion, constitutional, and content analysis of the United States, Israel, India, Greece, Uruguay, and Malaysia, weaving together historical and contemporary illustrations.

J. Christopher Soper is Distinguished Professor of Political Science at Pepperdine University. He received his PhD from Yale University and his MDiv from Yale Divinity School.

Joel S. Fetzer is Frank R. Seaver Professor of Social Science and Professor of Political Science at Pepperdine University. A graduate of Cornell and Yale Universities, he specializes in religion and politics and in migration studies.

Cambridge Studies in Social Theory, Religion, and Politics

Editors

David E. Campbell, University of Notre Dame
Anna M. Grzymala-Busse, Stanford University
Kenneth D. Wald, University of Florida, Gainesville
Richard L. Wood, University of New Mexico

Founding Editor

David C. Leege, University of Notre Dame

In societies around the world, dynamic changes are occurring at the intersection of religion and politics. In some settings, these changes are driven by internal shifts within religions; in others, by shifting political structures, institutional contexts, or by war or other upheavals. *Cambridge Studies in Social Theory, Religion, and Politics* publishes books that seek to understand and explain these changes to a wide audience, drawing on insight from social theory and original empirical analysis. We welcome work built on strong theoretical framing, careful research design, and rigorous methods using any social scientific method(s) appropriate to the study. The series examines the relationship of religion and politics broadly understood, including directly political behavior, action in civil society and in the mediating institutions that undergird politics, and the ways religion shapes the cultural dynamics underlying political and civil society.

Mikhail A. Alexseev and Sufian N. Zhemukhov, *Mass Religious Ritual and Intergroup Tolerance: The Muslim Pilgrims' Paradox*

Luke Bretherton, *Resurrecting Democracy: Faith, Citizenship, and the Politics of a Common Life*

David E. Campbell, John C. Green, and J. Quin Monson, *Seeking the Promised Land: Mormons and American Politics*

Ryan L. Claassen, *Godless Democrats and Pious Republicans? Party Activists, Party Capture, and the "God Gap"*

Darren W. Davis and Donald Pope-Davis, *Perseverance in the Parish? : Religious Attitudes from a Black Catholic Perspective.*

Paul A. Djupe and Christopher P. Gilbert, *The Political Influence of Churches*

Joel S. Fetzer and J. Christopher Soper, *Muslims and the State in Britain, France, and Germany*

François Foret, *Religion and Politics in the European Union: The Secular Canopy*

Jonathan Fox, *A World Survey of Religion and the State*

Jonathan Fox, *Political Secularism, Religion, and the State: A Time Series Analysis of Worldwide Data* Anthony Gill, *The Political Origins of Religious Liberty*

Brian J. Grim and Roger Finke, *The Price of Freedom Denied: Religious Persecution and Conflict in the 21st Century*

Kees van Kersbergen and Philip Manow, editors, *Religion, Class Coalitions, and Welfare States*

Mirjam Kunkler, John Madeley, and Shylashri Shankar, *A Secular Age Beyond the West: Religion, Law and the State in Asia, the Middle East and North Africa*

Karrie J. Koesel, *Religion and Authoritarianism: Cooperation, Conflict, and the Consequences*

Ahmet T. Kuru, *Secularism and State Policies toward Religion: The United States, France, and Turkey*

Andrew R. Lewis, *The Rights Turn in Conservative Christian Politics: How Abortion Transformed the Culture Wars*

Damon Maryl, *Secular Conversions: Political Institutions and Religious Education in the United States and Australia, 1800-2000*

Jeremy Menchik, *Islam and Democracy in Indonesia: Tolerance without Liberalism*

Pippa Norris and Ronald Inglehart, *Sacred and Secular: Religion and Politics Worldwide*

Amy Reynolds, *Free Trade and Faithful Globalization: Saving the Market*

Sadia Saeed, *Politics of Desecularization: Law and the Minority Question in Pakistan*

David T. Smith, *Religious Persecution and Political Order in the United States*

Peter Stamatov, *The Origins of Global Humanitarianism: Religion, Empires, and Advocacy*

Religion and Nationalism in Global Perspective

J. CHRISTOPHER SOPER

Pepperdine University

JOEL S. FETZER

Pepperdine University

CAMBRIDGE
UNIVERSITY PRESS

University Printing House, Cambridge CB2 8BS, United Kingdom

One Liberty Plaza, 20th Floor, New York, NY 10006, USA

477 Williamstown Road, Port Melbourne, VIC 3207, Australia

314–321, 3rd Floor, Plot 3, Splendor Forum, Jasola District Centre, New Delhi – 110025, India

79 Anson Road, #06-04/06, Singapore 079906

Cambridge University Press is part of the University of Cambridge.

It furthers the University's mission by disseminating knowledge in the pursuit of
education, learning, and research at the highest international levels of excellence.

www.cambridge.org
Information on this title: www.cambridge.org/9781107189430
DOI: 10.1017/9781316995280

© J. Christopher Soper and Joel S. Fetzer 2018

First published 2018

Printed in the United States of America by Sheridan Books Inc.

A catalogue record for this publication is available from the British Library.

Library of Congress Cataloging-in-Publication Data
NAMES: Soper, J. Christopher, author.
TITLE: Religion and nationalism in global perspective / J. Christopher Soper,
Pepperdine University, Malibu, Joel S. Fetzer, Pepperdine University,
Malibu.
DESCRIPTION: First [edition]. | New York : Cambridge University Press, 2018.
| Includes bibliographical references and index.
IDENTIFIERS: LCCN 2018012845 | ISBN 9781107189430 (hardback : alk. paper) |
ISBN 9781316639122 (pbk. : alk. paper)
SUBJECTS: LCSH: Nationalism—Religious aspects.
CLASSIFICATION: LCC BL65.N3 S67 2018 | DDC 201/.72—dc23
LC record available at https://lccn.loc.gov/2018012845

ISBN 978-1-107-18943-0 Hardback
ISBN 978-1-316-63912-2 Paperback

Dedicated to my wife, Jane, and my children,
Katharine and David
– JCS
Dedicated to the memory of Carl Frederick Fetzer
(February 2, 1937–July 28, 2016), dear father, grandfather,
husband, and father-in-law
– JSF
Dedicated in memory of Ted Gerard Jelen
(April 30, 1952–November 21, 2017), devoted scholar,
frequent collaborator, and long-time friend
– JCS & JSF

Contents

Figures

Tables

Preface

Like most scientific projects, this book began with an intriguing question: Why do most American churchgoers proudly display prominent US flags at the front of their sanctuaries and find little or no conflict between devotion to the American state and loyalty to Christ, while their theological cousins in places such as France or Germany generally avoid nationalistic symbols in their sanctuaries and can sometimes express quite critical views about their respective central governments? From an original plan to cover just a couple countries in the Atlantic region, this study morphed into the global, six-nation investigation you hold in your hands. Although such an approach probably suffers from our having less in-depth expertise in all the states of the world, let alone the various religious traditions within those countries, we trust that our intellectual audacity in broadening the range of cases has enriched the general international literature on this subject.

As coauthors, we each have our particular special interests and gifts. Chris completed most of the theoretical background and large-scale institutional argument. He also wrote the bulk of the American, Israeli, Greek, and Indian chapters. Joel focused on the quantitative, public opinion, and content analysis and also composed the Malaysian and Uruguayan chapters. But over almost a decade we have been toiling on this book, we sent each other innumerable drafts of our respective sections and constantly revised and reconsidered our approach as a whole.

Although this multi-country project required far less fieldwork than some of our earlier works, we did benefit from financial assistance from Pepperdine's Endowed Chair and Endowed Professorship programs as well as from several release times, Dean's Grants, and Seaver Research Grants. We would particularly like to thank Pepperdine's Vice-Provost for Research and Strategic Initiatives, Lee Kats, as well as Assistant Provost for Research, Katy Carr, and Divisional Dean Steve Rouse. In Payson Library, we are especially grateful to Melinda Raine and Melissa Pichette for processing countless new-book and ILL requests. Because we are not conversant in all of the languages spoken in the six countries used as case studies, we relied on several research assistants and a translation firm to render relevant documents into English. Our deepest appreciation thus goes out to Samir Fernandes, Joanna Siong N. Chen, Latifa Al Saud, Anitha K. V. Sampath, Carolyn Dapper, and Day Translations. Responsibility for the analysis and interpretations in this volume rests solely with us, however.

The quantitative analysis in this book relied heavily on many public-opinion surveys from around the world. Databases we examined include the 2003 International Social Survey Programme's National Identity II, 2004 American National Election Study, 2006 Latinobarómetro, 2008 European Values Study, 2010 Spring Pew Global Attitudes Survey, 2011 World Values Survey, 2013 Israel Democracy Index, 2013 Spring Pew Global Attitudes Survey, and 2013 International Social Survey Programme's National Identity III poll. The usual caveats about authors' responsibilities apply.

As we worked on this project, we became painfully aware of the breadth of our topic and of our limitations as scholars. We would therefore like to thank the following friends and colleagues who read chapters and helped us avoid glaring omissions or outright mistakes in our country case studies and generally strengthened the book: Ken Wald, David Leege, Scott Hibbard, George Th. Mavrogordatos, and Joseph Chinyong Liow. Lewis Bateman encouraged our proposed book when he was editor at Cambridge, and his successor, Sara Doskow, has been just as generous in her time and support of us. We would therefore like to thank both of them and the rest of the editorial team at Cambridge University Press who have been helpful and accommodating partners in our project.

Chris is thankful for the love and support given to him for many years from his wife, Jane, and children, Katharine and David. Over the years they have patiently listened to his dinnertime musings about religion and nationalism, but more importantly they teach him on a daily basis that we are made better by the commitments we make to the people around us.

The research and writing of this book took place during a particularly dark period in Joel's life, with the terminal illness and death of his father followed by a health crisis of his own. He is eternally grateful for the support shown by his family, church, and friends during these try-ing experiences. Eliseo Franco and the congregation at Ministerios en Su Presencia once again prayed Hno. Joel through a long series of personal trials. The second author also owes many thanks to Dr. Shahdad Arami, Dr. Rennie Cheung, and Rev. Jim Mockabee for their professional care, and he expresses much love and gratitude to his wife Christina and son Isaak for accompanying him on this journey and putting up with his many defects.

Sadly, as this book manuscript was about to go back to the publisher for the last time, our dear friend and colleague Ted G. Jelen passed away. We will always be grateful for his enthusiastic support for our research over the decades (including serving as a peer reviewer for this manuscript) and for his similar encouragement of generations of younger scholars in religion and politics. Ted was a pioneering, organizational genius and will be sorely missed.

A Theory of Religion and Nationalism

INTRODUCTION

It is difficult to imagine forces in the modern world as potent as nationalism and religion. Both provide people with a source of meaning, each has motivated people to extraordinary acts of heroism and unimaginable deeds of cruelty, and both serve as the foundation for communal and individual identity. Religion and nationalism are equally imagined communities that can both unite and divide people across space and time. Not only are the concepts politically and morally compelling; they are also intimately related to one another. In much of the world, one cannot analyze the topic of national identity without also scrutinizing religion. There is, however, no simple or straightforward pattern in how religion and nationalism interact. The relationship between religious and political institutions, or religious and national loyalties, has been a vexing one, and has historically run the gamut from deep contestation between religious and national allegiances to a fusion of them. The French and Russian revolutions are notable examples of conflicting religious and national identities, while the religious nationalism in postcommunist Poland, the rise of the Hindu-based Bharatiya Janata Party (BJP) in India, and even the state-sponsored Confucianism in China mark the opposite extreme. Religious nationalism has also been the source of a host of humanitarian catastrophes in regimes such as Hirohito's Japan and Milošević's Yugoslavia. The reemergence of religious nationalism in places as diverse as Hungary, Turkey, Myanmar, and even the United States suggests that the interplay between these two ideological systems remains as significant as ever.

Religion and nationalism are closely associated historically, theoretically, and empirically. Religion has historically been one of the strongest pillars of, and reasons for, nationalism and nation-state formation. Theoretically, nationalisms frequently appropriate religious language and concepts in forging a new, national identity. Even secular nationalism makes religious or quasi-religious claims about the land, the people, and the nation. Empirically, religious actors assume some position vis-à-vis the nation state and its nationalism. They can support, oppose, or be indifferent to the nationalism that is being promoted. The multiple lenses through which one can analyze the religion–nationalism nexus suggest both the complexity of the topic and that no single model can adequately explain the religion–nationalism link. Instead, we argue that religion can influence nationalism in varying degrees and that three models predominate: religious nationalism, secular nationalism, and civil-religious nationalism. The purpose of this chapter is to offer a theory that explains the emergence and continuing relevance of these three models.

While scholars vigorously debate and have offered important insights into the role of religion in the origin of nation states and of their nationalisms, what is largely missing from the literature is a theoretical framework to explain what are the differing models of religion and nationalism, how those models are defined and measured, why they emerge, and what explains the continuing nexus between civic and spiritual identities within states. Despite the prolific literature on both religion and nationalism, there is very little scholarship that systematically examines their interaction. As one analyst has aptly noted, "scholarship on the interplay between religion and nationalism is a relative novelty" (Abulof 2014:515).

The chapter opens with a review of the literature on religion and nationalism. Much of the seminal nationalism scholarship focused on the origins of the concept, and had less to say about contemporary manifestations of nationalism. Nonetheless, these works implicitly offer valuable insights on three models that will dominate our discussion: religious nationalism, secular nationalism, and civil-religious nationalism. A number of scholars have begun to tease out the theoretical implications of those different models, but have offered few insights on how they emerge and remain viable over time. We conclude the chapter by offering a framework for understanding the key variables that explain the emergence of one of the three models, and the factors that explain the stability or instability of each model over time.

NATIONALISM AND RELIGION IN HISTORICAL CONTEXT

The literature on nationalism is vast and continues to expand. These disparate works touch on the nexus between religion and nationalism in two respects. First, the literature considers what role, if any, religion plays in the origins of nationalism, and second, scholars have analyzed the role of religion in contemporary nationalisms. The seminal work on the origins of nationalism by theorists such as Eric Hobsbawm (1990), Ernest Gellner (1983), and Ben Anderson (1983) sees nationalism as historically constructed and as a product of modernization. Nationalism provided the unifying myth necessary to support the needs of sovereign states that emerged in the aftermath of the French and American revolutions. These modernists focus their attention on the role of language, the print media, and the educational system in creating this new national identity, and by their relative silence they implied that religion played little or no part in forming national consciousness. Gellner did note that it was a "curious fact" that nation-states were smaller than "pre-existing faith civilizations" (quoted in Hutchinson and Smith 1994:59), suggesting perhaps a point of possible contention between transnational religious or ethnic claims and national loyalties. For Gellner and most of these early scholars, however, nationalism was "invented," it jettisoned religion as a binding force among people, and it was thus understood as a secular phenomenon. In assessing modernist theories of nationalism, Anthony Smith (2003:21) rightly concludes that they "relegate religion and the sacred to the premodern past."

The rise of secular nationalism in the West provides some evidence for the value of a modernist approaches to nationalism (Kramer 1997). The states that emerged in Western Europe in the seventeenth and eighteenth centuries expanded concurrently with modernization and industrialization. Religion was politically important in the premodern, pre-sovereign state world, but as modernist theories argued, the appearance and rapid development of states based on territorial units and the political sovereignty of groups living within those places implicitly undermined the role of religion. The Westphalian political system subordinated religion to the state. What had been a "friendly merger" between religious and political authorities in the pre-state age, gravitated to what Toft, Philpott, and Shah (2011:58) describe as a "friendly takeover" of religious functions and authority by the state. In some cases, the takeover was anything but friendly, as in the case of the French Revolution's overt attack on the political powers of the Roman Catholic Church, or Bismarck's

Kulturkampf in the second German Empire a century later, which similarly tried to suppress Catholic political influence. Even the more benign forms of expanded state power nonetheless reduced the political salience of religion throughout the West.

Not only did the nation-state challenge the political power of religious groups, but the secular nationalism that emerged also posed an ideological threat to religion. Secular nationalism replaced ethnic and religious identity for national identity based on civic and secular norms (Spohn 2003:269). Instead of defining a community in terms of its ethnicity, common culture, or religion, civic identity was to be understood primarily in political terms. Secular nationalism also introduced the idea that loyalty to and identification with the nation superseded all other preexisting commitments (Marsh 2007; Dingley 2011:399). The implication of modernist theories of nationalism, and of the secular nationalism that they defined, was that nationalism replaced the influence of religion on political institutions and civic identities (Rieffer 2003:223). As Roger Friedland aptly put it, "the first European republic was understood as a usurpation of God's sovereignty" (Friedland 2001:127).

There is thus both an institutional and ideological component to the idea of secular nationalism. Institutionally it leads to the separation of church and state and the diminishment of the direct political power of religious organizations. The secular nationalism of the French Revolution led eventually to the diminishment of the political power of the Catholic Church. Much the same could be said for the attempt of political leaders in newly formed, postcolonial states who aggressively forged a secular national ideology. Leaders like Nehru in India and Atatürk in Turkey specifically attempted to limit the role of religion in national consciousness as they created a secular national ideology. Religious groups retained some formal role in politics, but it was a considerably diminished one by the standards of what Hindu nationalists in India or Muslim nationalists in Turkey advocated for their new state. For these modernizing state actors, secularism was seen as a necessary condition for political development (Hibbard 2010:44). Ideologically, secular nationalism presupposes that secular concepts of nation, rather than religious ones, provide meaning and shape souls (Joppke 2015:47). It is a form of nationalism that has no connection with any particular religious tradition or with religion more generally. The historical experience of Europe, where most modernist theories emerged, lent some credence to the idea that secular nationalism was historically inevitable.

The secular assumptions of modernist theories came under attack on several fronts. Ethno-symbolic theorists of nationalism like Anthony Smith and Adrian Hastings challenged the idea that the roots of modern nationalism were non-religious. Hastings (1997) argued that nationhood owed its existence to preexisting religious ties, while Smith asserted that political elites rediscovered "the myths, memories, traditions, and symbols of ethnic heritage" (Smith 1999a:9); as they forged new national identities (see also Smith 1986; O'Brien 1988). Rather than having their roots in religious decline, as modernist theorists presumed, Anthony Marx argued convincingly that Western European nationalisms were constructed "on the back of fanatical religious passion and conflict" (Marx 2003:193). In his account, the religious cleavages brought on by the Protestant Reformation made possible the confessional, exclusionary nationalisms that emerged in Western Europe. Others rejected the claim that nationalism was a modern construct. Philip Gorski (2000) demonstrated the key role played by Hebraic religious ideas in the premodern national consciousness in the Netherlands and England. Ariel Roshwald (2006) noted the ancient religious and ethnic foundation of contemporary political Zionism.

The different views of religion and nationalism were on full display as nationalism was transported to developing countries via colonialism. Postcolonial leaders such as Atatürk in Turkey, Nehru in India, the Shah in Iran, Azikiwe in Nigeria, and Kenyatta in Kenya made national appeals largely shorn of religion. Often western-educated, these rulers developed nationalist ideologies heavily inspired by European thinking and political models (Özdalga 2009), ideas which seemed to reflect the collective Zeitgeist of the time about religion and political modernization. Moreover, in many instances these political leaders feared the destabilizing effects of religious conflict in the emerging nation state (India and Nigeria) or they saw religious groups as a potential challenge to their political power (Iran and Turkey). The newly formed states, thus, were secular and political leaders made concerted efforts to minimize the political and moral appeal of a religiously based national identity. At least initially, historical developments around the globe seemed to be proving the point that secular nationalism was the norm in the modern world. However, in most of those places secularization did not exile religion from the state to the society. In the intervening decades, religion remained the popular basis for self-definition and political legitimation (Altunaş 2010; Omer and Springs 2013:4–9). The reemergence of religion in nationalist discourse was also a helpful reminder that the idea of secular nationalism is a fairly recent invention and might therefore not be historically inevitable (Juergensmeyer 2010:262).

Not only did these theories diverge on the issue of what role religion assumed in the origins of nationalism, but by implication they also parted company on the continuing relevance of religion for contemporary nationalism. Modernist theories presupposed the triumph of secular nationalism and the privatization and depoliticization of religion. In highlighting the vital role of religion in the origins of nationalism and the ideological basis for secular nationalism, however, ethno-symbolic theories implicitly raised the question of the continuing role of religion for national identity.

The final and arguably most decisive test to modernist theories, however, came from the political resurgence of religion in the past several decades. Contrary to the confident predictions of secularization theory that religion would disappear as a political force, religion's influence on politics has increased on every continent and within every major world religion over the past several decades. The politics of nationalism have been very much affected by this renaissance. Michael Walzer (2015) notes that the revival of religion as a political force in Algeria, India, and Israel represents the rejection of secular nationalism and the ascendency of religiously based alternatives to it. The nationalism of most postcolonial leaders was secular, but their subordination of religion would prove to be short-lived in many places. Religious groups and leaders such as the Ayatollah Khomeini in Iran, the early Anwar Sadat in Egypt, and more recently Recep Erdoğan in Turkey presented secular nationalism as a legacy of colonial rule and a foreign political model imposed by the West (Tamadonfar and Jelen 2014). Not only did political Islam provide a basis for opposing "foreign" influence, but it also offered a foundation for a newly formed nationalism. For many people in those countries, the modernizing, secular state which privatized religion had little purchase because religion provided a stronger basis for self-identification than did secular, nationalist values. The result was the rise of a religious nationalism in much of the developing world that hewed much more closely to the spiritual, cultural, and historical allegiances of the masses (Juergensmeyer 2008).

A similar dynamic occurred in Eastern Europe with the demise of the Soviet Union, the discrediting of communism as a unifying ideology, and the reemergence of religious nationalism to fill the political and ideological void. The political revolution in Poland owed much to that country's long and deep identification with the Roman Catholic Church, much as post-Soviet Bulgaria reinvigorated the strong links between national identity and the Eastern Orthodox Church (Zubrzycki 2006; Stan and Turcescu 2011). As different as they were in their political agendas, the Iranian Revolution, the Solidarity Movement in Poland, and postcommunist Bulgaria all used religion as a mobilizing force against secular states.

The spread of democracy also abetted the rise of religious nationalism in various parts of the world (Toft, Philpott, and Shah 2011:77). Democratization opened space for political activism; freed from the constraints of authoritarian regimes, religious actors were suddenly able to form political movements on the basis of religion. The political success of the Muslim Brotherhood in Egypt, for example, came partly as a result of their growing ability to participate in relatively free and fair elections. Their political success demonstrated that an electoral market existed for a more religiously focused political party. By the same token, democratization encouraged more secular political parties and their leaders to appeal to religious voters, thereby stimulating the rise of religious nationalism. These developments and many others were a helpful reminder that in many ways religion is "a natural competitor to the nationalism of the secular state" (Friedland 2001:128). Or to put it in the terms of this chapter, religious nationalism is a second model for the relationship between religious and national identities.

As with its secular counterpart, there are both institutional and ideological ramifications to religious nationalism. Institutionally, religious nationalism leads to formal links between politics and a particular religious group. Far from a separation of religion from the state as is presumed in secular nationalism, in this model religion and the state are formally intertwined in various ways. In Saudi Arabia, as an example, the version of Sunni Islam inspired by Muhammad ibn 'Abd al-Wahhab is the state religion and the law requires that all citizens be Muslim. Religious nationalism need not, however, lead to autocratic politics. The Republic of Ireland is a political democracy which has for decades granted the Roman Catholic Church a political monopoly over education and public morality issues, although church control over these issues is currently being challenged. Religious nationalism legitimates policy programs using religious values. Religious nationalists in India seek to redefine the Indian state as Hindu, and they justify their policy views in terms of the supposedly shared values of the state's Hindu majority. Ideologically, this form of nationalism "makes religion the basis for the nation's collective identity and the source of its ultimate value and purpose on this earth" (Friedland 2001:139). Instead of uniting people on the basis of secular political values, religious nationalism adopts sacred language to explain the nation's role in history (Marsh 2007:3). Religion is so important to this form of nationalism that it "adopts religious language and modes of religious communication" (Rieffer 2003:225).

As much as they differ in their orientations, theories of secular and religious nationalism share the assumption that there is an essential difference between civic and spiritual identities and that there is a potential for a competition between them. Secular nationalism presumes the triumph of national over religious identity, and religious nationalism counters with a model where religious identity supersedes or competes with secular national identity. However, scholars have offered a third prototype where nationalism is itself seen as a secularized form of religion. This theory borrows heavily from the sociological insights of Émile Durkheim (2001[1912]). In his sociological work, Durkheim argued that secularization was historically inevitable, but that something was needed to fulfill the socially integrative role performed by religion in a pre-secular society. The disappearance of religion left unmet needs for meaning and purpose, needs that had to be fulfilled in some other fashion. Given the myths and symbols associated with it, and the passions that it evokes, nationalism filled that void (Santiago 2009). Traditional religion might well disappear, Durkheim argued, but it would be replaced by an equally compelling commitment to nationalism and nationalist values. Or as Mark Juergensmeyer ironically notes about the contemporary context, "at the same time that religion in the West was becoming less political, its secular nationalism was becoming more religious" (Juergensmeyer 2010:263).

Scholars have also called into question the idea that secular nationalism was somehow non-religious, claiming instead that nationalism is itself essentially a form of religion. Smith (2000:811) argues that the rituals and symbols of secular nationalism are a "political religion" that fulfills many of the functions of traditional religion. Noting that secular nationalisms often legitimate themselves in such religious terms as "holy nation" and "chosen people," Gorski and Türkmen-Dervişoğlu (2013a:139) conclude that even "secular forms of nationalism are almost always parasitic on religious sources of identity." Others perceptively noted that the neglect of religion in modernist accounts of nationalism said more about the secular presuppositions of modernist theories than it did about the historical inevitability of secular nationalism (Gorski 2000:1459; Rieffer 2003:222; Brubaker 2012:15).

Robert Bellah offered a variation of this theory in his work on civil religion in America (Bellah 1967, 1975). Civil religion was "a collection of beliefs, symbols, and rituals with respect to sacred things" (Bellah 1967:3). Unlike secular nationalism, civil religion was not an attempt to usurp religion, but neither was it simply the marrying of nationalism with a particular religious tradition. Instead, American civil religion promoted the idea of a sacred link between God's purposes and the American nation. Moreover, religious and political ideas mutually reinforced each other and came together to form this new civil religion (Kurth 2007:121). What made these religious ideas unique, however, is that they were unifying rather than dividing, they stressed the points of spiritual commonality among the religious population as a whole, and they promoted national solidarity rather than division (Chapp 2012:30–8). The concept of civil religion is Durkheimean in the sense that this form of nationalism is providing some overarching sense of meaning and purpose. Like modernization theory, civil religion presumes that the modern state is in some respects replacing the role traditionally played by the church, but it challenges the secular presumption of modernist accounts in recognizing that the state retains a need for moral legitimacy, something that civil religion can provide.

The relationship between particular religions and national self-understanding is complex in civil-religious regimes. Civil-religious nationalism is rooted in the country's religious experience, but it nevertheless develops separately from it. It does not identify the majority religious tradition with the state, as in religious nationalism, but it also does not jettison any religious values from the national story, as in secular nationalism. Civil religion is, instead, a form of nationalism that creates a sense of solidarity and collective identity among the people based on shared religious and political values (Williams and Fuist 2014:931). As a concept, civil religion has proven to be quite popular and has been applied by scholars to countries as disparate as South Korea (Cha 2000), Chile (Cristi and Dawson 1996), and Israel (Liebman and Don-Yehiya 1983; see also Hvithamar, Warburg, and Jacobsen 2009). In their account of the Israeli case, as an example, Charles Liebman and Eliezer Don-Yehiya argue that Israel's civil religion borrows from ideas within traditional Judaism, but is not synonymous with it (Liebman and Don-Yehiya 1983:162).

What civil-religious theories get right, in our view, is that they implicitly reject the dichotomous framework offered in accounts of secular and religious nationalism, where a religious tradition is presented either as implacably irrelevant or absolutely central to a country's nationalism. Following the argument of Gorski and Türkmen-Dervişoğlu (2013b), we contend that it is better to think of religion's role in nationalism along a continuum. A religion can be more or less central as an ideological resource for nationalism, and the corresponding institutional links between religion and the state can be more or less strong. If secular and religious nationalisms represent opposing ends of the spectrum, civil-religious nationalism recognizes that there might be some middle ground between these opposing poles.

Civil-religious theory falls short, however, in its overarching claim that every regime fits this typology. In this reading, there is little theoretical difference between a French nationalism that canonizes the revolutionary values of liberty, equality, and fraternity, on the one hand, and modern Jewish Orthodoxy in Israel that advocates a religious nationalism based on its particular reading of the Torah and of Jewish history. Seen from the civil-religious standpoint, both are secularized forms of nationalism. We contend, however, that this generalization is overly inclusive. Broadly to classify the two forms of nationalism together misses important differences between them. Moreover, the role of specific religious traditions often disappears from the political scene in civil-religious theories. While the United States might be a case where civil-religious nationalism erases some of the distinctions among religious traditions, this situation is less evident in countries where religious actors and institutions have differing relationships with the state and its nationalism.

Civil religion offers a nationalist model that stands somewhere between secular and religious nationalism. Particular religious groups and traditions play a less central ideological and institutional role in civil-religious states compared to in religious-nationalist ones, but those same religious actors assume a more supporting role than in secular nationalism. Institutionally, the formal links between religion and the state are weaker in civil-religious regimes when contrasted with those with religious nationalism. Religious nationalism leads to a formal recognition of a religious tradition and multiple connections between that dominant tradition and the state. Secular nationalism, on the other hand, separates religion from the state and minimizes formal contacts between them. Civil-religious states, finally, manifest themselves as regimes of benign separation or of pluralistic accommodation where the state recognizes multiple religious traditions.

Table 1.1 offers an overview for the divergent religion–nationalism models reviewed. As is indicated in the table, secular, religious, and civil-religious nationalisms can be compared both ideologically and institutionally. The ideology variable indicates how closely the nationalism hews toward a religious tradition, while the institutional variable notes

TABLE 1.1. *Models of religion and nationalism*

Model	Religion–state ideological links	Religion–state institutional links
Secular nationalism	Weak to nonexistent	Separation
Religious nationalism	Strong (with a particular group)	Multiple religion–state contacts (to a particular group)
Civil-religious nationalism	Supportive (to religion in general)	Benign separation or pluralistic accommodation

the formal connections between religion and state in the variant models. Thus, secular nationalism is marked by weak to nonexistent ties to religious identity in national consciousness and a formal separation of religion from the state. By contrast, religious nationalism forges strong connections to a particular religious group both ideologically and institutionally. Civil religion lies somewhere between the two in that religion is supportive of nationalism, but it is not linked to a particular religious tradition. Institutionally this form of nationalism can manifest itself either in a formal, but benign separation of church and state or in a policy accommodation to multiple religious traditions.

Thus far we have attempted to tease out the theoretical implications of the religion and nationalism literature. For the most part, those accounts presume the monopolizing dominance of one of the three nationalism models (secular, religious, or civil religious). What we have argued, however, is that states differ in how closely national ideas are ideologically and institutionally linked to religious ones. Recognizing that multiple forms of nationalism exist, a few scholars have begun systematically to analyze what differentiates them. In his influential work, Mark Juergensmeyer (1994, 2010; see also Friedland 2001) juxtaposes religious and secular nationalism as competing ideologies of order. Secular nationalism, particularly via colonialism, relegated religion to the private sphere and sought to keep it out of political life. Religious nationalism is a response of religious elites to a loss of social and political influence, and the failure of secular nationalism to bridge the gap between public values and the political community. As we will note in our Israel and India chapters, there is much to be said for Juergensmeyer's account of religious nationalism. However, his binary categories of secular and religious nationalism leave little room for models that fall somewhere between those opposing extremes. The United States, as we will demonstrate, seems an ill fit for either secular or religious nationalism. Moreover, his account presumes a link between religious nationalism and violence, which has clearly been in evidence in some countries of the world. However, our Greece chapter will show that states with religious nationalism as a model can be stable and relatively free of violence based on religion.

In her article, Barbara-Ann Rieffer (2003) posits the existence of three nationalist models: secular nationalism, religious nationalism, and instrumental pious nationalism. She also outlines some of the distinctive features of the three models. As an example, Rieffer argues that religious nationalism tends to occur in religiously homogenous territories, where that land has some religious value, and where there is an external threat to the group from a different religious tradition (226). Secular nationalism, by contrast, is "devoid of religious sentiment and overtones" (231), while religion plays a supportive but not leading role in instrumental pious nationalism. In many respects, Rieffer's three models mirror our own. Her work, however, looks only at the role of religion in the origin of nationalist movements. It does not consider the continuing relevance of religion in a country's nationalism, how the variant models lead to alternative institutional frameworks, or what factors might explain how those models change over time.

Rogers Brubaker (2012) offers four "approaches" in the relationship between religion and nationalism: religion and nationalism as analogous phenomena, how religion explains certain aspects of nationalism, how religion is a part of nationalism, and religious nationalism as a form of nationalism. Brubaker's account is intended, however, as an overview of the literature rather than a theoretical examination for how divergent models of religion and nationalism emerge. In a similar vein, Eastwood and Prevalakis (2010:97) provide four "classes or families of views" on the relationship between religion and nationalism: nationalism as a form of religion, nationalism as a replacement of religion, nationalism causing the displacement of religion, and religious nationalism as a subtype of nationalism. Their article is mainly interested in the ideological implications of the four models; they have very little to say about the institutional ramifications of each. They briefly note "substantial variation" on the political settlement between religious and national worldviews (from state churches to French-style separation), but this is included as a supplementary question that needs greater scholarly attention.

Finally, Gorski and Türkmen-Dervişoğlu (2013a; see also Gorski and Türkmen-Dervişoğlu 2013b) offer the tripartite models of secular nationalism, religious nationalism, and public religion. As we noted above, they also provide a framework which understands religion's role in nationalism on a continuum. Gorski and Türkmen-Dervişoğlu also take into account the key role that contingent factors play in the development of and challenges to each of the models. In particular, they examine the strategic alliances between religious and political elites, the demographic makeup of the country in question, and the institutional autonomy and resources of religious elites. While Gorski and Türkmen-Dervişoğlu offer valuable insight, their work offers only a brief sketch of the interaction of these variables in the different models of religion and nationalism. We intend more fully to develop the three models and examine in some detail how they operate in different countries.

KEY FACTORS IN THE EMERGENCE OF RELIGION–NATIONALISM MODELS

At the risk of simplifying complex historical and political phenomena, we contend that four key dynamics shape the kind of religion–nationalism model a state adopts and retains: the role of religion in the pre-state formation period, the constitutional status of religion in the new order, the country's demographic makeup at the point of state formation, and the social and political power of religious groups at the point of state formation. The relationship among these four historical variables underpins how and why nations fall into one of three basic models: religious, secular, or civil-religious nationalism.

The first variable separates regimes based on the role of religious groups in the nationalist project. Specifically, it examines the degree to which religious groups consent to or contest state-sponsored nationalism. At one end of the spectrum are states where religious groups understand and experience nationalism as an affront to their religion and its interests, and these traditions therefore oppose it. In India, for example, there were Hindu nationalist organizations that opposed the developing secular nationalist model that was promoted by Nehru and other leaders in the Congress Party. At the other extreme are those cases where religious groups implicitly or explicitly consent to the newly formed nationalism, and thereby support it. While there was some diversity among religious groups in the United States during the Revolution, by and large the churches supported the independence movement.

The second variable similarly looks at founding moments in a country's history, but in this case we focus on how religion is legally or constitutionally linked to the state. The drafting of a Constitution, we contend, is a regime-defining moment that creates institutional and symbolic path dependencies that shape policy and national self-understanding going forward. As with our first variable, regimes fall somewhere along a continuum from those that have an officially established religion and multiple links to a particular faith codified in law or in the Constitution, to those with a formal separation of religion from the state and few if any institutional connections.

The third variable is a demographic one measuring states on a measure of their degree of religious diversity, from those that are religiously uniform to those that are religiously diverse. The final variable places states on a continuum from those where religious groups assume a strong social and political role at the point of state formation to those where religious groups are socially and politically weak. We contend that clear patterns emerge in the three religion–nationalism frames based on the combination of these four factors.

It is important to note that these three models are ideal types in the Weberian sense of that term. It is rare for a state to embody every feature of one of the three models in its purest form, but the prototypes offer an analytical tool to understand the relationship between religion and nationalism in countries around the world. Nor are the models exhaustive. The Islamist movement ISIS provides a religious rationale for a transnational political empire that extends well beyond contemporary nation-state borders. The political religion of Nazi Germany and Pancasila as the philosophical foundation of the Indonesian state are still other models in the nexus between religion and nationalism. Nonetheless, secular nationalism, religious nationalism, and civil-religious nationalism remain the dominant ways in which religion and nationalism interact, and it is these three ideal types that we will analyze.

Arguably, the most important variable in regimes of religious nationalism is that they are marked by high levels of religious uniformity (Rieffer 2003:225; Gorski and Türkmen-Dervişoğlu 2013a:140; Rubin 2013:498). For obvious reasons, religious nationalism is most likely to be constructed in places where a critical mass of the population identifies with one religion. Historically, many European states reflected this model as state churches reproduced the religious culture that developed along the confessional lines brought on by the Protestant Reformation. This does not mean, however, that a mono-religious culture is a sufficient condition for religious nationalism. The modern Turkish state promoted a secular-nationalist vision although the overwhelming percentage of the nation adheres to Sunni Islam.

This model also emerges in states where the religious population has consented to the new nationalism precisely because national and religious identities are so closely fused. Support from religious groups for the nationalist project thereby minimizes points of potential conflict between state and society. Religious nationalism also occurs when religious groups are socially and politically strong and have some degree of institutional autonomy from the state (Friedland 2001:144; Toft, Philpott, and Shah 2011:32–9). This independence enables religious groups more effectively to affect the political process and to demand that the state be religiously based. Given those factors, it is not surprising that religious nationalism is also characterized by a formal political role for religion. Political elites have little choice, and possibly little incentive, to challenge the institutional establishment of religion. In this model, a special relationship develops between the state and the dominant religious group. This manifests itself on such issues as religious education in the schools, religiously based national holidays, public benefits to a particular religious group, and a formal role for the main religious group in shaping public policy.

One example of religious nationalism is postcommunist Poland, where the state erected a new nationalism by alluding to the very old and strong connections in the country to the Roman Catholic Church (Zubrzycki 2006). The leading role assumed by Catholic leaders in the democratization movement demonstrated both the power of organized religion in Poland and its relative independence from the Communist state. The Polish state that emerged after the fall of the Berlin Wall granted the church political rights in the new order, including the return of religious education to the public schools and the criminalization of abortion (Byrnes 2002:27–30). In accordance with a 1998 concordat, the government and the Roman Catholic Church meet regularly to discuss church–state relations. More than half of Poland's official holidays are Catholic, including Epiphany, Easter, Whit Sunday, Corpus Christi, Assumption Day, All Saints Day, and Christmas. In Ireland, nationalist discourse has long equated being Irish with being Roman Catholic (Inglis 1998). Ireland's 1937 Constitution formalized this relationship in its recognition of "the special position of The Holy Catholic and Apostolic Church as the guardian of the Faith professed by the great majority of citizens," and in various provisions that provided state support for Catholic institutions.

The parallel religious nationalism in Greece, where an estimated 95 percent of the population self-identifies as Greek Orthodox (United States Department of State 2014), rests on a similar premise. While Greece has thousands of years of history, the establishment of the modern Hellenic state is linked with its war of independence from the Ottoman Empire from 1821 to 1832. The first constitution adopted in 1822 was liberal and democratic in most of its features. Nonetheless, it forged a strong link between the state and the demographically dominant Greek Orthodox Church. Article I affirmed that "the religion of the state is the orthodox religion of the Eastern [Greek] Church." Constitutional changes over the next century reflected political dynamics on the ground, but what was consistent in each of those constitutions was the formal establishment of the Greek Orthodox Church, the granting of numerous subsidies to the Church, the public recognition of various Orthodox religious events as national holidays, and the implicit understanding that Greek and Orthodox identity were virtually one and the same (Mavrogordatos 2003; Chrysoloras 2004).

Secular nationalism, on the other hand, develops in very different cultural and political contexts. An aggressive form of this model emerges in places like Turkey where religious groups are culturally strong and contest the dominant nationalism because they experience it as an affront on religion. Islamic religious leaders challenged Atatürk's secular nationalism in Turkey in the early twentieth century because they concluded that the new order would restrict and/or seek to control the power and privileges of the mosque (Kuru 2009:Chapter 7). However, secular nationalism can also emerge in places where religion is culturally and institutionally weak, such as contemporary Sweden or Uruguay, where religion is not powerful enough to serve as the basis for the state's nationalism. The social and political power of religious groups similarly varies in secular nationalist states. In many instances, religious groups are strong and secular nationalism is a form of state control over a potential foe (Bruce 2002:57). In still other cases, religious groups might be so institutionally and organizationally weak that the state can effectively ignore those voices. The end of the Soviet occupation of Estonia did not lead to the development of an Estonian religious nationalism as only a small percentage of Estonians are religious. While the Lutheran Church was a rallying point during the later period of Soviet occupation, this religious institution was not itself politically powerful, and its role as a locus of dissent was brief. In this instance, secular nationalism was not so much a response to a perceived threat from the church, but a recognition that religion can effectively be ignored as a part of the national consciousness and institution building. Institutionally, secular nationalism leads logically to some form of religion–state separation. This model can manifest itself in a benign separation that preserves religious liberty but keeps the state at arm's length from religion, or as an assertive separation where the state seeks to diminish or to control the political role and power of key religious groups (Kuru 2009).

India and Uruguay are examples of these opposing types of secular nationalism. India had a highly religious culture when it gained independence from Britain, and political leaders set about the task of drafting a new Constitution. India experienced the bloody partition with Pakistan largely on religious grounds just as it was forming the new state. Nehru and other leaders of the Congress Party reasoned that religious (and caste) cleavages could undermine the state-building project, and so they minimized the state's religious character in the drafting of the new Constitution and promoted secular rather than religious nationalism as the basis for political unity, a decision that would eventually lead to a counter mobilization among Hindu nationalists (Chiriyankandath 2008; Tejani 2013). The basic structure of India's 1948 Constitution was secular, though that word itself was omitted from the original preamble but added two decades later after Prime Minister Indira Gandhi declared a state of emergency. The preamble now affirms that India is a "sovereign, socialist, secular [Hindi "laukik"/लौकिक], democratic Republic." Secular nationalism came to Uruguay, on the other hand, not as an effort to restrain the political power of the Catholic Church, but because religion has been historically weak in Uruguay. Under the leadership of President José Batlle y Ordóñez, the 1918 Constitution officially separated church and state. Religious freedom was preserved, but there were no formal institutional links between the state and religious groups. Religious groups, in particular the Roman Catholic Church, were simply not powerful enough to force an alternative arrangement. Those institutional relations have largely remained intact in the intervening decades as the social role of religion has, if anything, diminished. At present, nearly half of Uruguay's population (47 percent) professes no religion, and most of those who do identify as religious are not particularly active.

Civil-religious nationalism borrows features from the alternative secular and religious models. Like its religious nationalism counterpart, civil religion forms where religious groups consent to the emerging nationalism. At least for most religious adherents, civil-religious nationalism is not experienced as an attack on religion, and so they do not fundamentally challenge it. It differs from religious nationalism, however, in that countries with this model are marked by religious diversity. Given the relative heterogeneity, a uniform religious nationalism tied to a single tradition cannot prevail, but the allure of civil religion is that the nationalism uses enough generic religious symbols and language to forge a strong link between the nation and multiple faiths. It is a form of nationalism that "claims to speak on behalf of a religious community" without being identified with a single religious group (Gorski and Türkmen-Dervişoğlu 2013a:140). Civil-religious nationalism also diverges from religious nationalism insofar as religion does not occupy a central position in the national movement. Religion is a supportive element that acts to unite the population in the nationalist cause, but its role is secondary to other groups and factors (Rieffer 2003:229).

In their institutional forms, on the other hand, civil-religious regimes more nearly mirror those of secular nationalism. What these states do not have is an officially established religion, and in the case of the United States, there is a formal separation of religion and state. The First Amendment to the Constitution famously opens with the words "Congress shall make no law respecting an establishment of religion," and in practice this moratorium on a nationally established religion would eventually be followed by similar bans in each of the individual states. In other instances, however, civil-religious regimes create a form of pluralistic accommodation that recognizes a formal role for multiple religious traditions. Because of their diverse nature, no single religious group has the political power to impose a mono-religious nationalism on the nation, but religious groups are strong enough that the state does not actively oppose them. The extent to which religious laws and beliefs are implemented in policies and governing institutions is much weaker in a civil-religious regime than in a state with religious nationalism as its model.

The United States is the clearest example for civil-religious nationalism. Religious groups generally played a supportive role in the nationalist movement. Americans were divided along denominational lines, but the various Protestant churches who represented the vast majority of the religious population accepted the nationalist project. Those groups and traditions were socially and politically important in American politics, but they were diverse, and not one of them was able to shape political outcomes. Religion was not the basis for the new constitutional order, but neither was it ignored or opposed. The institutional separation of religion from state that emerged was not, therefore, a hostile one as in the case of many secular nationalist regimes. Nor did such an institutional separation mean that religious groups were unable to engage in politics or have a decisive political role through the shaping of cultural values. Instead, separation was understood and experienced largely as a way of preserving the integrity of religious groups. African Americans and Native Americans were excluded from the nationalist frame, and the political loyalties of religious newcomers (Catholics, Jews, Mormons, and Muslims) were similarly questioned. Over time, however, formerly excluded groups were enfolded into the civil-religious nationalism and believers from multiple religious traditions (not simply the dominant ones) supported the nationalist project.

Table 1.2 outlines the patterns that can be identified in the three models along our four variables. As the table indicates, religious nationalism emerges in a religiously uniform context. The dominant tradition advances and supports the religious nationalist project, and that religious tradition is politically and socially strong. The result is a formal establishment of that tradition. In a secular nationalist regime, by contrast, religious groups, whether weak or strong, contest a secular nationalist model. Demographically, it can manifest itself in states with a dominant religious tradition or in a religiously diverse nation. Either way, however, a formal separation of religion from the state is the institutional form of secular nationalism. Finally, religious groups are diverse in civil-religious regimes, but they consent to the civil-religious nationalism. While there is no formal establishment of religion, the institutional form (either separation or pluralistic accommodation) is experienced not as an attack on religion but as a support to it.

TABLE 1.2. *Variables in the emergence and maintenance of religion–nationalism models*

Model	Religion and nationalist project	Institutional links	Demographics	Religious role
Religious nationalism	Consensual (for a particular group)	Establishment	Religiously uniform	Strong
Secular nationalism	Contested	Separation	Various	Strong or weak
Civil-religious nationalism	Consensual (for multiple religious traditions)	Separation or pluralistic accommodation	Religiously diverse	Moderate

KEY FACTORS IN THE MAINTENANCE OF RELIGION–NATIONALISM MODELS

The development of one of the three religion–nationalist frames does not, however, determine its success or stability over time. The initial religious–nationalist models are not static, and numerous contingent variables can destabilize the religious–nationalist frame over time. Chief among these variables are how the losers in the initial battle over the nationalist narrative respond to their defeat, demographic changes over time, and how political actors challenge or coopt religious groups. To varying degrees, secular nationalism was imposed from above in both Turkey and India, despite or because of the opposition of Muslim nationalists in the former and Hindu nationalists in the latter. Far from solving the dilemma of alternative notions of nationalism in its initial years, however, the original secular nationalism did not prevent the continued struggle over national identity between secular and religious elites. At times, political elites have reaffirmed the secular nature of the state and increased efforts to control religious life. Sensing a threat to the status quo, Indira Gandhi therefore used her powers during the period of emergency rule in the 1970s to press for the addition of the words "secular" and "socialist" to the preamble to India's Constitution. More recently, however, both countries have witnessed the rise to power of religiously based nationalist movements, the Justice and Development Party in Turkey and the BJP in India. Both parties self-consciously promote a nationalist vision that is much more closely linked to religion, and in both countries political elites have concluded that they can benefit politically from an effort to coopt mass-based religious movements.

This leads to a second vital factor in the stability of the nationalist model over time: the role of political elites. Scott Hibbard (2010), Michael Walzer (2015), and Nadav Shelef (2010), among others, have persuasively argued that political elites in countries as diverse as India, Egypt, Algeria, and Israel have abetted the rise of religious nationalism in an attempt to coopt religion for their own political ends. Debates about the role of religion in the state were not new in any of those places; what changed over time was the commitment of state elites to secular or civil-religious nationalism based on their calculations of the political benefits of advocating religious nationalism. What political elites discovered is that the moral language and a sense of transcendence within religious traditions make them uniquely capable of providing political legitimacy to temporal regimes. Religion, in short, can be very useful to political leaders who have every reason to seek spiritual sanction for their actions (Hibbard 2010:6).

In an effort to manipulate religion for their own political purposes, state elites encouraged the rise of religious nationalism in states where the social conditions at the mass level encouraged it. The political power of these movements was a function of both their popular appeal and the new orientation of state elites to religious nationalism. This is a particularly salient factor in political democracies, where political leaders can ill afford to be indifferent to the religious values of the masses. Because he did not face the voters in free and fair elections, Atatürk could impose his secular nationalist vision on the religious mass from above. As Turkey democratized, a market emerged for religious nationalism and political leaders forged strategic alliances with religious leaders that undermined the state's commitment to secular nationalism. The result in Turkey and in India, therefore, is that the secular nationalism forged at each country's founding is in the process of transitioning to religious nationalism.

Nationalist narratives can also be destabilized by the perception (real or manufactured) of external or internal threats to the state and by political elites' response to these challenges (Rieffer 2003:226). As Smith (1999b:338) notes nationalism "sharpens the cultural and social boundary between the nation and its neighbors." National identity is a primary factor in demarcating the community from outsiders, and conflict, or the fear of conflict, with those neighbors can reinforce this demarcation. Most of Israel's founders advocated a secular or a civil-religious nationalism that sought to downplay the specifically Jewish features of the new state. Over the next several decades, however, Israel has gone to war with neighboring states that are predominantly Islamic. Political elites have used this conflict to strengthen arguments for the religious character of Israel. In this case external conflict reinforces the importance of religion as an identity marker for citizens of Israel, and in the process the inherited nationalist model has been challenged.

External threats can, alternatively, reinforce the inherited nationalist model. As we noted above, Greek nationalism has been closely linked with Orthodoxy since the country's independence from the Ottoman Empire in the early nineteenth century. Over the next century and a half, the religious basis for this nationalism has been strengthened by persistent conflict between an overwhelmingly Orthodox Greece and a largely Muslim Ottoman Empire and then Turkey. The conflict, in short, has buttressed the Orthodox foundation for Greek national identity. The immigration of religious newcomers to the United States, or of home-grown religious movements, has periodically threatened the country's civil-religious nationalism. Roman Catholics, Jews, and Mormons, among others, have at different points in American history had their loyalties questioned. President Trump's rhetoric about immigrants gen-erally, and Muslim immigrants in particular, is the latest example of how politicians have targeted groups because of their faith, and by implica-tion offered a much narrower religious nationalism. As we will note later in the book, however, up to this point in American history the immi-gration of new religious groups has *strengthened* rather than weakened America's civil-religious nationalism. Religious newcomers have eventu-ally been enfolded into the national story, thus strengthening the under-lying model.

Nationalist models can also be tried simply by demographic changes. We highlighted postcommunist Poland as a regime of religious national-ism and noted some of the strong institutional links between the Catholic Church and the state as evidence for this claim. In recent years, however, the Church's political privileges have come under attack, as has its virtual monopoly role in shaping social and moral public policy (Byrnes 2002). The secularization of Polish society, were it to accelerate, might further undermine a national identify built on Catholic sensibilities, though it would presumably take a long time. Similarly, British nationalism is tied historically to religion, but religion is less central now than it was even a century ago. The secularization of British society, the weakening of Christian practices and traditions, and the gradual demise of the power of the Established Church of England means that Britain is moving to a model of secular nationalism.

The point is that regimes of religious, secular, or civil-religious nation-alism can be unstable if the underlying conditions change enough. Certain factors help explain the emergence of each of the three models, but their maintenance over time has much to do with the particular histories of individual countries. The origin of a particular model is often contested, resolving these disputes can be a never-ending process, political leaders may conclude that there is some benefit in coopting religious movements, external or internal threats can arise which advance an alternative nation-alist frame, and thus the underlying conditions that led to the original model can change.

Figure 1.1 demonstrates a few examples for how changing underlying conditions can influence the nationalism model embraced by a state. The foundation of the Swedish state is linked to the reign of Gustav Vasa

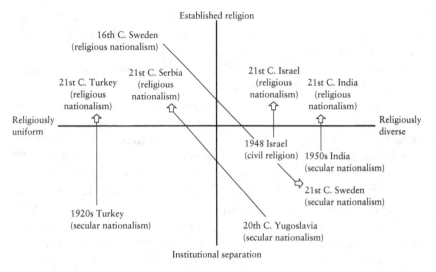

FIGURE 1.1. *Change in religion–nationalism model*

(1523–60) who confiscated Catholic property, concentrated power in the hands of the monarch, and nationalized the church. The establishment of the Church of Sweden (Lutheran) forged a strong bond between religion and national identity. Much had changed five centuries later, however. What had been a religiously uniform Lutheran country had become pluralistic as Lutherans (60 percent) competed with self-described agnostics (20 percent), atheists (11 percent), Muslims (6 percent), and various smaller traditions in what has become a much more diverse religious environment. In this context, a religious nationalism tied to a single tradition has less ideological power, and in the year 2000 the country voted to disestablish the Church of Sweden, with the acquiescence of the Church. What had once been a model of religious nationalism has been gradually transformed into a prototype of secular nationalism brought on in large measure by demographic transformations at the mass level. At the other extreme, the secular nationalism of Cold-War Yugoslavia has transitioned into religious nationalism in the now-separate Republic of Serbia after the "ethnic cleansing" of the civil war. During the war, people were targeted because of their religion, which reinforced the importance of that identity for them. Moreover, while Yugoslavia was religiously pluralistic, Serbia was religiously monolithic. As the underlying conditions changed, therefore, Yugoslavia and then Serbia evolved from secular to religious nationalism.

Demographically, Turkey looks much the same now as it did when it was officially recognized as the Republic of Turkey under the 1923 Treaty of Lausanne. The country was and remains overwhelmingly Sunni Muslim, though there are a significant number of Alevis, who belong to a liberal branch of Shia Islam, and who may or may not be ethnically Kurdish. What has changed in recent decades, however, is relations at the elite level between religious and political authorities. Religious leaders largely opposed Atatürk's state-imposed secularism in the early twentieth century and spent decades seeking the political power necessary to over-turn it. As the country democratized, political leaders had a growing elec-toral incentive to mobilize voters on the basis of religion. The election of Recep Erdoğan, founder of the Islamist Justice and Development Party, as Prime Minister in 2003 altered the political landscape. During his ten-ure as Prime Minister and President, Erdoğan rescinded a longstanding ban on head scarves in public institutions, established more control over the more secularly minded judiciary, and increased the number of reli-gious schools and the role of religious instruction in education. What had once been a regime of separation is moving toward a regime of religious establishment. Coincident with this transition is an effort to transform Turkish national understanding from one rooted in secular nationalism to one more aligned with its religious constituency.

India and Israel are experiencing a similar transition to religious nation-alism although from different original models. Both were religiously diverse at their founding and today. In both cases, however, political elites have electorally mobilized the majority religion and strengthened the reli-gious self-understanding of the state and its policies.

In her account of nationalism and religion in postcommunist Poland, Geneviève Zubrzycki (2006) insightfully observes that there is continuity and change inherent in the relationship between that country's religion and its nationalism. She describes the link between them as being "in con-stant motion" (222) as political and religious leaders create, define, and redefine the nation through the interpretation of key religious symbols and events. However, she also argues that while malleable, interpreta-tions of the Polish nation are "constrained within the boundaries of more or less durable narrative structures and sets of symbols" (216).

In his perceptive account of civil-religious nationalism in the United States, Philip Gorski (2017) highlights the relative stability of that nation-alist frame over time. Nonetheless, he notes that civil-religious nationalism has been challenged throughout American history by those advocating reli-gious or secular nationalism as alternative frames for the American nation.

In a similar manner we argue that contingent factors affect the stability of the model of religion and nationalism over time, but that those original structures are not entirely malleable. Instead, those initial formations create, if not a truly determinative path-dependent process, at least guideposts that shape subsequent debates about that nation's original model. Chief among those limitations are constitutional arrangements. The disestablishment of religion in the American Constitution limited the scope of action for those who have wanted, at various times throughout American history, to impose a religious nationalism on the state. Advocates of religious nationalism in India face a similar constraint given that country's secular constitution, though they have been quite adept at manipulating the language and logic of secularism for their political purposes. While England's religious nationalism seems a thing of the past given that country's secularizing trends, the establishment of the Church of England which was a manifestation of that religious nationalism centuries ago remains largely embedded in the country's laws and its public values.

We contend that these patterns are broadly predictive, but not determinative. None of the models guarantees an absence of conflict between religious and nationalist claims. Instead, each model can lead to stable or unstable outcomes depending on factors unique to each case. To illustrate our theory, subsequent chapters will analyze two countries from each of the three ideal types. The first member of each pair will represent a stable version of this model, while the second example will show signs of instability, or of moving away from one model toward another. In stable cases, religion and nationalism peacefully coexist, and even reinforce one another, and contingent variables support rather than undermine the original model over time. In unstable cases, on the other hand, religion becomes a key variable in political mobilization, religion and nationalism (for some groups) work at cross purposes, and contingent variables undermine the original model. Such stability or instability does not necessarily imply the absence of economic or political turmoil, or even that there are no controversies about the religious meaning of the nation. It simply suggests different levels of support for the status quo religion–nationalism arrangement.

CASE SELECTION

To illustrate our theory, we will analyze two countries from each of the three ideal types. The first member of each pair will represent a stable

version of this model, while the second example will show signs of instability, or of moving away from one model toward another. For the civil-
religious ideal type, we investigate the United States (stable) and Israel
(unstable). Greece (stable) and Malaysia (unstable) illustrate religious
nationalism. Lastly, Uruguay (stable) and India (unstable) stand in for
secular nationalism. Each of our cases is a liberal democracy or at least
a semi-democracy/hybrid regime. The importance of candid responses
to public opinion polls and of honest expression of elite views in the
content analysis makes an open, minimally democratic research environment essential for this project. Additionally, one of the variables we use to
assess the stability of each model is political mobilization along religious
lines, and this factor is particularly salient in electoral democracies.

The United States and Israel represent our civil-religious model. Both
countries were religiously diverse at the founding of the state. In the
United States, the main religious traditions largely supported the nationalist project on both civic and religious grounds. The constitutional order
created, however, did not establish a particular religion (at least at the
national level), and the formal ties between religion and the state were
few. Once solidified, these political structures and cultural patterns created a path-dependent process that shaped future understandings of religion and nationalism in the United States, even in the face of profound
social and political changes. Immigration and racial diversity, in particular, have posed serious threats to the model.

Israel is admittedly a unique case in many ways. We place it in the civil-
religious category, however, for various reasons. It was demographically
diverse, both between Jewish and non-Jewish residents and among the
different strands of Judaism. Like American Christians, Israeli Jews were
divided religiously, but both religious and secular Zionists supported the
establishment of the state of Israel. Of course, only Jews had a significant
voice in the structure of the resulting state, but the eventual institutions
that they founded accommodated the diverse religious traditions present
in the new country. In contrast with religious nationalism, the arguably
civil-nationalist model of Israel did not formally recognize only Judaism
at the expense of Islam, Christianity, and the Druze religion even if non-
Jews were politically disadvantaged. The Israeli framers hoped that multireligious accommodation would help maintain inter- and intra-religious
peace. However, contingent factors since the founding have destabilized
the original model. The constitutional status of religion in Israel has
become deeply divisive. Changing demographics have further inflamed
the relationship between religion and nationalism. Persistent tensions with

Israel's neighbors have created a larger market for religiously based political parties, while at the same time the secular, socialist voices that helped moderate religious nationalism at the founding have gradually weakened.

Greece and Malaysia represent the stable and unstable versions, respectively, of religious nationalism. Demographically, they differ insofar as Greece is overwhelmingly Orthodox Christian while Malaysia is much more diverse. Institutionally, they are more similar, however, in that each has a constitutionally established religion. In its hundreds of years of experience as a democracy, Greece has experienced tremendous political instability, yet its model of religious nationalism has been remarkably consistent. Moreover, contingent factors in the country's history have reinforced the power of that original model. Most notable among those new variables were the population exchange with Turkey along religious lines that made Greece even more religiously homogenous than it had been at the founding, and periodic conflict with "Islamic" Turkey that similarly reinforces religious identity for Greeks.

The roots of Malaysia's unstable religious nationalism go back to the disconnect between the country's institutional arrangement and its religious and ethnic demographics. Although Muslim Malays constitute only a bare majority of the population, the country's founders imposed established Islam on the people. Given this incompatibility between religious establishment and spiritual diversity, Malaysia continues to be wracked with conflict – sometimes violent – over the religious or ethnic nature of the state. All of the aggrieved members of nonestablished religions thus threaten to overturn the status quo arrangement and transform Malaysia's religious nationalism into secular nationalism.

Finally, Uruguay and India are our examples of stable and unstable secular nationalism. In both nations, the constitutional structure separates the government from specifically religious affiliations and limits the formal points of interactions between religion and the state. The process by which the countries adopted this secular structure differed, however. In Uruguay, a low level of religious affiliation and a corresponding weak Catholic Church meant that little opposition to a nonreligious polity developed, and the nationalism that emerged relied little on religious identity. Uruguay's secular nationalism has faced few demographic or political challenges, and the model has proved stable since its final formation in 1918.

In India, by contrast, nationalist elites promoted secular nationalism as an answer to the destabilizing effects of the country's deep religious cleavages. The country was strongly religious and spiritually diverse, and religion was and remains a source of intense political conflict and violence. Founding political leaders promoted a liberal constitution that protected religious freedom, guaranteed citizens the right to establish and maintain religious institutions, prohibited the state from raising taxes for specifically religious ends, and barred state-run schools from religious teaching. India's secular nationalism, however, was contested from the founding by religious groups who wanted a Constitution that would align more closely with the spiritual sensibilities of the population. Particularly since the 1980s, the Hindu-nationalist BJP has exploited those tensions for self-interested political ends, and demographic challenges remain as threatening today as they did in 1950. In contrast to Uruguay's situation, the conditions on the Subcontinent have not allowed India's model of secular nationalism to enjoy stability.

RELIGION AND NATIONALISM IN MASS PUBLIC OPINION AND RELIGIOUS PERIODICALS

Our theory also makes certain assumptions about the relative role of a religious ideology in forging attitudes toward the state. Without question, an ideological conflict exists between the transnational claims of the world's major religions and the specific, territorial allegiances promoted by nationalism (Katzenstein and Byrnes 2006). Each of the world's major religions claims that believers are bound together by a shared commitment to a set of religious doctrines and to coreligionists (wherever they might be). Christian ethical principles and social teaching represent a transnational commitment (Cavanaugh 2011) that has, at times, expressed itself in church statements that qualify the allegiance that adherents should feel to the nation-state (Ferrari 2006). The Islamic ideal of the *Ummah* – or "community of believers" – presupposes identification with fellow believers beyond the borders of a nation (Özdalga 2009). Even an ethical system like Confucianism teaches that adherence to a set of values and practices is more important than one's loyalty to the state (Fetzer and Soper 2013). Tensions between these opposing claims are likely to be the greatest for religious elites who are the bearers of the tradition and most likely to resist incorporation into any state ideology (Bruce 2002:84). For all adherents, however, there is always the potential for what Aviad Rubin (2013) describes as a bifurcated loyalty between a commitment to religious laws and norms, on the one hand, and loyalty to the state, on the other.

While the transnational claims of religious groups from disparate traditions can lead believers to qualify their allegiance to the state, we argue that what drives the emergence of this "bifurcated loyalty" is not the religious ideology by itself but the nationalism model promoted by the state. Generally speaking, what religious groups want is recognition for their faith and a national identity that fuses civic and religious loyalties. In some cases, this recognition comes as religious nationalism, while in others it is manifest in civil-religious nationalism. We hypothesize that the nationalist model in a given state are a more powerful predictor of attitudes than are the ideological claims of different religious traditions. Allegiance to the state (i.e., levels of support for patriotism/nationalism) among religionists will largely mirror the religious-nationalism model a state adopts and the status of the religious group within the state. To be more specific, we hypothesize that members of the majority faith are likely to express pro-nationalist sentiments in states with religious nationalism as its model, though this archetype runs the danger of alienating members of minority faiths and undermining their levels of patriotism. Thus, we predict that those who identify with the Greek Orthodox majority in Greece and with Sunni Islam in Malaysia are more likely to express patriotic sentiments than are persons who identify with the minority nonreligious or religious communities. Religion can create a bifurcated loyalty, in short, but it is less likely to do so for members of the religious majority when the state adopts and/or manipulates that religious tradition for its own ends.

States with secular nationalism as their model, by comparison, will either breed anti-state hostility or religion will be a nonfactor in explaining levels of nationalism. Throughout much of the twentieth century, Sunni Muslims rejected Turkey's secular nationalism and fought for a state grounded on Sunni religious principles. In such a context, we hypothesize that religiously devout Sunni Muslims would have lower levels of nationalism than secular Turks. As the Turkish state embraces more religious principles, however, the roles might well be reversed. Once again, the religious ideology remains constant, while state policies and the attitudes of political elites change. In other states with secular nationalism, however, religion is not so much opposed as it is ignored. Thus, Estonia's secular nationalism was not forged to counter the power of religion, but was instead constructed in a context in which few people were actively religious. In Estonia religion will have no bearing on predicting levels of individual nationalism. Looking at our cases, we predict that in both Uruguay and India, countries that forged a model of secular nationalism, religious identification should have no bearing on levels of nationalism.

Finally, we predict that civil-religious states will encourage high levels of nationalism for disparate religious traditions. The power of a civil-religious model is that it creates a strong link between nation and faith for multiple traditions. In the United States and Israel, therefore, we suggest that religious identification (irrespective of tradition in the United States and for the various Jewish groups in Israel) will increase levels of individual nationalism.

To test this claim, each of our country chapters will analyze mass-level public opinion surveys to test the relationship between levels of nationalism by religious groups and regime types. We will also use the public opinion data to test the stability or instability of the country's model of religion and nationalism. The model is stable if levels of nationalism correspond with our predictions about public opinion. For example, we suggest that religion should not be a predictor of levels of patriotism in a country with secular nationalism, precisely because those countries do not link national and religious identity. However, if there are indications at the mass level that religion is a variable in levels of nationalism, as in India for example, then the model is unstable. By contrast, a civil-religious regime is stable to the extent that levels of national devotion are similarly high for all relevant religious groups, while it is unstable if there are divergent patterns among religious groups on levels of nationalism.

In addition to public opinion data, we also test our theory through a content analysis of the periodicals of the leading religious organizations in each of our six countries. The purpose of this analysis is to determine if the primary religious groups in each of the six countries support the nationalist project in the ways that our theory predicts. As with the mass level data, we predict that the dominant religious tradition is likely to support religious nationalism in regimes with that model (Greece and Malaysia) while religious minorities will oppose it. In secular nationalist countries (Uruguay and India), by contrast, there should be no distinctive pattern in support for the state among religious groups. Finally, in civil-religious regimes (United States and Israel) we predict that the periodicals of multiple religious groups will be favorable toward the state. Once again, we will also use this data to indicate if the original model is stable or unstable, based on the observed attitudes of the major religious groups in each country.

CONCLUSION

The relationship between religion and nationalism is extraordinarily complex, both historically and in contemporary politics. Scholars of nationalism have diverged on what role, if any, religion played in nationalist movements, and those early debates have shaped understandings for how religion interacts with nationalism in the modern world. While the patterns between religion and nationalism are diverse, and have much to do with the unique history, culture, and political context in every country of the world, we nonetheless contend that three dominant paradigms prevail: religious nationalism, secular nationalism, and civil-religious nationalism. We further claim that it is the interplay among four key dynamics that shape the kind of religion–nationalism model a state adopts and retains: the role of religion in the pre-state formation period, the constitutional status of religion in the new order, the country's demographic makeup at the point of state formation and beyond, and the social and political power of religious groups in that state.

2

United States: Stable Civil-Religious Nationalism

INTRODUCTION

In a 2015 presidential campaign rally in South Carolina, then-candidate Donald Trump called for a "total and complete shutdown of Muslims entering the United States until our country's representatives can figure out what the hell is going on" (Johnson 2015). As if to demonstrate that this was not simply campaign bluster, President Trump followed through on this promise by issuing an Executive Order shortly after taking office that would have suspended the entry of immigrants from seven Muslim-majority countries for at least 90 days, barred refugee admission for 120 days, lowered the number of refugees admitted, and postponed the admission of Syrian refugees indefinitely. A few days later, Trump indicated in an interview that he would also prioritize the resettlement of Christian refugees over members of other religious groups.

One of the core claims in our book is that countries have a dominant model for the interaction of religion and nationalism. In the case of the United States, as we will see in the pages below, the framework is that of civil religion, an ideology which at its best unites people of diverging religious traditions into a shared set of political commitments and values. President Trump's Executive Order challenged our civil-religious obligations by explicitly dividing Americans (or potential Americans) along religious lines. However, in a rare show of unity, leaders across the religious and political spectrum challenged the moral legitimacy of Trump's order. In the religious realm, Mainline Protestant, Evangelical Protestant, Catholic, Mormon, Jewish, Muslim, and Pentecostal groups opposed the order, and in their statements they typically referenced the sacred teachings of their divergent religious tradition, and the shared values of America's civil religion (Jenkins 2017).

This vignette suggests the strength and the fragility of American civil religion. American history, public opinion, and even our politics note the close link between nationalism and religion in the United States. The question is, why? We argue that a key factor in determining the relationship between religion and nationalism within a nation state is the role and status of religion at the point of state formation. Specifically, we are interested in three interrelated aspects of religion as a new state forms: the role of religion in the ideology of the emerging political elite, the constitutional status of religion in the new order, and the country's demographic makeup at the point of state formation. In the United States, each worked to advance a civil-religious nationalism, as opposed to a nationalism linked to a particular tradition or to a secular vision.

Religious elites in the United States largely supported the political break from England, and even provided spiritual rationale for political independence. In contrast with a country like France, there was no significant anticlerical component to the American Revolution. Since it was not a danger to the emerging state, religion could be infused in the national ethos and secular nationalism never found a strong voice in the new American Republic.

The constitutional order created, however, did not establish a particular religion (at least at the national level), and the formal ties between religion and the state were few. For both prudential and ideological reasons, most framers opposed official ties between church and state, but they fully supported the idea that religious values and practices would aid the new nation. This encouraged the development of nationalism based on widely shared cultural values that linked the cause of the nation and the cause of religion together. In the United States, religious persons trained themselves to see their spiritual mission in nationalistic terms, but they did so without the complications inherent in a constitutional system that formalized those connections. Freed from that constraint, and the political conflicts inherent in it, religion could work its magic at a cultural level to become what de Tocqueville famously described as "the first" of America's political institutions.

Finally, while a large percentage of Americans were Christians at the founding, they were divided into multiple denominations, a trend that would only be exacerbated as the decades progressed. The multiplicity of sects, along with a political culture that encouraged the formation of many more, meant that religious leaders sought points of cultural and moral agreement with their religious counterparts. As a consequence, a nonsectarian nationalism formed that proved to be relatively open to religious newcomers.

Once solidified, these political structures and cultural patterns created a path-dependent process that shaped future understandings of religion and nationalism in the United States, even in the face of profound social and political changes. A remarkable aspect of that story is the degree to which religious interpretations of the country's mission – along with implicit or explicit assertions about which religious groups could or could not be good citizens – have expanded over time. The result has been that new religious groups have been enfolded into the canopy of the country's sacred mission. But much of this process was unplanned. At different moments in American history, religious majorities have questioned the patriotic bona fides of Roman Catholics, Lutherans, Jews, Mormons, and Muslims, not to mention African Americans and Native Americans. Religious majorities periodically sought to use the political process to institutionalize their particular values, and they questioned whether religious outsiders could be socialized into American values. However, constitutional norms limited the opportunities for political mischief by the religious majority, while the rhetoric of religious liberty proved to be a cudgel that could be used by religious minorities to stake their claim as both religious and American. And even though these challenges threatened to undermine the model, the ultimate effect was to strengthen even further the bonds between these two institutions.

The purpose of this chapter is to outline relations between religion and nationalism in the United States. We offer a historical overview of this process and an analysis of contemporary public opinion data on questions related to their interaction on the most salient nationalistic project of the United States over the past decade: the War in Iraq. We contend that patterns established at the time of state formation continue to be of crucial importance to contemporary understandings of religion and nationalism.

RELIGIOUS ELITES AND NATIONALISM AT THE FOUNDING

In a sermon from 1785, Samuel Wales, a Congregational Minister and Professor of Divinity at Yale, spoke for most Americans when he said: "true patriotism is a branch of that extensive benevolence which is highly recommended by our holy religion" (Wales 1785:850). For Wales, religious faith and national commitments reinforced each other. In theory and often in practice, American nationalism is premised on the conception that membership in the political community follows from the acceptance of certain fundamental values and institutions. This civic notion of nationalism excludes prescriptive criteria to define what it is to be an American. Such a conception, however, has to acknowledge that religion, which can be a very prescriptive category, was important at the nation's founding and remains important today. How, then, did a liberal, ideas-based conception of nationalism take hold in a nation filled with religious persons of particular persuasions?

The answer to that question at the founding was that civic norms and religious values reinforced each other, and they did so under the common banner of civic republicanism. As Mark Noll argues, there was at the founding a widespread assumption "that republican principles expressed Christian values and hence could be defended with Christian fervor" (Noll 1992:116). The republican idea of the corrupting influence of unchecked powers mirrored complaints against the national church coming first from the Puritans and later from the fast-growing dissenting sects, republican notions of natural rights found parallels in the Protestant commitment to religious liberty, and both traditions emphasized the importance of freedom, individual choice, and civic virtue (Noll 2002: chapter 4; Witte and Nichols 2011:33–36). In a 1780 sermon, Congregational minister Samuel Cooper suggested that the free republic which America had recently established matched that which God had created with the Israelites:

The form of government originally established in the Hebrew nation by a charter from heaven, was that of a free republic ... Even the law of Moses, though framed by God himself, was not imposed upon the people against their will; it was laid open before the whole congregation of Israel; they freely adopted it, and it became their law, not only by divine appointment, but by their own voluntary and express consent.

(Cooper 1780:634)

While this might be a creative interpretation of God's covenant with the Israelites, it nonetheless demonstrates how religious elites effortlessly understood political values in religious terms.

The language of and commitment to religious and political liberty similarly made its way into religious rhetoric. In his 1784 Thanksgiving sermon, Presbyterian minister George Duffield linked republican and Christian values when he affirmed about America: "Here has our God erected a banner of civil and religious liberty" (Duffield 1784:783). In the minds of religious leaders, political and religious liberties were theological requirements as much as they were a political necessity. As Congregational minister Samuel Cooper contended, "a Constitution that respects civil and religious liberty in general ought to be regarded as a solemn recognition from the Supreme Ruler himself of the rights of human nature" (Cooper 1780:636). Time and again, these religious leaders bonded the cause of nation and religion together, and in so doing they established a pattern that generations of religionists would largely follow. Far from challenging each other, patriotism and religious faith were knit from the same cloth.

There were some loyalists, particularly among the Anglican clergy, and a small number of pacifists who questioned both the revolution and God's purposes for the new nation (Noll 1992:122). At their 1774 annual meeting, for example, the Quakers affirmed that they were "indebted to the King and to his royal ancestors, for the continued favour of enjoying our religious liberties ... and we discourage every attempt which may be made by any to excite disaffection or disrespect to him" (quoted in Gaustad 1982:238). Others offered the contrasting visions of religious nationalism married to a particular tradition, or secular nationalism devoid of any religious content (Gorski 2017:16–30).

Those voices, however, were outliers in a sea of religious support for the Revolution. Representative of this religious perspective was the leadership provided by John Witherspoon. Witherspoon was elected to the Continental Congress in 1774 and signed the Declaration of Independence. He later became a professor and then the President of Princeton where he trained numerous political leaders in the new Republic, including James Madison. In a 1776 sermon, Witherspoon "embraced the opportunity of declaring my opinion without any hesitation, that the cause in which America is now in arms, is the cause of justice, of liberty, and of human nature" (Witherspoon 1776:549). Support among the leading clergy for the American Revolution also helped the United States to avoid the fate of the Catholic Church in revolutionary France. In contrast with its French counterpart, the American Revolution was not anticlerical, anti-church, or anti-religious. By the time the revolution had been won, even the dissenting religious voices had largely been drowned out.

The orthodox Christian view that God works through history provided another way for religious leaders to offer a spiritual interpretation for the nation's founding and destiny. In his 1784 Constitution Day sermon, Congregational Minister Samuel McClintock asserted that "the divine hand hath been signally displayed in the events and occurrences which led to it [the revolution]" (McClintock 1784:798). In a similar vein, Samuel Wales reasoned that "a proper view of all of our various blessings will lead us to conclude that we are indeed the most highly favored people under heaven. God hath not dealt so with any other nation" (Wales 1785:840). Given such claims, it is hardly surprising that there was little space between civic and religious notions of what it meant to be an American.

The practical effect for most churches in the early years of the Republic was that they preached a seamless message of national and religious purpose. Typical of this attitude was a Pastoral Letter from the Presbyterian Synod of the Carolinas (1790) that urged members of its churches to "revere the government under which you live ... teach your children the constitution of your country; inform them that we, and they with us, were in the design of our enemies, Pharaoh's bond-men, and that the Lord brought us out of Egypt with a mighty hand." The Congregational Minister John Lathrop (1799) echoed this sentiment in his Fast Day Sermon when he noted: "as we are bound by the law of God, to love our neighbors as ourselves, so we are bound to love our country." It was thus largely taken for granted by most American Christians that good citizenship was a religious virtue.

Religious and political elites further reinforced the symbiotic relationship between spiritual and national commitments when they linked national prosperity with virtue. In a Thanksgiving Day Address, Lathrop also confirmed that "political liberty depends on national virtue" (Lathrop 1787:878). This perspective was largely shared by the Founders, many of whom were Deists rather than orthodox Christians. They may not have believed in a personal God, but they certainly saw the benefits of a union of religion and political values. John Adams expressed such a perspective in an 1811 letter to his friend Benjamin Rush: "religion and virtue are the only foundations, not only of republicanism and of all free government" (Adams 1856). Article 3 of the 1787 Northwest Ordinance made a similar point in justifying the creation of schools in the Northwest Territories: "Religion, morality, and knowledge, being necessary to good government and the happiness of mankind, schools and the means of education shall forever be encouraged" (Northwest Ordinance 1787).

RELIGIOUS DEMOGRAPHICS AND EMERGENT NATIONALISM

As we noted in the previous chapter, religious nationalism is most likely to occur in religiously monolithic countries where religion is socially and politically strong. By these measures one might have expected America to develop this kind of nationalist frame. America was relatively religious; although only an estimated 17 percent of the population were formal church members in 1776 (Finke and Stark 1989), this figure underestimates the true religiosity of the society. At a cultural level, Christianity was much more influential than official membership statistics might imply and "helped to define the context of American political life" (Wald and Calhoun-Brown 2007:39). America was also, by one measure, religiously homogenous as the overwhelming majority of Americans were Protestant. Moreover, some states developed the kind of close alliances between religion and the government that is symptomatic of religious nationalism. Taxes in Massachusetts, for example, supported the established Congregational Church and those who declined to support the state church went to jail. Philip Gorski (2017:58) notes that America "teetered back and forth between civil religion and religious nationalism," and he concludes that religious nationalism is "but a small stream within the revolutionary torrent" (61).

It remained a small stream in part because of religious demographics. While Protestantism largely prevailed, Americans were very much divided into the differing camps of Congregationalists, Presbyterians, Baptists, and Episcopalians, each with between 15 and 20 percent of all religious adherents. There were also a smaller number of Methodists and Roman Catholics, and an even smaller number of Quakers, Lutherans, and Jews. Thus, demographic conditions in the United States encouraged the formation of civil-religious nationalism across multiple traditions, rather than a religious nationalism that promoted a single branch even of the Christian faith. The nationalism that emerged would therefore be shorn of religiously prescriptive ties, a marked contrast with those countries that had an established church with its implicit understanding that membership in a particular tradition was a prerequisite for genuine nationalism.

Moreover, Christian leaders promoted points of cultural and political agreement among their coreligionists of different denominations. In his 1776 sermon, Witherspoon urged his listeners to reject "a furious and angry zeal for the circumstantials of religion, or the contentions of one sect with another about their peculiar distinctions." The "surer marks of the reality of religion [is] when a man feels himself more joined in spirit to a true holy person of another denomination, than to an irregular liver of his own" (Witherspoon 1776:554). In a sermon preached before a convention of the Episcopal Church, William Smith (1784:826) recommended a focus on the "evangelic grace of [Christian] charity" which united fellow believers rather than "in all the doubtful questions over which Protestant churches have been puzzling themselves." He further noted that what the country most needed was "the pious assistance and united support of all her true sons, and of the friends of Christianity in general" (Smith 1784:829). While acknowledging a "diversity of sentiment" among religionists in America, the Congregationalist minister Samuel Cooper similarly urged a "happy union of all denominations in support of our government" (Cooper 1780:656).

Founders such as Washington and Adams made similar claims. In his Farewell Address, Washington reminded Americans that the patriotism that united them should be stronger than the religion that might divide them: "The name of American, which belongs to you in your national capacity, must always exalt the just pride of patriotism more than any appellation derived from local discriminations. With slight shades of difference, you have the same religion, manners, habits, and political principles" (Washington 1796). Seen in the right way, Washington suggests, all religions are essentially the same, and they preach from the same prayer book of patriotism. The point is that there were precious few religious or political elites pushing for a more narrow religious nationalism.

The Second Great Awakening challenged this tidy consensus. This movement introduced a much more personalistic Protestantism that was evangelistic and promoted moral reform. As Martin Marty (1976) put it, the religious landscape of the country moved from emphasizing belief to concentrating on behavior. Such a perspective, at least in the short run, was religiously divisive: Evangelical "true believers" seemed to be trying to sort Americans into warring camps of the faithful and infidels. This effort could similarly have easily undermined the unifying force of America's civil-religious nationalism. Yet at a political level, even those who advocated such a "Christian politics" remained remarkably ecumenical in whom they viewed as allies.

One of the most controversial sermons of the early nineteenth century was Ezra Stiles Ely's *The Duty of Christian Freemen to Elect Christian Rulers*, which he gave on July 4, 1827. In that homily, Ely called for the establishment of a Christian political party, counseled his listeners to vote against Deists, and urged his audience to "promote Christianity by electing and supporting as public officers the friends of our blessed Savior" (Ely 1827:552). Ely's target was the incumbent President and likely Unitarian, John Quincy Adams (Kabala 2013:45). By Ely's light a Unitarian could not be a true friend of Christianity, and in his mind it was the duty of faithful Christians to reject suspect Unitarians as political leaders. Nonetheless, Ely managed to include in his politically acceptable camp "all who profess to be Christians of any denomination" (Ely 1827:556). Restrictive he might have been, in short, but Ely's nationalist vision nonetheless embraced nearly all of the Protestant denominations of the time. Moreover, the winning denominations in the Second Great Awakening were precisely those that shared his vision, while those he was excluding were dying out as a viable electoral bloc. Thus, during this initial challenge to the model, the unifying features of civil religion prevailed in the end.

While the Framers tied notions of civic virtue to religion, it was a generalized religion, not religion in its particularistic forms that the framers had in mind (Monsma 2012:45–58). The rather indiscriminate nature of this fusion encouraged religionists of varying denominations to define themselves into the national ethos rather than out of it. The result was the development of a civil religion where faith and patriotism were two sides of the same coin. As Hugh Heclo (2007:32) notes, Americans were constructing a "public religion, speaking of God in a way that unified rather than divided." It was a public religion where denominations dropped their doctrinal distinctions and absolutist claims. Only in this way could Christianity, which had historically been the locus for so much religious and political conflict, be "made safe for democracy" (Heclo 2007:64).

RELIGION IN THE CONSTITUTION

The status of religion in the new state reflected this civil-religious nationalism. Religion is hardly mentioned in the Constitution that was ratified in 1789. Article 6 forbids religious tests for holding public office, and in gesture to Quakers and others who believed that the Bible forbade the swearing of oaths, the Constitution allows those taking the oath of office to "affirm" rather than "swear" their allegiance (Gaustad and Smidt 2002:126). Other than that, religion is not cited in the Constitution. Nor is there any evidence that religion was a topic at all among the delegates at the Constitutional Convention in Philadelphia that drafted the Constitution (Larson and Winship 2005). The First Amendment, which was added shortly thereafter, famously forbids Congress from making a law "respecting an establishment of religion, or prohibiting the free exercise thereof." While the Constitution disestablished religion at the national level, a few states maintained established religions after the ratification of the Constitution, others restricted elected offices to Protestants, some maintained tax support for ministers, and many applied the concept of religious liberty selectively (Gaustad and Schmidt 2002:131). Over time, however, such overt religiously discriminatory policies dissipated, religious tests for public office at the state level were largely abandoned, tax support for ministers disappeared, and by 1833 all states had dropped their religious establishments.

The First Amendment was both a practical response to demographic reality and a principled commitment to religious liberty. As we noted above, given the nation's pluralism an established church was impractical, and the framers well understood how politically explosive any movement in that direction would have been. Moreover, a growing number of religious and political thinkers advocated the spiritual virtues of both religious liberty and of church–state separation. Many American Protestants had chafed at the powers accorded the established Church of England, and from the more secular side thinkers like Jefferson and Madison famously defended disestablishment and religious liberty in their debates on Virginia's "Bill for Establishing Religious Freedom" (Sikkenga 2010).

The First Amendment was not, however, an attack on religion; nor was it meant to denude the role that most religious and political leaders assumed that Protestant Christianity would play in the new nation (Neuhaus 1984). Over the next several decades, in fact, Protestant values deeply shaped public policy on such matters as Sunday closing laws, the promotion of education, and public morals, to name a few. A religious establishment was neither plausible nor attractive to most, but unity under a common Christian morality was. This allowed for the creation of what James Kabala (2013:2) describes as a "quasi-official non-sectarian Protestant Christianity." This unofficial religion shaped both public policy and the national values of the country's civil religion.

None of this is to minimize the very real points of political conflict that developed among religious groups in America. The dominant religious traditions at the founding (Congregationalists, Presbyterians, and Episcopalians) faced intense competition from religious upstarts like the Methodists, Disciples of Christ, and various Baptist groups (Hatch 1989). To stem the tide, the majority traditions often turned to the state to try to restrict their religious competition (Finke and Stark 2005). Had those efforts prevailed, a more restrictive understanding of religious nationalism might have developed. Over time, intense political persecution would no doubt have soured the Baptists and the Methodists on the political project and led them to reject a necessary connection between their religious and patriotic commitments. But in the end, the state proved unwilling or unable fully to suppress the religious newcomers, and in short order they became the new dominant traditions and civil religion as the basis for religious nationalism survived.

IMMIGRATION AND THE CHALLENGE TO CIVIL-RELIGIOUS NATIONALISM

An even more disruptive challenge to this civil-religious nationalism came from the immigration of large numbers of Roman Catholics, Lutherans, Jews, and other minority groups in the nineteenth century (Smith 1997:349–57). America's civil-religious nationalism was relatively open at the founding, but it was implicitly Protestant. Given the religious makeup at the time this was hardly surprising. While there were a few Roman Catholics and Jews at the time of the Constitution's ratification, the country was overwhelmingly Protestant, albeit of various denominations. The Second Great Awakening had demonstrated that these sects could divide religiously while remaining unified in their abstract national feeling. How would the status quo Protestant majority see new religious groups fitting into America's nationalism, and how would religious believers outside of this largely Protestant consensus experience this civil-religious discourse?

Some religious and political leaders responded by asserting the Protestant character of the nation's religious mission, and a more particularistic religious nationalism. Immigrant Catholics and Jews, along with the homegrown Mormon movement, could not be good citizens or patriots, some claimed, because their religion inculcated in them values inconsistent with republican government. Republicanism required everything that Protestantism provided: educated citizens committed to liberty, self-government, and church–state separation. By contrast, these other religions supposedly produced citizens with little education, mixed loyalties, and no firm commitment to or familiarity with republican principles. Because of their large numbers, Roman Catholics bore the brunt of this charge. An editorial from an Amherst New Hampshire newspaper, *The Farmers' Cabinet*, expressed precisely this fear: "Romanism sends into every city, town, and village, its forked-tongued priests; it commands its devotees to make a reservation in all its oaths of allegiance, in favor of the Holy Mother Church, it nurtures treason under the guise of religion" (*The* Farmers' Cabinet 1853). In a similar vein the *New Englander and*

Yale Review reported that "It [Roman Catholicism] is associated with the most arbitrary principles of government, and with sweeping and bloody persecutions. Their ecclesiastical system owns for its head a foreign potentate" (New Englander and Yale Review 1844:234).

One of the most popular and representative nativist works of the nineteenth century that expressed this religious nationalism, the Reverend Josiah Strong's *Our Country*, was published by a bastion of American Protestantism, the American Home Missionary Society. In that work, Strong argued that the main perils facing the country's future were immigration, Mormonism, and Romanism. What particularly concerned Strong about the latter was its purported rejection of what he called the "foundation stone(s) of our free institutions": liberty of conscience, religious liberty, free speech and church–state separation (Strong 1885:48). All of this led Strong to conclude that there were "irreconcilable differences between papal principles and the fundamental principles of free institutions" (Strong 1885:53). The Right Reverend William Goswell Doane, Episcopal Bishop of Albany, worried about American Catholic political loyalties: "And if the question ever came, which God forbid, between their yielding obedience to the American republican principles, or obedience to the Roman authority, large numbers of them would be almost compelled to surrender political loyalty to what they thought the higher law" (Doane 1894:38).

Simply perusing the titles of books and tracts from that era demonstrates the degree of animosity directed toward the Roman Catholic Church. Thomas E. Watson, the Populist Party vice-presidential candidate in 1896 and later a Senator from Georgia, penned a book with the not-so-subtle title *The Roman Catholic Hierarchy: The Deadliest Menace to American Liberties and Christian Civilization* (Watson 1912). Melville Grant's (1921) early twentieth-century volume *Americanism vs. Roman Catholicism* was so popular that it went through three editions. Writing under the auspices of the American Protestant Historical Society, Saxby Vouler Penfold (1926) used the title of his book to affirm *Why a Roman Catholic Cannot be President of the United States*. When it was not lynching or otherwise terrorizing African Americans, the Ku Klux Klan (KKK) found time to target Roman Catholics as well. Early in his tenure as Imperial Wizard of the Ku Klux Klan, Hiram Wesley Evans (1924) wrote a tract entitled *The Public School Problem in America: Outlining Fully the Policies and the Program of the Knights of Ku Klux Klan*, in which he detailed the threat posed by Catholic education and praised the alternative offered by the KKK.

American Jews faced similar accusations. Suspicion of Jewish loyalties was a common anti-Semitic trope, but it was relatively muted in the United States when Jews were few. The immigration of a larger numbers of Jews in the nineteenth century, however, brought the assertion of the supposed divided loyalties of the Jews more to the forefront. Debate about the "Jewish Question" led Goldwin Smith, himself an immigrant from England, Professor of history at both Oxford and Cornell Universities, to argue – in the pages of the prestigious *North American Review* – that "it is impossible that a man should be heartily loyal to two nationalities at once; and so long as a trace of Jewish nationality remains the Jew cannot be a thorough American" (Smith 1891:142). For Smith and many other anti-Semites, Jews were a "parasitic race ... [that] retains a marked and repellent nationalism of their own" (Smith 1891:137).

Such prejudiced views were freighted with grave political implications. One of the more prominent if short-lived groups was the anti-immigrant and anti-Catholic Know Nothing Party. The group advocated dramatic restriction on Catholic immigration, supported limitations on alcohol, and promoted policies that would have required civil servants to be native-born. The party swept to state-wide victory in Massachusetts in 1854 and secured 40 percent of the vote in Pennsylvania in the same year. Millard Fillmore, the preferred candidate of most of this alliance, likewise garnered over 20 percent of the popular ballots in the 1856 presidential election (Anbinder 1992). The overwhelming success of the Blaine Amendments further threatened to divide Americans of different religions in the years after the Civil War. This state legislation prohibited any funding of parochial – especially Catholic – schools (DeForrest 2003). The religious divisions, in short, were real, and they manifested themselves in social movements and divisions between the political parties of the day (Kleppner 1970; Higham 1988).

In hindsight, it is easy to dismiss these overwrought nativist claims, but from their standpoint there was some degree of plausibility to them. Protestants had married republican and religious claims. In that union, religious liberty, opposition to established churches, and the sovereignty of the people were both civic and religious values. There was, to be sure, nothing inherent in interpreting the faith in that way, and in many ways these Protestants were abandoning their Calvinist heritage with its emphasis on the sovereignty of God, rather than the sovereignty of the individual (Noll 1992:355). Nonetheless, in making the connections between religious and republican values, these Protestants knit together a civil-religious nationalism that required adherence to particular political principles; religious traditions that did not naturally embrace them would have their patriotic bona fides questioned. Moreover, implied in this critique was an assumption that the distinct religious practices of these newer communities made them resistant to assimilation.

This assertion put religious immigrants in an impossible bind. They could question republican values in light of their religious commitments and thereby reinforce claims that they were insufficiently patriotic, or they could embrace those political norms at the risk of losing the distinctiveness of their religious tradition. At the elite level, some highlighted the tension. *The Syllabus of Errors* issued by Pope Pius IX in 1864 catalogued a series of propositions the church had condemned throughout the nineteenth century. Among the doctrines proscribed by the church were the separation of church and state, religious liberty, and freedom of conscience. As John Noonon notes, "what is incontestable is that in absolute terms, without qualification as to context, the pope pronounced freedom of conscience and freedom of religion to be pernicious errors" (Noonan 2005:149). Conservative views in the American church had a strong voice at the end of the nineteenth century. One way that this expressed itself was in terms of sympathy for "Romanist" versus "Americanist" values. Thomas Scott Preston, vicar general for Archbishop Corrigan of New York, contended in a letter that "here in New York we are loyal Catholics. We are devoted to the Holy See, we do not believe in the great folly and absurdity of Americanizing the Catholic Church. We propose to Catholicize America" (quoted in Byrne 1995:313).

A similar concern was expressed in portions of the American Jewish community. Arthur Ruppin, an early Zionist thinker, lamented that the typical Jewish immigrant to the United States "submits himself absolutely to the influence of American culture, which in a few decades, or at least in one or two generations, lures him away from Judaism, or at any rate weakens its hold that a formal profession is all that remains" (Ruppin 1913:12). In a 1917 sermon titled *Crisis*, Reformed Rabbi James G. Heller similarly noted that "assimilation and intermarriage, alienation and indifference, have grown with alarming rapidity in exactly those countries where freedom has come to the Jew" (Heller 1917). Orthodox Jewish leaders were even more insistent that American Jews had lost their way in embracing American values (Cohen 2008:112–117). In expressing these concerns Catholics and Jews did not see themselves as undermining American nationalism, instead they were implicitly questioning the compatibility of their faith with some of the political values and social norms of America's civil religion.

Anxieties about a possible conflict between religious and national identity were, however, expressed by only a small number of religious leaders; the overwhelming majority of religious newcomers married their spiritual and nationalistic values. Like Protestants before them, Catholic and Jewish religious leaders rejected the claim that there was anything intrinsic in their faith that qualified their patriotism, and they embraced many of the republican values that Protestants claimed they could not naturally support. In response to the charge that Catholics rejected church–state separation, for example, John England, the First Catholic Bishop of Charleston asserted that "the decision upon the question of the expediency as to the form of government for temporal or civil concerns is one to be settled by society and not by the church" (England 1837). In terms of the claim that Roman Catholics owed their ultimate allegiance to the pope, a letter from the *Catholic Telegraph* signed simply by "a Catholic" stated that "it must be apparent that any idea of the Roman Catholics being in any way under the influence of any foreign ecclesiastical power, or indeed of any church authority, in the exercise of their civil rights, is a serious mistake" (Catholic Telegraph 1842). John Ireland, Archbishop of Saint Paul, stated:

there is no conflict between the Catholic Church and America. The Church is the mother of my faith, America is my country, the protectress of my liberty and of my fortunes on earth ... When I assert as I now solemnly do that the principles of the Church are in thorough harmony with the interests of the Republic, I know in the depths of my soul that I speak the truth.

(Ireland 1905:10)

Orestes Brownson (1852:381), a prominent transcendentalist and Catholic convert, even suggested that Roman Catholicism provided a firmer foundation for the preservation of Republican values than did Protestantism: "the Roman Catholic religion is necessary to sustain popular liberty, because popular liberty can be sustained only by a religion free from popular control, above the people." In this way, Catholic leaders were reinforcing what Alexis de Tocqueville (1969[1830]:288) had observed in American Catholics nearly a half century earlier. Finally, while there were clear divisions among the American church hierarchy, few of them embraced the papal condemnations in the *Syllabus of Errors*, and many of them worked to reassure Americans of their loyalty to American political principles (McGreevey 2003:118–120). In doing so, they were setting a trajectory by which the church would eventually embrace those values, though it would take nearly a century for that position to be fully incorporated by the Church.

The response of American Jewish leaders was overwhelmingly to fuse religious and national sentiment. A study of nineteenth-century rabbis in the United States (Cohen 2008) demonstrates that Jewish clergy promoted American values and worked to show the compatibility of Americanism and Jewish identity. Rabbi Isaac Mayer Wise, a Jewish immigrant and one of the founders of Reformed Judaism, understood his religious reform efforts as part of a larger project to Americanize Jews (Gaustad and Smidt 2002:214). At a conference of reformed leaders that he chaired in 1885, Wise helped to adopt the Pittsburgh Platform that articulated the principles of Reformed Judaism. One of the planks of that platform stated "we consider ourselves no longer a nation, but a religious community" (Pittsburgh Platform 1885). The implication was that Jews were no more a separate nation than any other religious community in the United States. In answer to his own rhetorical question "does the Jewish religion forbid patriotic sentiments and actions?" Rabbi Isaac Schwab defied "any one to prove it from the Bible or the Talmud" (Schwab 1878:4).

Religious leaders spared no effort to demonstrate their fealty to American values and to America. In his work entitled *American and Catholicism*, Catholic Church historian Frederick Joseph Kinsman (1924:152) noted that "the Catholic body is sometimes looked upon as an alien element in the land," but he assured his readers that "Catholics cannot be, and never have been, otherwise than wholeheartedly loyal to America ... It is assumed [by Catholics] that American institutions are in conformity with the law of God." The B'nai B'rith commissioned a statue on religious liberty that it dedicated to the people of the United States on Thanksgiving Day 1876, and placed at Fairmount Park in Philadelphia. Twenty-nine years later, also on Thanksgiving Day, American Jewish leaders celebrated the 250th anniversary of the settlement of the first Jews in the United States. In his address at the celebration Lee M. Friedman, President of the American Jewish Historical Society, commented that "not merely as Jews, but as American citizens, we have gathered here tonight to testify to the underlying loyalty and altruistic patriotism of the Jewish citizens to the great American ideals of liberty and democracy" (American Jewish Historical Society 1906). Echoing Heclo's argument noted above, religion was made safe for American democracy by denuding it of its distinctive features that might have challenged the spiritual affirmation of patriotism, and of America's civil-religious nationalism.

While some politicians found fertile electoral ground in nativist rants and in promoting a Protestant religious nationalism, others reached the opposite conclusion and extended their hand out to Catholics and Jews.

As part of the celebration for the 250th anniversary for Jews in America, congratulatory letters were read to the assembled audience from the Mayor of New York, the Governor of New York, former President Grover Cleveland, and current President Theodore Roosevelt. In his letter, Roosevelt wrote that "the Jews of the United States have become indissolubly incorporated in the great army of American citizenship, prepared to make all sacrifice for the country, either in war or peace, and striving for the perpetuation of good government and for the maintenance of the principles embodied in the Constitution" (American Jewish Historical Society 1906).

Nativism and religious nationalism also failed because they made interlocking claims that were not easily reconciled. On the one hand, nativists asserted that Catholics and others posed a danger to American values, at the same time that they affirmed the value of religious liberty which presumably guaranteed Catholics and others the right to practice their faith. This inconsistency offered an avenue for new religionists to affirm American values and thereby to challenge nativists on their own grounds. An editorial from the *Catholic Telegraph* intoned that "every enlightened patriot and every sincere admirer of that best of earthly blessings, the undisturbed and secured possession of civil and religious liberty, must behold with deep regret and melancholy foreboding for our country ... the spirit of sectarian prejudice" (*Catholic Telegraph* 1835). The same Thomas Scott Preston who had defended "Romanist" values later noted that "the Constitution of the United States guarantees to every citizen the perfect freedom of religion; and that great charter must fail and pass away err any State can frame laws which abridge or take away that freedom" (Preston 1870:8). The suggestion in both cases is that nativists are the enemies of religious liberty (and by implication of American values) because of their zeal to deny that right to Roman Catholics.

In his aptly titled work from 1878, *Can Jews Be Patriots?* Rabbi Isaac Schwab (1878:14) similarly argued that "the foreigner having settled in that land and interwoven his interests with those of the native citizens, will just as heartily be devoted to it as they, provided we have equal rights and liberties untainted by sectarian prejudice." It is the sectarianism of the nativists and of the Protestant religious nationalists, Schwab suggests, that threatens religious liberty, though he also implies that the denial of that right to Jews might understandably qualify their commitment to the new land. The point is that religious outsiders consistently used the power of religious liberty rhetoric to assert their right to be understood as fully American.

Public schools remained a contentious site of controversy among religious groups. We already noted the success of the Blaine Amendments around the country at the end of the nineteenth century. After America entered the First World War, anti-German (and by implication anti-Lutheran and anti-Catholic) hysteria spread. Many states banned the teaching of German in public schools, while Ohio, Iowa, and Nebraska went even further and forbade the teaching of German in public or in private schools, a law that the Supreme Court would overturn in its 1919 decision *Meyer v. Nebraska* (Capozzola 2008). In its opinion the court highlighted the Constitutional/American values of liberty and the right to worship God according to the dictates of one's own conscience. A few years later in *Pierce v. Society of Sisters*, the court similarly overturned an Oregon law mandating that all children attend public school through twelfth grade. Even when they lost the political battle, religious minorities nonetheless used the language of constitutional rights to assert their position. Like many school districts around the country, the Chaddo Parish School Board in Louisiana proposed religious exercise in its public schools in the early twentieth century. In an address opposing that policy which he titled "Is this a Christian Country?," Rabbi Moses Jacobson argued that the policy was "in direct conflict" with the state and federal Constitution, and that it was "not as a Jew, but as an American that I am opposing this measure" (Jacobson 1913). For more than a half century Jacobson's argument fell on deaf ears, but he articulated his opposition to this policy in terms of widely shared constitutional values.

We noted earlier in this chapter the key role played by religious elites, the constitutional status of religion in the new order, and the country's demographic makeup at the point of state formation as factors that contributed to civil-religious nationalism. Even in the midst of political battles brought on by widespread immigration, those same factors continued to reinforce that civil-religious model. The country was even more religiously diverse at the turn of the twentieth century than it had been at the turn of the nineteenth, thus undermining a nationalist ideology linked to a particular religious tradition. While clearly open to diverse interpretations, the Constitution nonetheless limited the capacity of the religious majority to forge particularistic links with the state or to restrict the rights of religious minorities. Even a "conservative" Supreme Court would overturn policies that had the effect of abandoning those religious rights. Finally, religious elites from the newer traditions fused their religious and national identities much as their Protestant forbears had done. The result was that religious immigrants abandoned any notions that their religious identity necessarily trumped or challenged their national one.

TRIUMPH OF CIVIL-RELIGIOUS NATIONALISM FROM THE COLD WAR TO THE WAR ON TERROR

In a 1952 speech before the Freedoms Foundation, President Eisenhower famously quipped that "our government has no sense unless it is founded in a deeply felt religious faith, and I don't care what it is." Eisenhower was not so much advocating a superficial religion, as he was suggesting that religion was part of the American creed that myriad American faiths could embrace and contribute to that creed, and that in so doing religion could unite Americans around a common understanding of their place in history. What began as a nonsectarian Protestant nationalism at the time of the nation's founding, became by the end of the 1950s a civil-religion that embraced Catholics and Jews (Chapp 2012:18–32).

No period in American history more fully institutionalized this civil-religious nationalism than the decade of the 1950s. Among the highlights of this ten-year stretch was the passage of a congressional proclamation calling on the president to set aside a day for national prayer, which every president has subsequently done. Congress passed a law that added the phrase "In God We Trust" to postage stamps and to paper money for the first time in the country's history, while another law added the line "under God" to the Pledge of Allegiance. The National Prayer Breakfast was established in 1953, and Eisenhower set a precedent followed by all future presidents by attending and speaking at the event (Kruse 2015:chapters 2–5).

At the time, none of these actions was politically controversial, and religious leaders of all the major traditions embraced them. They were perceived not as sectarian attempts to divide Americans, but as lowest common denominator spiritual affirmations to unite them. The various forms of public religiosity during the period included the participation of myriad religious groups, thereby reinforcing what Kevin Kruse (2015:74) has described as the "postwar emphasis on ecumenical religious senti-ment." The 1950s also marked a surge in religious observance, and one without a partisan cast to it (Putnam and Campbell 2010:83–5). Without question, the shared external threat of "atheistic communism" united religionists of all stripes and in that respect the Cold War did much to reinforce America's civil-religious nationalism. However, the seeds of that response had already been sown decades before, both at the point of the nation's founding and during the supposed "immigrant threat." The Cold War thus strengthened rather than created this civil-religious model.

Furthering solidifying the unifying potential of this model was the changing role of Roman Catholics in American politics. At the mass level, nothing proved more symbolically important than the election of the country's first Roman Catholic President, John F. Kennedy, in 1960. While it seems ironic from a twenty-first century standpoint where Evangelical Protestants chafe against the policy implications of church–state separation, numerous Protestant leaders actively opposed Kennedy's election and reignited concerns about the incompatibility of Catholic and American values, including the principle of church–state separation. In his famous address before the Greater Houston Ministerial Association, Kennedy tried to put those fears to rest when he affirmed, "I believe in an America where the separation of church and state is absolute – where no Catholic prelate would tell the President (should he be Catholic) how to act." Kennedy's election, assassination, and the outpouring of public grief over a new American martyr limited any subsequent political mobilization along anti-Catholic lines.

Concomitant with this change at the mass level were developments among Catholic elites. As we noted earlier in the chapter, leaders of the American church in the eighteenth and nineteenth centuries demonstrated their fidelity to core American principles. However, they did so within a Catholic Church whose doctrine opposed such key ideals as popular sovereignty, religious freedom, and church–state separation. Like many of their American Catholic predecessors, Avery Dulles (Carey 2010) and John Courtney Murray made a strong case for the compatibility of Catholic principles and American values. Murray described the First Amendment's religious clauses as "articles of peace" which provided a practical and theological solution to the "problem of religious pluralism" that has been "good" for both religion and for Catholicism (Murray 1960:56ff). The American Catholic, he asserted, is "entirely prepared to accept our constitutional concept of freedom of religion and the policy of no establishment" (Murray 1960:47). Murray also endorsed civil-religious nationalism when he noted that the American government "does indeed represent the commonly shared moral values of the community. It also represents the supreme religious truth expressed in the motto on American coins: 'In God we trust'" (Murray 1960:74). The Second Vatican Council affirmed many of Murray's ideas.

Civil-religious nationalism did not mean, however, that political divisions based on religion disappeared. In fact, the political unity around religion during the 1950s proved to be short-lived as the public schools once again became the location for deep political divisions among religionist who found themselves on opposing sides on issues such as prayer and bible reading in public schools (Wuthnow 1988:173–214). As with the immigrant challenge of the previous century, politicians were only too willing to demonize their enemies and paint them as un-American for their failure to accept "God's will" for the public arena. The rise of the religious right reinforced the political cleavage based on religion. What was distinctive about this new religious cleavage, however, was the degree to which it was cross-denominational and even cross-religious. Republicans and Democrats offered opposing moral visions and mobilized divergent religious coalitions. The Republicans reached out to white Evangelicals and conservative Catholics, while the Democrats organized members of black churches along with liberal Protestants and Catholics (Leege and Kellstedt 1993:3–25).

Nonetheless, contestants in this culture war could read into the American narrative a position consistent with their civil-religious impulse. The tradition is malleable enough so that different partisan groups can appeal to distinct elements of the civil-religious model. For example, in relatively good faith one side can appeal to Thomas Jefferson's line about church–state separation as the best guarantor for religious liberty, while the opposing camp will cite George Washington on the centrality of religion for the political enterprise. As we will note in the next section, Democratic President Barack Obama was likewise almost as likely to mention "God" in his presidential statements as was his Republican counterpart and the darling of the religious right, George W. Bush. Even as they bitterly divided along partisan lines over controversial social issues, in short, at a deeper cultural level, the two presidents and their respective religious constituencies were able to define themselves into and under the civil-religious canopy. Of course, as Americans in the twenty-first century increasingly abandon traditional religion, a model based on generic religiosity may well face a new kind of challenge.

After the terrorist attacks of September 11, Muslims became the latest "threat" to the civil-religious nationalist model. Like religious newcomers before them, they encountered questions about the compatibility of their religion with American values. We noted at the beginning of this chapter President Trump's Executive Order to ban the travel of persons from majority Muslim countries. The rhetoric around Muslim Americans and nationalism mirrors that of religious minorities before them. There is also some mass level data indicating support for a more restrictive religious nationalism. Thirty-nine percent of the respondents in a 2016 survey (Democracy Fund Voter Study Group 2017) indicated that it was somewhat or very important to be a Christian to be an American, one half of the respondents in a 2017 survey (Pew Research Center 2017b) said that they did not think that Islam was "a part of mainstream American society," and nearly half (44 percent) believed that there is a "conflict between Islam and democracy."

Perhaps nothing better personifies the power of anti-Muslim sentiment than the fact that President Obama spent much of his eight-year presidency rejecting the charge that he was Muslim and that he was born overseas. Donald Trump won the presidency while openly questioning both Obama's professed faith and his actual birthplace. Despite Obama's repeated affirmations that he was a Christian, nearly one third (29 percent) of all respondents in a 2015 poll and almost a majority of Republicans (43 percent) indicated that they believed Obama to be a Muslim (Agiesta 2015).

However, more than eight in ten respondents in the 2016 survey (84 percent) said that accepting people of diverse racial and religious backgrounds was important to being American. Even more important is that American Muslims are overwhelmingly adopting democratic norms and rejecting all forms of extremism. While nearly half (48percent) of American Muslims in the Pew survey indicated that they had experienced some form of religious discrimination in the previous year, 92 percent said that they were "proud to be an American," 88 percent noted that they had a lot or something in common with most Americans, and half said that someone had expressed support to them because they were Muslim. Thus, in all likelihood, the civil-religious model will eventually incorporate Muslims in the same way that it came to include Catholics and Jews.

The other contemporary challenge to American civil religion is political and demographic. As we will see in the country chapters that follow, political leaders often have an incentive to mobilize voters along religious lines. The politicization of religion, in turn, can undermine a nationalist frame that tries to incorporate believers of disparate traditions. The United States has hardly been immune from this kind of politics. What makes the current situation unique, however, is the rapid growth in the percentage of Americans who are religiously unaffiliated, and the emergence of a new kind of religious polarization between the two major parties. In two decades, between 1996 and 2016, the percentage of Americans who rejected any religious identity grew from 12 to 26 percent (Jones and Cox 2016). During that time, white Evangelical Protestants became the most reliably Republican voters and the largest religious block within the party. Simultaneously, the religiously unaffiliated became the most consistently Democratic voters and equally an important constituency within that party (Green and Dionne 2008).

While the major American parties have always been divided by religion, in the past it was between different kinds of religion, rather than between religion and no religion. Religious voices in both parties could disagree on any number of policy issues but comfortably find themselves within the larger civil-religious discourse. This new religious–secular divergence provides both opportunities and constraints for politicians. President Obama made frequent use of religious language in his public speeches (see Figure 2.1). Moreover, he retained the somewhat controversial White House Office of Faith-Based and Neighborhood Partnerships that had been created by George W. Bush.

Nonetheless, Obama's core "religious" constituency was arguably those with no religion. As we will note below, secular Americans express lower levels of nationalist sentiment. It could be that for these Americans, the civil-religious frame is itself too religious, and Obama's use of that rhetoric was alienating in a way that it was not for previous generations of Americans. Moreover, these secular Americans advocated policies on health care reform, same-sex marriage, and religion in public schools that opponents came to label as anti-religious. Thus, Obama found himself between the proverbial rock of those in the Democratic Party that

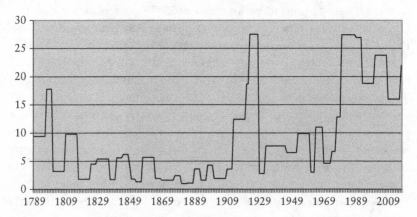

FIGURE 2.1. *Percentage of references to "God" or "Providence" and "Nation" in presidential documents*
Source: Presidential Documents of the UCSB American Presidency Project Database

wanted more faith outreach and those who wanted less. The challenge for Democratic politicians going forward will be to recapture a civil-religious discourse that can unify religious and secular Americans.

President Trump, on the other hand, demonstrated that Christian, nativist appeals could win both a presidential election and the support of an overwhelming percentage of white, Evangelical voters. Trump's religious nationalism promoted a narrower vision than the civil-religious discourse he inherited. Both symbolically and rhetorically, President Trump has excluded Muslim Americans, and to a lesser extent secular Americans, from his nationalist frame. Most evident was President Trump's proposed Muslim ban, but just as significant in its own way was when the Trump White House broke a decades-long tradition by not hosting a reception for Eid al-Fitr, which marks the end of the holy month of Ramadan. It was as if President Trump was trying symbolically to exclude Muslim Americans from the nationalist frame. The President has shown fidelity to white Evangelical Christians who helped elect him by embracing policies and a rhetoric that separates religious from secular Americans. In remarks at the 2017 Family Research Council's Values Voter Summit, Trump noted that "the American Founders invoked our Creator four times in the Declaration of Independence – four times. How times have changed. But you know what, now they're changing back again. Just remember that." He also vowed that his administration is "stopping cold the attacks on Judeo-Christian values" (Trump 2017).

The religious cleavage between the parties could reinforce this trend, particularly if Republican politicians sharpen those divisions through their rhetoric and their actions. It is possible that Republican politicians going forward might similarly distinguish between "good" and "bad" Americans based on whether or not they are religious, or even Christian, the inevitable result of which would be to undermine the country's unifying civil religion and move the country more toward a model of religious nationalism, albeit a highly unstable one.

A final challenge to the civil-religious tradition has been the country's history of racial discrimination. While African Americans and Native Americans might theoretically have been included in the religious frame of American nationalism, both groups were for most of American history specifically excluded from the political and social rights enjoyed by their white religious counterparts. It stands to reason, therefore, that these ethnic minorities might reasonably conclude that they were not invited to the civil-religious party. Nor did it seem to matter that the overwhelming majority of African Americans and a large fraction of Native Americans were Christian, since white Americans principally defined those groups in racial rather than religious terms. Symptomatic of this critical view is the title of the famous address given by Frederick Douglass in 1842, "What to the Slave Is the Fourth of July?"

Nonetheless, political activists have used the values of American civil religion (including religious values) to highlight the inconsistency between what America affirms in its civil-religious nationalism and what it practices. Edward Blum (2016) shows that black anti-slavery activists in Massachusetts used the language of Christian nationalism to call for the abolition of slavery in that state. In his address, Frederick Douglass pointed out that slavery was the "great sin and shame of America" precisely because it was inconsistent with the Declaration of Independence, the Constitution, and the Bible, each of which were key documents of American civil religion (Douglass 1852). A century later, Martin Luther King Jr. would famously say that his dream of racial equality was "firmly rooted in the American dream." The issue of race and civil religion, therefore, is complicated. The values of civil religion were not powerful enough to overcome the country's racial animus, yet those norms have also been embraced by racial minorities as they challenge deviations from American ideals.

PUBLIC OPINION AND NATIONALISM

We have argued that civil religion emerged in the United States for historical reasons and that it encouraged religious believers to marry their religious and national commitments. The data for this claim, however, have come primarily from religious and political elites. Elite cues are important, of course, but if our argument is sound we should be able to show a similar set of attitudes among the mass public. We next turn our attention to an empirical analysis of how the general public fuses nationalist and religious values. While a number of scholars have noted the importance of civil religion in American politics (Bellah 1967; Chapp 2002; Müller-Fahrenholz 2007; Murphy 2009; Gorski 2017), there have been very few empirical analyses of religion and American national identity.

Two exceptions to this lacuna in the literature are works by Shelton (2010) and Wright and Citrin (2009), both of which make use of the same database that we are going to analyze for our research: the General Social Survey/International Social Survey's "National Identity" module. Based on his analysis, Shelton concludes that most racial, religious, and ethnic groups show pride in American culture. His definition of support for American culture, however, is very broad and includes attitudes toward American political and economic institutions, cultural and athletic achievements, the nation's ethnic characteristics, and its civic characteristics. As we note below, it is these latter that we are interested in (civil characteristics) as we think they best capture views of nationalism. Wright and Citrin, on the other hand, expand their analysis to multiple surveys. One of their conclusions is that "Christian" definitions of nationalism are more prevalent in the United States than in other advanced democracies.

Using data from the 2003/4 National Identity Survey we created a nationalism scale consisting of six items ($\alpha = 0.653$). The questions asked the respondents about how close one feels to America, how proud one is to be American, and whether the American way of life should be adopted by other countries. The final three questions gauged how much respondents agreed with statements on whether they would rather be a citizen of America than any other country, whether there were some things about America that made them feel ashamed, and if they are often less proud of America than they would like to be. When all the items were added together, they formed a scale ranging from seven to twenty-eight.[1]

As Table 2.1 confirms, Americans are highly nationalistic. While religious groups do differ a little on nationalism, religious people in general rank higher on this scale than do the non-religious. Despite historical conflicts and contemporary disagreements among Mainline Protestants, Evangelical Protestants, and Roman Catholics, they all exhibit nearly

TABLE 2.1. *Nationalism by religious tradition*

Tradition	Mean
Mainline Protestant	21.38
Evangelical Protestant	21.35
Roman Catholic	21.29
Other Christian	20.90
Mormon	22.30
Jewish	21.60
Non-Judeo-Christian	19.45
Not Religious	19.30
All Respondents	20.96

Source: 2004 International Social Survey Programme, National Identity II, United States subsample.

indistinguishable levels of (high) nationalism. Although Mormons and Jews have at least in the past experienced religious prejudice at the hands of American nationalists, today they actually top the chart in identifying with this nation. This result confirms our argument earlier in this chapter that America's civil religion has gradually expanded to incorporate formerly excluded religious groups. Those with no religious identification, on the other hand, have lower nationalism scores, perhaps suggesting secular Americans still feel excluded from the traditional American narrative of civil religion.

As we noted in the previous section, America's civic nationalism has proved to be malleable over time. While they certainly have faced discrimination at the hands of the religious majority, religious outsiders have by and large embraced national values and become part of the religious mainstream. A slight exception were the periodic efforts by some religious elites (particularly Catholic and Jewish) to raise questions about the compatibility of Americanism (variously understood) and faith. Table 2.1 suggests that those elite questions have fallen on deaf ears at the mass level.

To explore further the roots of the fusion of religion and nationalism, we performed a multivariate regression interpreting this nationalism scale. Overall, the results of Table 2.2 suggest that religious people – regardless of tradition – are more nationalistic than secular respondents after one controls for other socioeconomic variables (e.g., ethnicity, income, education, age, gender, etc.).[2] This effect holds for the long-standing, dominant Mainline and Evangelical Protestants but also for more recent arrivals or religious minorities such as Catholics, Jews, and Mormons. In fact those groups smallest in number and that have faced the most persistent exclusion in American society, Jews and Mormons, rank highest in nationalism. This finding further confirms our argument that nationalism seems to be understood in religious terms in the United States but that this religiously tinged "patriotism" is not exclusive to a particular spiritual tradition. This table also includes a variable for religious attendance, but it failed to reach statistical significance when interviewees of all religious backgrounds were mixed together. However, Table 2.2 confirms that race remains a significant challenge to American civil-religious nationalism. Being African American substantially reduces nationalist sentiment when all other variables are held constant. Native Americans also appear to be less nationalistic, though the small number of those respondents in the survey meant that the coefficient did not reach statistical significance.

TABLE 2.2. *Religious and other determinants of nationalism*

Variable	Coefficient	Standard error
Jewish	2.668*	0.716
Mainline	2.083*	0.403
Evangelical	2.190*	0.364
Catholic	2.058*	0.366
Mormon	3.064*	0.785
Other Christian	1.138	0.618
Non-Judeo-Christian	−0.002	0.561
Religious attendance	0.047	0.050
Education	−0.546*	0.092
Income	5.875*	0.000
Woman	−0.575*	0.204
Age	0.024*	0.007
Asian	0.347	0.596
Latino	0.923	0.673
Native American	−1.763	1.138
African American	−1.196*	0.341
Urbanicity	−0.249*	0.073
Immigrant origin	0.150	0.371
West	0.334	0.300
South	0.664*	0.235
Constant	19.981*	0.524
N	1,017	
R^2	0.164	

*Denotes an effect that is significantly different from 0 at the 5 percent level for Ordinary Least Squares model.
Source: 2004 International Social Survey Programme, National Identity II, United States subsample.
Note: All regressors are dummy variables except for religious attendance (range = 1–8), income (500–165,000), age (18–88), education (1–5), and urbanicity (1–7).

To unpack the true influence of religiosity on nationalism, Table 2.3 performs a parallel regression for each of the major religious groups for which we have a sufficient number of respondents (i.e., Catholics, Mainline Protestants, and Evangelical Protestants). As the estimate for religious attendance indicates in the third column of coefficients, religious practice only matters among Evangelicals. To unpack this result further, we also divided this group up by ethnicity and found that this positive

TABLE 2.3. *Effect of religious attendance on nationalism by religious tradition*

Variable	Catholic	Mainline	Evangelical	White Evangelical	Black Evangelical
Religious attendance	−0.005	−0.177	0.169*	0.192*	0.093
Education	−0.572*	−0.588*	−0.422*	−0.549*	−0.179
Income	4.925	8.339	3.104	5.263	−3.205
Woman	−0.438	−0.285	−0.645*	−0.339	−1.072
Age	0.022	0.028	0.014	0.013	0.015
Asian	0.297	−1.281	−0.185		
Latino	1.044		−2.306		
Native American	−4.565*		−0.814		
African American	0.339	−0.698	−2.251*		
Urbanicity	−0.254	−0.260	0.016	0.080	0.001
Immigrant origin	−0.501	1.861	1.186	−1.198	3.203*
West	0.355	0.191	0.696	0.423	1.886
South	0.142	0.851	0.926*	0.832*	1.596*
Constant	22.697*	22.596*	21.091*	20.963*	18.689*
N	261	154	331	236	80
R^2	0.099	0.139	0.162	0.088	0.206

*Denotes an effect that is significantly different from 0 at the 5 percent level for OLS model.

Source: 2004 International Social Survey Programme, National Identity II, United States subsample.

Note: All regressors are dummy variables except for religious attendance (range = 1–8), income (500–165,000), age (18–88), education (1–5), and urbanicity (1–7).

effect only held for whites. In predominantly Anglo-evangelical congregations, parishioners are likely hearing cues directly from the pulpit and over church dinners, thus reinforcing the nexus of nationalism and religious identity. Other religious Americans, in contrast, seem not to be getting the same overt messages during services or social hours. Rather, the link between national and religious identities appears to originate in the act of identifying with a spiritual tradition, whatever it is. By accepting the currently dominant norm of being religious in the United States, one also embraces the national ethos of a strong psychological link to the state. For most Americans, not even the act of attending a religious service matters as much as simply affiliating with a faith community.

The exception to this pattern is among African Americans and Native Americans. Among all Catholics, Native Americans are dramatically less nationalistic than their non-indigenous Catholic counterparts. Similarly, among all Evangelicals, African Americans are distinctly less nationalistic. Indeed, there is no relationship between religious attendance and nationalism for African-American Evangelicals.

SUPPORT FOR THE IRAQ WAR

In addition to measuring abstract nationalism in the United States, we wished to look at a more concrete, applied version. We therefore settled on attitudes toward the Iraq War, perhaps the most important nationalism project of the past three decades. In general, foreign policy attitudes are less stable and informed than are opinions on domestic policy (Holsti 1994). There is, nonetheless, a rally-round-the-flag effect when America goes to war (Mueller 1994:70). The data on religious attitudes toward foreign policy and war is quite limited. Wald and Calhoun Brown (2007:199–201) find little difference among religious groups on most foreign policy questions. However, they discover some divergence on support for the War in Iraq, with Mormons, Evangelical Protestants, and Hispanic Protestants the most supportive, and Muslims, Black Protestants, and Jews the least supportive. The question that we used asked respondents was whether they believed the Iraq War was "worth the cost." This survey was conducted in the fall of 2004, a year and a half after the war had begun and late enough for opposition to the action to grow.

As Table 2.4 notes, by this point only 40 percent of all respondents still supported the American intervention. For the most part, however, religious respondents were more likely to endorse the effort. Once again, the historically dominant Protestants remained enthusiastic, as did Roman Catholics. As with our general measures of nationalism, Mormons were the most positive group about this enterprise. However, Jews were less supportive than the average respondent.

As we found for general measures of nationalism in Table 2.2, Evangelical Protestants were significantly more likely to support the war in Iraq. However, this relationship did not hold for any of the other religious traditions. More frequent religious practice, on the other hand,

TABLE 2.4. *Support for Iraq War by religious tradition*

Tradition	Mean
Mainline Protestant	0.406
Evangelical Protestant	0.441
Roman Catholic	0.414
Other Christian	0.234
Mormon	0.514
Jewish	0.300
Non-Judeo-Christian	0.144
Not religious	0.357
All respondents	0.400

Source: 2004 American National Election Study, Time Series version.

seems to have boosted enthusiasm for the conflict. Although we do not include a separate table for the effects of religiosity among separate religious traditions (cf. Table 2.3), the results for war-related attitudes are similar to those for generic nationalism. Highly practicing white Evangelicals, for example, appear more supportive of US intervention in Iraq ($b = 0.186$, $p = 0.091$), as do very devout Catholics ($b = 0.171$, $p = 0.072$). Among mainline Protestants and African-American Evangelicals, in contrast, the effect of religious attendance did not achieve statistical significance (Table 2.5).

Overall, identifying as a religious person seems make one more nationalistic and, for most traditions, more likely to agree with a major nationalistic enterprise: for the US case, the Iraq War. Within a particular religious grouping, frequent interaction with other members of one's faith often also appears to drive both nationalism and militarism.

RELIGION AND NATIONALISM IN RELIGIOUS PUBLICATIONS AND PRESIDENTIAL STATEMENTS

Our quantitative findings reinforce our argument about the power of civil religion in the United States, both within the culture at large and in the pews. What is less clear is the degree to which religious elites have consistently supported this connection between national and religious identities. Religious elites are generally more steeped in the teachings of their respective tradition and more engaged in its practices than are the

TABLE 2.5. *Religious and other determinants of support for Iraq War*

Variable	Coefficient	Standard error
Jewish	−0.337	0.476
Mainline	0.297	0.253
Evangelical	0.517*	0.228
Catholic	0.196	0.227
Mormon	0.593	0.507
Other Christian	−0.303	0.590
Non-Judeo-Christian	−0.668	1.055
Religious attendance	0.161*	0.051
Education	−0.008	0.004
Income	0.037*	0.013
Woman	−0.184	0.142
Age	−0.008	0.004
Asian	−1.054	0.563
Latino	−0.420	0.303
Native American	0.378	0.536
African American	−1.657*	0.253
Urbanicity	−0.037	0.065
Immigrant origin	0.124	0.221
West	−0.074	0.197
South	0.585*	0.171
Constant	−0.457*	0.388
N	999	
Nagelkerke R^2	0.137	

*Denotes an effect that is significantly different from 0 at the 5 percent level for dichotomous logit model.
Source: 2004 American National Election Study, Time Series version.
Note: All regressors are dummy variables except for religious attendance (range = 1–5), income (0–23), age (18–90), education (0–7), and urbanicity (1–5).

average lay persons. This greater exposure to the tradition might lead elites to be more aware of the potential points of conflict between fidelity to the faith and support for American nationalism. We noted previously in this chapter that religious leaders have been more likely than parishioners to challenge the intimate nexus between religion and American civil religion. Many Catholic bishops urged their parishioners to strengthen the distinction between Catholic and American values at the end of the nineteenth century, while a number of Orthodox Jewish leaders questioned the compatibility of their faith with the political values and social norms of America's civil religion in the early twentieth century.

To analyze elite attitudes, we conducted a content analysis of leading religious periodicals for four main religious traditions in the United States: Roman Catholic, Mainline Protestant, Evangelical Protestant, and Jewish. American religious practice is exceptionally diverse, but those four groups represent a sizeable percentage of the American religious population. For each group we identified a publication as representative for the tradition as a whole. For example, we selected the *Reformed Judaism Magazine* because Reformed Judaism is the largest group within the American Jewish community. Similarly, *Southern Baptist Life* is the publication of Southern Baptist Convention, which is the largest Protestant denomination in the United States and is closely identified with Evangelical Protestantism. *Episcopal Life*, which was later renamed the *Episcopal News Monthly*, is the official voice for a denomination that has historically been among the nation's most prominent and is closely associated with Mainline Protestantism. The Roman Catholic Church, however, is so large and so internally divided that we selected publications that broadly represent the more conservative (*National Catholic Register*) and more progressive (*National Catholic Reporter*) wings of the church.

As for our public-opinion data, we focused attention on attitudes toward both abstract nationalism and the War in Iraq. We first located relevant texts (e.g., editorials, letters to the editor, commentaries, and op-eds) within each publication by generally using a Google-type electronic (most journals) or manual (*Episcopal Life*) search for at least the words "United States," "nation," and one of the terms "defend," "chosen," "patriot," "patriotism," "war," "allegiance," "country," or "fight" (for generic nationalism; we also excluded texts on "abortion") or "war" and "Iraq" (for the Iraq War) in all issues from 2001 to 2011. For some sources, we needed to tweak the search criteria slightly to exclude irrelevant items and include substantively important narrative (e.g., we omitted anything from a regular column in the *National Catholic Reporter* because the column was not relevant for our purposes even though it often mentioned our search terms). Figure 2.2 summarizes the results of our content analysis of the five publications. In this bar graph, "negative" is for articles expressing disapproval of the state and its actions without making any qualifying patriotic statements or for those pieces contending that the values of the church should trump those of the government. "Neutral" pieces discussed the nation without making any apparent

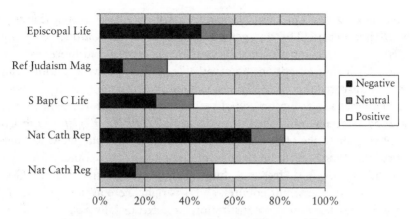

FIGURE 2.2. *Abstract nationalism in religious publications*

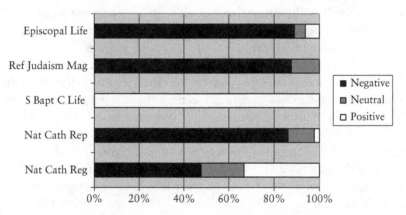

FIGURE 2.3. *Support for the Iraq War in religious publications*

value judgments. And "positive" essays in some way expressed patriotism or praised American values. In Figure 2.3, meanwhile, "negative" represents a passage suggesting that the war in Iraq was not just and should not be supported. "Neutral" indicates that the piece suggests believers carefully consider the ethical aspects of the war but that the author takes no decisive stance one way or another. A "positive" quotation claims the war was just and should be supported or, regardless of the morality of its origins, the war should be supported and fought righteously in the future.

On abstract nationalism, religious elites are generally very pro-American. As Figure 2.2 indicates, there was a much higher percentage of positive than negative statements in the *Reformed Judaism Magazine*,

Southern Baptist Life, and *National Catholic Register* during this ten-year time period. The one genuine outlier was the *National Catholic Reporter*, where anti-nationalistic statements outweighed more positive ones. With that exception, however, elite attitudes toward nationalism largely mirrored those of religious persons more generally, both of whom are nationalistic. Symptomatic of such an expression of nationalism was a 2007 interview published in the *National Catholic Register* with US Ambassador to the Holy See, Francis Rooney. In that interview, Rooney noted that "the bottom line is that the United States is a country founded on the big ideals of freedom, human dignity, respecting people. God made us, God made our country, and it is right there in the Declaration of Independence and the Constitution" (quoted in Lilly 2007). In 2011, Mark Shea, a columnist for the same publication, noted that "independence day is, for us Americans, the primordial celebration of our beginning as a people. It is the original celebration of American patriotism, and patriotism is a good thing ... So it's a fine thing to celebrate patriotism toward ones country" (Shea 2011).

Attitudes of religious elites toward the War in Iraq, on the other hand, demonstrate a much different pattern. We noted in our review of public opinion that Evangelical Protestants were the most supportive of the war effort, a result that was confirmed in our content analysis. There was not a single statement in *Southern Baptist Life* during this ten-year period that was coded as negative toward the war (see Figure 2.3), despite the fact that the war itself was supported by only 40 percent of Americans by 2004. Characteristic of such support was a 2002 opinion piece by Scott Simon (Simon 2002) titled "Even Pacifists must Support this War." In it, Simon argued that "it seems to me that in confronting the forces that attacked the World Trade Center and the Pentagon, American pacifists have no sane alternative now but to support war." Two years later when it became apparent that the war would not easily be won, Joni B. Hannigan (2004) reminded her readers in an article titled "Soldiers Need U.S. Support ... And Faith in God," that "America's freedom did not come without loss of life."

For every other religious publication, on the other hand, negative comments about the war by religious elites were much more common than positive ones. As Figure 2.3 indicates, more than 80 percent of the comments about the War in Iraq during this ten-year period were negative in *Episcopal Life, Reformed Judaism Magazine*, and *National Catholic Reporter*. To be sure, most of those negative statements were about the progress of the war itself, and this is admittedly a not ideal indicator of support for civil-religious nationalism per se. It is quite possible to be critical of a national policy, like the War in Iraq, and still be loyally patriotic. Prior to the start of the war, Auxiliary Bishop of Detroit Thomas J. Gumbleton (2002) argued in an article in the *National Catholic Reporter* that the imminent invasion of Iraq is "so contrary to the way of Jesus that you would think all the Christian churches would rise up and say: No, we can't do that. We have to find a different way." A 2003 article by Tom Roberts (2003) in the same publication lamented that "our politicians regularly seek God's blessing on America, particularly in times of war. Perhaps it would be appropriate also to beg God's mercy." Finally, a 2003 editorial (National Catholic Reporter 2003) challenged the war in light of American values: "Historically, U.S. ideals have set our nation apart. However, in a matter of months, the Bush administration has broken with our beloved past to recklessly set off along a path of peril, of empire building ... This is not the America we grew up with and learned to love."

A similar pattern emerges in analyzing official statements by religious bodies about the War in Iraq. The most supportive of the American effort was the Southern Baptist Convention. Between 2002 and 2006, leaders of the church meeting at the annual Southern Baptist Convention passed three resolutions that dealt with the War on Terrorism and the War in Iraq, and two others that dealt with attitudes toward the American military and President Bush. The 2002 resolution "On the War on Terrorism" determined that "we wholeheartedly support the actions of the United States government, its intelligence agencies, and its military in the just war against terrorist networks" (Southern Baptist Convention 2002). A year later in "On the Liberation of Iraq" the convention confirmed that "we believe Operation Iraqi Freedom was a warranted action based upon historic principles of just war ... [we] affirm President George W. Bush, the United States Congress, and our armed forces for their leadership in the successful execution of Operation Iraqi Freedom" (Southern Baptist Convention 2003). In 2006, the Convention passed a resolution "On Prayer for the President and Military" which linked the religious and national cause: "whereas our nation is currently engaged in a global war on terrorism, and our military is fighting against a determined and fanatical enemy that is threatening the liberty and security of our nation and the world ... [we] resolve that we express our profound appreciation for our president, who confesses his faith in Christ and values the efficacy of prayers" (Southern Baptist Convention 2006). In short, for leaders of the Southern Baptist Convention the War in Iraq was just, it promoted American values like freedom and liberty, and it deserved the wholehearted support of the American public, particularly the Christian part of the American public who could lend both their voice and prayers for the national effort.

At the other end of the spectrum were resolutions passed during the same time period by the General Convention of the Episcopal Church. The Convention meets every three years and is the highest legislative body of the Church. In contrast to the resolutions of the Southern Baptist Convention, the Episcopal Church did not initially conclude that the War in Iraq met the criteria for a just war, but instead "urged dioceses and congregations to study and better understand the Just War theory and pacifism as they apply to the situation of the United States in responding to contemporary international conflicts" (Acts of Convention of the Episcopal Church 2003). Three years later, the Convention abandoned whatever ambiguity was implied in its 2003 action with a resolution titled "Oppose the War in Iraq and Support Nonviolent Means to Ending Conflict." The resolution stated that conditions for just war "had not been met in the national government's decision to attack the nation of Iraq," it resolved that "our government's participation in the war in Iraq has resulted in individual and global injustices," and it called upon all Episcopalians "as an act of penitence, to oppose and resist through advocacy, protest, and electoral action the continuation of the war in Iraq" (Acts of Convention of the Episcopal Church 2006). Thus, whatever initial hesitancy the church exhibited about whether the war met the criteria of a just war, by 2006 church leaders concluded that the war was unjust, and it called Americans, including American Christians, to acts of repentance and activities to end what was an unjust war.

Somewhere in the middle, but probably leaning more closely toward the Episcopalians, was the American Roman Catholic Church. The famous 1983 pastoral letter of the American Bishops, *The Challenge of Peace*, applied just war doctrine to the moral problem of nuclear proliferation, and since then the church has consistently raised similar questions about American military intervention in various places around the world. However, the largest number of major statements over the past several decades was on the War in Iraq (Powers 2009:73). Writing as President and on behalf of the United States Conference of Catholic Bishops, Bishop Wilton Gregory wrote to President Bush in September of 2002 to "express our serious questions about the moral legitimacy of any preemptive, unilateral use of military force to overthrow the government of Iraq" (United States Conference of Catholic Bishops 2002). Unlike their Southern Baptist and Episcopalian counterparts, the American Catholic Bishops never took a definitive stand on whether this was a just war. But, the language of a statement issued on the eve of the war in 2003 suggested strong moral reservations about the conflict. The bishops expressed their concern about "precedents that could be set and the possible consequences of a major war of this type," and they reminded military and political leaders that the "moral and legal constraints on the conduct of war must be observed" (United States Conference of Catholic Bishops 2003).

At the elite level, thus, Roman Catholic and Episcopal Church leaders challenged American policy and implicitly urged fellow believers to qualify their support for this war on religious grounds. However, these appeals seem to have fallen on deaf ears, or at least they appear not to have qualified the patriotic feelings for people in the pews. In the Evangelical world, by contrast, there was very little distinction between pro-American sentiments of both church leaders and members.

Up to this point the content analysis has looked at religious elites' attitudes toward the nation. Next, we wish to examine political elites' views of religion. If our hypothesis about America's civil religion is correct, we would expect political leaders to link religious and national identities. To test this claim, we performed a content analysis of all presidential statements (e.g., State of the Union addresses, signing statements, proclamations, speeches, and news conferences) for each chief executive through the first year of Trump's term. We conducted numerous searches using various terms linked to religion or nationalism. As our civil-religious model predicts, generic/inclusive language is far more common among American presidents than is language specific to a particular religious tradition. For example, a search for "Christian" and "nation" yielded 1,393 hits, while a parallel inquiry for "God" and "nation" identified 11,047 statements. We therefore focused on searches by president for any statement that included the terms "nation" and "God." In the United States, politicians wishing to reinforce the "God-and-country" sentiment typically use these two words in public addresses.

As Figure 2.1 suggests, Presidents have employed such rhetoric throughout America's 200-plus-year history. For example, just under 8 percent of John Adam's ninety total statements contained both of those words. Thus, in his 1799 "Proclamation Recommending a National Day of Humiliation, Fasting, and Prayer," Adams (1799) closely connect the nation's religious and political purposes when he encouraged "acts of humiliation, penitence, and prayer ... to the Author of All Good ... for the countless favors which He is still continuing to the people of the United States, and which render their condition as a nation eminently happy when compared with the lot of others." A century later, nearly 5 percent of William McKinley's 255 pronouncements include both terms. And in the 1970s, Gerald Ford registered just over 6 percent in this category. Ford (1975) concluded his remarks at the 1975 National Prayer Breakfast by seeking "God's continued blessing and God's continued guidance for our country and all its people whose servants we in government strive to be." Such civil-religious terminology is ubiquitous in American politics.

Figure 2.1 also demonstrates a steep rise in such discourse beginning in the early twentieth century and continuing until today. Thus, almost a quarter of all of Calvin Coolidge's statements in the 1920s referenced "God" and "nation," more than one quarter of Ronald Reagan's did in the 1980s, and even Barack Obama followed this pattern at 18 percent. Some might interpret this trajectory as evidence that civil-religious commitments are more robust now than they were at the nation's founding. Alternatively, it is likely that earlier presidents did not have to be so explicit in such references because of the country's overwhelmingly Protestant Christian affiliation. It is no surprise that some of the largest spikes in the data come when those implicit connections are being challenged and dispute between rival political forces. The early twentieth century saw the rapid rise of immigration into the United States and a previously unexperienced level of religious diversity. As we noted earlier in the chapter, this religious diversification threatened America's civil religion, but the concept eventually expanded to include substantial numbers of Catholics, Jews, and other religious newcomers. Another notable rise occurred during the Cold War, when the external threat of Communism led to increased religious discourse. The more recent increase in this "status-politics" rhetoric is likely tied to the political rise of the Christian right and its union with the conservative wing of the Republican Party (Luker 1984; see also Gusfield 1963). The appeal is powerful enough, however, that Democratic presidents also find themselves adopting this language.

CONCLUSION

Our historical and quantitative findings reinforce our argument about the power of civil religion in the United States, both within the culture at large and in the pews. Americans almost naturally link their nationalistic ideology with their religious point of view. It would seem that it has always been this way; the relative power of religious traditions wax and wane, new groups emerge and old ones decline, yet the connecting thread between religion of virtually any stripe and the American nation remains strong. From the standpoint of civic peace and political legitimacy, this civil religion has proved stable, enduring, and strong.

This is not to suggest, however, that this civil-religious model will inevitably endure. As Philip Gorski (2017) notes, religious nationalism and radical secularism have competed with civil religion throughout American history. Those counter-narratives challenge the civil-religious model. Religious nationalism offers a much narrower, more prescriptive religious frame to define American nationalism, while its secular counterpart imagines no place for religious language in discourse about the nation. Those alternative frames have not prevailed in the past, but each is growing in social and political significance now. One analyst (Carlson 2017) has even suggested that we are "losing our civil religion." While cognizant of those dangers, we remain hopeful that the American past will be a prelude to its future and that the nation will recapture the unifying value of our civil-religious heritage.

Endnotes

1. While the number of indicators might suggest the utility of exploratory factor analysis, we chose to adopt this additive scale because we are specifically interested in only one dimension of nationalism, that of the relatively uncritical "patriot" in each country. Outside of the United States, moreover, the paucity of data usually precludes such item-by-item analysis because the surveys contain at most one or two questions measuring nationalism. We acknowledge, however, that a few citizens in each state might express "loyal opposition" to the nation. An American might object to the frequent police killings of unarmed African American men, for example, because such actions violate US norms of the equality of all people.

2. Table 2.2 and the following regressions assume that religion causes nationalism (and the arguably related partisanship) but not vice versa. A critic might point to the 2016 election of Donald Trump, however, as evidence that that white American Christians often are "patriots" or Republicans first and only secondarily hold to a religious identification or particular theological principles. National loyalty or party allegiance would therefore be influencing religious affiliation instead of religion causing nationalism. While we acknowledge the plausibility of this argument, statistically

modeling such a theory would require simultaneous equations or a related technique that would probably not be tractable using the relatively generic datasets publicly available for the six countries in this book. We still maintain, moreover, that religious socialization occurs before political socialization and that religion is more likely to influence feelings toward the nation than national identification and political partisanship are to affect religious identity.

3

Israel: Unstable Civil-Religious Nationalism

INTRODUCTION

In remarks during a visit to Tel Aviv's Independence Hall in May of 2014, Prime Minister Benjamin Netanyahu said that he intended to present a new basic law to the Knesset that would "provide a constitutional anchor for Israel's status as the nation-state of the Jewish people." The bill he eventually proposed would have ensured a Jewish demographic majority in Israel, established Hebrew as the only official language (Arabic is also an official language), and recognized Jewish religious law as a legitimate source of law for certain issues. Leaders of Arab political parties and the Labor Party opposed the proposal, and even his own Justice Minister, Tzipi Livni, objected on the grounds that the law would lead Israel to "subjugate [its] democratic values to its Jewish values" (Ravid, Lis, and Khoury 2014). While the law also affirmed the country's democratic political principles, many interpreted Netanyahu's words as an effort to add another complicating factor in peace talks between Israelis and Palestinians. The subsequent controversy surrounding his proposal underscores the degree to which Israel's national identity has been a perennially contested issue since the nation's founding more than sixty years ago. And at the forefront of much of that debate have been tensions around competing conceptions about religion and nationalism.

Israel is an interesting case in which to analyze the development of nationalist ideology and its link with religion because political elites proposed all three models as the state was being formed (secular, religious, civil religious model). Moreover, the constitutional status of religion in Israel was and remains deeply divisive, and demographic factors have further inflamed the relationship between religion and nationalism. The most salient cleavages have been among Jewish and between Jewish and non-Jewish citizens of the state who are separated over whether Israel should be a Jewish state, and between Orthodox and secular Jews who largely agree on the Zionist project but disagree on what it should mean. Demographic divisions within the Jewish majority and between Jewish and non-Jewish citizens of the state reinforced those splits, and subsequent changes in the state's population have only strengthened those divides. The state's ongoing security concerns, wars with her Arab neighbors, and party-political variables have further inflamed separate visions for what constitutes Israeli nationalism.

Even before the establishment of the State of Israel, Jews were divided into varying Zionist camps, each with different understandings of the kind of nationalism that a Jewish state would promote. Political elites sought to neutralize these tensions in the regime's early years, but the pragmatic decisions that they made reinforced persistent controversy over the state's religious identity. In short, the roots of the contemporary tension around matters of religion and state, or religion and national loyalties, were formalized at the moment of state formation. The contested nature of Israel's model of religion and nationalism has led to differing levels of patriotism among different religious traditions. There is a civil religion in Israel, but it has proven to be an unstable one over time. The country thus contrasts with the United States, whose civil-religious model has been relatively stable. We argue that the instability in Israel's model arises from political pressures from different quarters toward either religious nationalism or secular nationalism. These pressures in turn came from the religious diversity at the state's founding, which also gave rise to ambiguous institutional links between the government and religious groups.

The purpose of this chapter is to outline relations between religion and nationalism in Israel. We offer an historical overview of this process and an analysis of contemporary public opinion data on questions related to their interaction on the most salient nationalistic project in Israel over the past several decades: Jewish settlements in the West Bank. We contend that patterns established at the time of state formation continue to be of crucial importance to contemporary understandings of religion and nationalism, and that those divisions are reflected in popular attitudes toward the state.

ELITES AND NATIONALISM IN THE FOUNDING PERIOD

The first key factor in determining how religion and nationalism interact within a state is to analyze how political and religious elites understood those relations during the period of state formation. The principal division that we are interested to uncover is whether or not religion was a unifying or divisive element among founding elites. In the case of Israel, the place and status of religion in national self-understanding was contentious; divisions emerged between Jewish and Arab residents on whether or not the state should be Jewish and among Jews on what a Jewish state meant.

In contrast with a country like the United States, where political independence coincided with or even preceded a nationalist ethos, the roots of Jewish nationalism occurred centuries before the formation of the state of Israel. Those roots included a common history and a sense of ethnic and religious particularity. It was not until the late nineteenth century, however, that these shared qualities expressed themselves in nationalist terms through Zionism. In its simplest terms, Zionism was a philosophical and political movement that aimed to safeguard the Jewish people from persecution and extinction as a people (Kolatt 2008; Shindler 2008:10). It emerged in a highly nationalist age, and one that witnessed the rise of ethnic nationalisms throughout Europe (Sternhell 1997:10).

From its inception, Zionism divided the world's Jews in a bewildering number of respects. First, not all Jews supported the political aim of Zionism, although they had different reasons for opposing it. Many orthodox Jews rejected Zionism for theological reasons. They precluded Zionism on the grounds that it was a secular political project and they contended that only God could bring about the ingathering of the Jewish people. At the other end of the religious spectrum were Jews in the West whose religion was increasingly privatized and practiced through Reformed Judaism, if at all. Their goal was the cultural and political acculturation of Jews into their respective societies. Leaders of the American Jewish Committee, as an example, initially opposed Zionism, considered it un-American, and were more likely to believe that assimilation could be a reasonable goal for Jews in political democracies (Urofksy 2009:490–3). It was not that Judaism would disappear in the United States in this vision, but Jews would blend their culture with that of the American society of which they were a part.

An equally significant divide arose among Jews who supported Zionism, but parted company on whether they understood this nationalism in secular, cultural, or religious terms (Conforti 2010). For leaders like Theodor Herzl and many others in Western Europe and the United States, Zionism was primarily a political project. As Herzl famously argued in his *Der Judenstaat* (1896), hatred of the Jews was an inevitable fact of life. Jews were everywhere a minority, and even sincere efforts on the part of Jews to assimilate to the cultures around them had been met by hostility. Only an ingathering of the world's Jews and the formation of a Jewish state could solve this dilemma. The nationalism implicit in Herzl's political Zionism was civic and secular. His Zionism focused more on shared political values than on Jewish culture, history, or religion (Don-Yehiya 1998:267–8). The Labor Zionists who were the heirs of this Herzlian vision largely associated Zionism with the implementation of Jewish ideals of social justice.

Other Zionists, particularly those in Eastern Europe, chaffed at Herzl's relative silence on the cultural aspects of Zionism. Led initially by Achad Ha'am, these cultural Zionists advocated a nationalism that would blend together the linguistic, cultural, and historical aspects of Judaism. Ha'am famously countered Herzl's political vision by claiming that he was striving for "a Jewish state and not merely a state for the Jews" (Sachar 1996:58–66). A Jewish state, Ha'am argued, had to be connected in a meaningful way to the historical and cultural experiences of Jews, and not simply be a replication of European, socialist values which he thought Herzl advocated (Halkin 2016a). A Jewish state should promote Hebrew as the historical language of the Jewish people and advance the intellectual heritage of Judaism. If Herzl's nationalism was civic and implicitly secular, the nationalism of Ha'am and his followers was historical and cultural. This nationalism was not, however, specifically religious, but instead offered a Judaism in a "semi-secularized form" (Halkin 2016b). The Jewish religion was surely a part of that tradition, but it was not synonymous with it. This movement persisted through the Bundist movement in Russia.

There was a more specifically religious nationalism advanced by some orthodox Jews. As we noted above, many orthodox Jews were non-Zionists (Haredi), but a smaller number (Mizrahi) supported Zionism and interpreted the movement in religious terms (Blackstone, Matsubayashi, and Oldmixon 2014:121–5). One of the leaders of this wing of Zionism was Rabbi Abraham Isaac Kook. Kook would later become the founding chief rabbi of Israel during much of the British Mandate and the "spiritual godfather of Religious Zionism" (Mirsky 2014:2). While Kook was an extraordinarily complex thinker whose political ideas are hard to generalize, he was nonetheless one of the first prominent orthodox rabbis to interpret the Zionist ideal in theological terms. The national identity advocated by these Zionists was clearly religious.

The other important Zionist group of note were the Revisionists. Founded by Ze'ev Jabotinsky in a split with the mainstream Zionist organization in 1925, the Revisionists contended that a Jewish state must be established as soon as possible. They abandoned the socialist values of Labor Zionism, and focused instead on the use of power forcefully to bring about a Jewish state. Jabotinsky founded the Jewish Legion as a military force that staked a claim to Palestine by fighting for it (Halkin 2014:92). The position most closely associated with Revisionism was the idea that Jews had a right to all of Palestine, including Jerusalem, as the historic home of the Jewish people.

In short, even before large numbers of Jews began immigrating to Palestine in the early decades of the twentieth century, they had competing visions for what kind of state they were promoting, and different models for the link between religion and nationalism. Political Zionism emphasized a civic and secular nationalism rooted in the principles of the Enlightenment and the French Revolution, cultural Zionism advocated a nationalism based on common practices and historical experiences, Revisionism justified a maximal Jewish state for purposes of self-defense and self-preservation, while theological or religious Zionism promoted a religious nationalism. The shared goal of a Jewish state united these differing streams, but tensions among them were never far from the surface.

Charles Liebman and Eliezer Don-Yehiya make a telling observation that divergent models of civil religion have competed with one another throughout Israel's history (Liebman and Don-Yehiya 1983:28). This was particularly the case during the Yishuv (pre-state) and early state formation periods as camps emerged that promoted the alternative models of secular nationalism, religious nationalism, and cultural nationalism. The respective nationalisms perceived a different role for religion in the eventual new state of Israel.

Labor Zionism dominated among the early Jewish settlers in Palestine, although they were internally divided into left- and right-wing camps based on their relative commitment to socialist values (Ram 2008:63). The leaders of this wing controlled the politically powerful Mapai Labor Party, they were not religiously observant, they rejected a formal political role for religion in the Yishuv and the newly created state, and they advanced a civic nationalism based on labor-socialist values (Don-Yehiya 1998:274). David Ben-Gurion, Executive Head of the World Zionist Organization, a founder of Israel, and the country's first prime minister, repeatedly articulated labor- and work-related themes in his description for what an eventual Jewish state would look like (Ben-Gurion 1987). In a 1917 speech that he delivered in New York City, Ben-Gurion noted:

it is a Homeland that we seek, where we may cast off the curse of exile, attach ourselves to the soil ... and renew our native life ... The true right of a country springs not from political or court authority, but from work. The real conquest of the Land through labor – that is the transcendent duty which faces the nation's pioneers, the builders and guardians of the land.

(Ben-Gurion 1954:4–6)

As we will note below, Ben-Gurion eventually decided to accommodate orthodox groups in the new State of Israel to ensure unity in the Zionist cause, but his nationalism gave ideological preference to the secular values of class, worker, and pioneer. As Don-Yehiya notes (1998:274), Labor Zionism functioned as "kind of secular religion" during the Yishuv and early state period, but over time this socialist version of Zionism weakened.

The second nationalist model, religious nationalism, broadly united the various orthodox groups. Although they were divided into the Zionist (Mizrahi) and non-Zionist (Haredi) positions, they shared the overriding conviction that religious law (Halacha) had to be the basis for any legitimate Jewish state (Rubin 2013:53). Not surprisingly, it was this group that advocated most vigorously a formal political role for religion in the new Jewish state. Religious nationalism was a minority position in the Yishuv and the Orthodox camp was deeply divided and lacked an organizational structure to match that of the labor movement (Rubin 2013:506). As Ken Wald has noted (2002:107), the relative weakness of the Orthodox community made it easier for Ben-Gurion to justify his decision to recognize the Jewish character of the new state of Israel. Like many of the secular founders of Zionism, Ben-Gurion assumed that modernity would undermine religious orthodoxy. Ironically, it has been Ben-Gurion's nationalism based on socialist values that has dissipated over time, while that of religious nationalism has grown.

Finally, revisionism provided a third broad nationalist model based on the conquest of the Land of Israel. The movement's foremost political objective was to establish a Jewish state with a Jewish majority on both sides of the River Jordan (Sachar 1996:183–8). While the leaders of the movement were largely secular Jews, they believed that the religious and cultural aspects of Judaism could help to preserve the unity of the Jewish people. In contrast with the religious nationalists, they opposed a state governed by Halacha, but revisionism also diverged from the secular nationalism in supporting the integration of religious practices in public life and in the promotion of Jewish cultural traditions (Liebman and Don-Yehiya 1983:59–61). In terms of its understanding of the role of religion in Jewish nationalism, revisionism marked a compromise between secular and religious nationalism, and in many respects it has come to dominate popular understandings of the link between nationalism and religion among Jewish citizens of Israel, particularly within the Likud Party.

It is important briefly to note that Arabs living in Palestine were not partners to the Zionist cause. As we will note below, secular nationalism seemed, at least rhetorically, most open to Arabs. To the degree that it expressed the "universal" socialist values of class and worker instead of the particularistic religious and cultural values of Judaism, secular nationalism might have been a unifying nationalist model for Jews and Arabs living in Palestine. But, socialist values hardly proved to be universally significant, and they proved insufficient for the needs of a state that needed some sacral legitimation for its endeavors (Sternhell 1997:7). Moreover, the early Yishuv leaders, including Ben-Gurion, hoped to establish a Jewish state with as small an Arab minority as possible (Morris 2014:20). This is precisely what occurred after the War of Independence and the much-debated transfer of Arabs outside of the borders of the new Israeli state. From the standpoint of the remaining Arab population in Israel, therefore, even a relatively benign civil-religious nationalism seemed very much to exclude those who were not at least culturally Jewish.

At the point of political independence, in short, alternative nationalist models, with different understandings for the role of religion in the national ethos, competed for dominance. In this regard, it is instructive briefly to compare the political experiences of the United States and Israel on religion and nationalism at the point of state formation. Lerner (2013:614) makes an important distinction between political cultures that are religiously diverse and those that are religiously divided. The former are marked by a wide variety of religious groups, while the latter are characterized by deep and ongoing conflict around religion. In this sense, the United States was and is religiously diverse, but it is not religiously divided. To be sure, an overwhelming majority of citizens at the point of state formation in the United States were Christian, yet they were divided into a dizzying array of religious denominations, and that diversity has only grown over time. Despite that diversity, however, religion has most often been a unifying factor in national identity. That has been the political genius of America's civil religion. Israel, on the other hand, has been marked both by religious diversity (among Jews and between Jews and Arabs) and it is religiously divided. Religion has been at the forefront of political controversy throughout the country's history, and rather than providing a unifying thread for nationalist sentiment, religion has been a source of ongoing division. Nowhere has that division been more evident than in political debates about the role of religion in the newly created State of Israel.

DEBATES ON RELIGION IN THE BASIC LAW

A second aspect in determining how religion and nationalism interact within a state is to focus on the political arrangements around religion at the point of state formation. Broadly speaking, states vary on a continuum from those where the state is intimately involved in regulating religious life to those where the government is not much involved with religion at all (Fox 2008). Israel's founders were deeply divided on the question of religion. There was a religious group that wanted political life shaped by Jewish law, a secular camp that wanted a strict separation of religious and political life, and a third group that advanced a compromise between the opposing poles. Each of these positions also implicitly advanced alternative nationalist visions.

Those tensions emerged as Israel's founders drafted, debated, and eventually signed the Declaration of the Establishment of the State of Israel on May 14, 1948. Meeting under the auspices of the People's Council whose purpose was to declare Israel's independence, the thirty-seven delegates represented all the major Jewish factions, and while they were unanimous in their support of the document, the debate among them underscored conflicting nationalist ideals.

Delegates of the left-leaning Mapam and Communist parties promoted a secular nationalist model. The use of the term "Rock of Israel" in the Declaration was a subject of controversy among various delegates. Several Jewish religious leaders wanted a clear reference to God in the Declaration, specifically the phrase "the Rock of Israel and its Redeemer," while others, most notably Aharon Zisling of the left-leaning Mapam Party, threatened to refuse to sign the Declaration if such language was included. During the debate about the phrase, Zisling argued:

Let not those who believe oblige those of us who think differently, and we do believe in our own way – to say 'I believe' without faith in our hearts. The phrase here is "with trust in the Rock of Israel." Why impose that expression on us? ... Let us not besmirch our credo. This version imposes an expression upon us which we do not accept.

Quoted in Lorch 1993:50)

Presumably, Zisling's objection was to a religiously based nationalism. Ben-Gurion negotiated a compromise that retained the phrase "the Rock of Israel," but dropped the term "and its Redeemer."

Meir Wilner, leader of the Communist Party of Israel, offered another amendment that underscored his preference for secular nationalism. During the debate, he noted that his party supported the declaration, but he proposed that a clause be included that would condemn the British mandate. Specifically, he wanted the Declaration to include the following:

The alien mandatory administration did its utmost to hinder the independence of both Jews and Arabs in order to separate them and incite conflict and it is primarily responsible for the war being waged against the Yishuv.

(Quoted in Lorch 1993:47)

While there is not a word per se about religion in Wilner's proposal, it implicitly promotes the idea that nationalist unity could be won if Jews and Arabs understand their shared history as victims of imperialist policy. His proposal did not pass.

A second nationalist model was that of religious nationalism. Represented most clearly by delegates of the Mizhrahi, a Zionist religious party, these delegates wanted a much more specific link between the Jewish religion and the state of Israel in the Declaration. One of their delegates, David Pinkas, argued that what was missing from the document was "the historical basis on which our existence as a nation in Israel exists." He therefore proposed that the Declaration include the "following few words" that would "tell the whole story."

The Land of Israel is the land which was set aside for the Jewish people, as stated in the law (Torah) and the books of the Prophets, and is the birthplace of the Jewish people, there its character was shaped.

(Quoted in Lorch 1993:52)

Pinkas also took exception to Zisling's proposal to drop any reference to "the Rock of Israel" in the document. Trying to negotiate a doable compromise, Ben-Gurion suggested that "each could believe in his own way" concerning the phrase "the Rock of Israel." But, he begged his fellow delegates "that you do not require me to put this phrase to a vote" (quoted in Lorch 1993:53), because of a likely concern that such a vote would divide them on the crucial question of declaring the state's independence.

The revisionists did not directly participate in the debate about religious language in the Declaration, but they advanced arguments that demonstrated their commitment to the territorial integrity of "the land of Israel." Herzl Vardi of the Revisionists proposed excising the paragraph that indicated Israel's support for the resolutions of the United Nations regarding the land of Israel. His concern was that such language implied an eventual partition of the land, while he and his fellow Revisionists "support the principle of Jewish independence in the whole land of Israel" (quoted in Lorch 1993:49). Similarly, Zvi Segal of Hatzohar objected to language in the Declaration indicating Israel's support for the United Nations General Assembly Resolutions which "contain the hint of an agreement to partition" (quoted in Lorch 1993:75). While the revisionists did not link the importance of the land to any specific religious content, the phrase "land of Israel" had religious meaning and could be sacralizing in a vision of a unified land state on both sides of the River Jordan.

For all of the debate about its religious content and character, it is important to note that the Declaration also promoted democratic political principles. Specifically, the document confirmed that Israel would "ensure complete equality of social and political rights to all its inhabitants irrespective of religion, race, or sex."

Three days after the passage of the Declaration, and in the midst of a war with five Arab states, the first session of the Provisional Council of States was held. In addition to discussions about a proposed bill to deal with the political and military crisis, Ben-Gurion opened the floor for members to make additional statements on the Declaration. Shmuel Mikunis of the Communist Party once again introduced the idea that the British mandatory authority was responsible for creating strife between Arabs and Jews "in accordance with the imperialist principle of divide and rule" (quoted in Lorch 1993:76). He also suggested that the Jewish character of the Declaration threatened to undermine the unity of Israeli citizens:

With all due respect for the Declaration of Independence, which mentions the equal rights of citizens of the State of Israel irrespective of nationality or religion, the fact remains that we have a large Arab minority and its specific rights as such should have been noted.

(Quoted in Lorch 1993:77)

Following those words, Zvi Lurie, a member of Mapam, promoted the idea that working class, socialist values might unite Arabs and Jews of the new nation:

Mapam will spearhead the struggle for attaining an alliance with the Arab masses both inside and outside of Israel, for achieving full equality for all the citizens of the country, be they Jew or Arab ... for establishing a cooperative Socialist front comprising the proletariat, the peasants and the progressive intelligentsia, and for upholding the integrity of the Land of Israel on the basis of consensus, tolerance and equality.

(Quoted in Lorch 1993:78)

In hindsight it seems highly naïve that socialist values might in fact have united Arabs and Jews into a shared secular nationalist vision, yet it was nonetheless one that was strong within left-wing elements of the labor movement.

Religious Zionists also expressed some reservation about the Declaration, or at least wanted to be on record with what they thought they were advancing when they had signed it. David Lowenstein of Aguda, the political party of the Haredi community, noted that the "secular form and content of the Declaration has deeply wounded my feelings and those of all religious Jews." He went on to note that he signed it to prevent "an internal rift within Israel," but he wanted to be transparent about its limitations in terms of religion:

It ignores our exclusive right to the Land of Israel, based on the greatest of all covenants, made between God and Abraham our father ... It also ignores the special character of our holy and promised land, which was destined for the Jewish people not solely in order to establish a sovereign state but primarily in which to live a holy and pure life. In defining the character of the State of Israel there is nothing to indicate that it will be based on the laws of our Holy Bible, and that it will aspire to fulfill all its commandments and laws.

(Quoted in Lorch 1993:76)

As might be expected, Revisionist delegates in the Provisional Council advanced a nationalism based on the promotion of strong security in the face of Israel's many enemies. Commenting on the political situation shortly after the second of what would eventually be three truces in Israel's War of Independence, Baruch Weinstein of Hatzohar argued that "we should not only refuse the return of the Arabs to our conquered territory but initiate Jewish urban settlement immediately ... We must settle our conquered areas in order to confront the world with facts. If you began with revisionism you must continue in that direction and go on to expanding the borders as well" (quoted in Lorch 1993:251). Once again, the nationalism of the Revisionists was not explicitly religious, but as would become clearer in later decades, territorial expansion for security concerns overlapped with territorial expansion for religious reasons.

The intersection between these positions was even more apparent in a Knesset debate on the annexation of the West Bank by Jordan in December 1948. Menachem Begin, a member the right-wing revisionist Herut Party, accused the government of "handing over Jerusalem, Rachel's Tomb, Hebron, Bethelem, Shechem, Gilead and Bashan to a foreigner, an enemy, an oppressor." These sites, he contended, "have been historically hallowed for 120 generations, and for which the blood of millions have been shed" (quoted in Lorch 1993:576). Josef Burg, of the Religious Front, continued along similar lines when he noted that "the Jews who still believe in God and His promises continued to believe in all of Jerusalem, Rachel's Tomb, Hebron and the whole country when they were in the diaspora" (quoted in Lorch 1993:586). For Begin those sites were important for historical and security reasons, while for Burg they had a religious meaning.

Alternative nationalisms similarly emerged in the debates among members of the First Knesset on a host of issues. Secular nationalism arose most strongly from members of the left-wing Mapai Party, the Maki/Israeli Communist Party, and Women's International Zionist Organization (WIZO)/Union of Hebrew Women for Equal Rights in Eretz Israel. Ben-Gurion's Mapai Party won a plurality of seats (46) in the first Knesset but he reached out to the members of the National Religious Party (NRP) rather than the left-wing parties to form a governing coalition. In fact, the NRP would be part of the labor establishment for several decades. This was too much for Mapam's Meir Ya'ari who lamented that Mapai had abandoned its commitment socialist values:

If freedom and democracy involve imposing the laws of *Shulhan Aruch* (religious precepts) on all the citizens of the state, both religious and secular, how can we expect democratic freedom and social progress from this Cabinet ... Can socialism be achieved by a coalition which resembles those found in France and Italy, based on clericalism?

(Quoted in Lorch 1993:386–8)

Anticipating political debates about the state's twin commitments to democratic values and Jewish principles, Rachel Cohen of WIZO commended Ben-Gurion for his "declaration of full equality for women," but she expressed concern for how those rights might be protected if religious leaders were empowered to govern in the area of personal status: "now that the laws of the state have been established on the basis of progress, we cannot accept legal discrimination against women" (quoted in Lorch 1993:417). Beba Idelson mirrored that view when she asserted that women "must have equal rights" which included the "sacred right to defend themselves even in rabbinical courts" (quoted in Lorch 1993:410). Socialism, equal rights, progress, and labor were the hallmarks of the secular nationalism promoted by some.

This nationalism, however, competed with that of religious nationalism, encouraged most strongly by members of the National Religious Party (NRP) and of the Sephardic and Oriental Communities. Zecharia Glosca of the Yemenite Association lamented that he and his fellow religious Zionists had been labeled "clericalists with its derogatory connotation." For him it was quite simple: "Nationalism and religion in Judaism are one and the same thing" (quoted in Lorch 1993:418). Rabbi Kalman Kahana of the NRP was dismayed that Ben-Gurion, when he presented the Cabinet and its proposed policies to the Knesset, had not commented "after the Lord [who] has delivered us from our enemies ... without which we would not have reached this point." He further noted that "our presence in the Cabinet is possible only if the law of marriage and divorce in the State of Israel are the rabbinic law" (quoted in Lorch 1993:416).

As he often did, Ben-Gurion tried to find some middle ground between what he saw as the extremes of religious and secular nationalisms. He punted on the specific question of the power of rabbinical courts in the area of family law by saying that his Cabinet was not "prepared to introduce a law concerning civil marriage and divorce, because at this time it would cause a rift within the Jewish nation" (quoted in Lorch 1993:438), thereby placating religious parties who would eventually retain that power. But, he also affirmed that the "equality of rights and obligations, which we have mentioned, will require every man and woman, and every Jew, Moslem and Christian court to recognize that women are equal in everything" (quoted in Lorch 1993:438). In truth, political Zionism generally, and Ben-Gurion specifically, never really knew what place, if any, the Jewish religion had in their brand of nationalism.

The lack of consensus among Jewish groups on religion was particularly evident in debates on the drafting of a Constitution. The Declaration called for the election of Constituent Assembly that would write a Constitution, presumably codifying relations between religion and the state. That proved to be an impossible task, however, because of deep disagreements between secular and religious parties on the state's religious identity, a divide as we have noted that was decades if not centuries in the making (Yanai 1996:111; Elazar 1990:20; Lerner 2009:445). At the end of the 1950 Knesset debate on the Constitution, a compromise was reached in which Israel would not have a formal Constitution, but the Knesset would pass a series of Basic Laws that would have quasi-constitutional status. Among those is the 1982 Basic Law on Human Dignity which identifies Israel as a "Jewish and democratic state," thereby codifying the country's complex self-understanding (Blackstone, Matsubayashi, and Oldmixon 2014:123).

Even before Israel became a state in 1948, leaders of the Zionist movement sought to tamp down potential conflict around religion in the new state. As he had done repeatedly in the past, Ben-Gurion compromised on religious issues in an attempt to placate Orthodox Jews, win their support for the nationalist project, and neutralize conflict around religion. The most obvious example of this was the "status quo" letter that he wrote to the World Zionist Organization in 1947 on behalf of Jewish Agency for Palestine which outlined his understanding of religion in the new state (Cohen and Susser 1996). In that letter, Ben-Gurion reaffirmed the legitimacy of the millet tradition that prevailed under both the Ottoman Empire and during the British Mandate with regard to religious issues. In both cases, religious communities had key roles in education and family law. At the same, however, Ben-Gurion advanced some practices that recognized the Jewish character of the new state including a guarantee that Shabbat would be the legal day of rest in Israel and that only kosher food would be served in state-run kitchens. The letter also anticipated Israel's subsequent commitment to being a democratic state. Ben-Gurion noted that the new state would have Jewish and non-Jewish citizens and that it would "advance full equal rights to all citizens and the absence of coercion or discrimination in matter of religion" (Status Quo Letter 1947).

At least in the short term, the agreement succeeded in avoiding a *Kulturkampf* around religion even before the state had formed (Peleg 1998; Shindler 2008:78–80). Ben-Gurion won the support of orthodox groups and he built a political coalition between his Labor Party and the National Religious Party, a union that would prevail for decades. In terms of public policy, this accommodation has meant that Israel is a democratic state, but one in which there is more government involvement with religion than in any other political democracy and personal law prevails for various confessional communities (Fox and Rynhold 2008).

There are numerous ways that the state accommodates religion, including granting religious courts the power to control marriages and divorce, providing public money to religious schools, the official recognition of the Sabbath as the day of rest for Jewish citizens, the former policy of universal exemption from military service for all Yeshiva students, the creation of a government ministry to administer religious life for the various faith communities, among others.

Ben-Gurion's compromise formed a middle path between those who wanted a purely religious state and those who wanted a decidedly secular one (Cohen and Rynhold 2005:728). In terms of the nationalism that we have been discussing, it sought to advance a civil-religious nationalism that married democratic political norms with the cultural symbols of traditional Judaism. As Shapira (2014:174) rightly notes, Ben-Gurion sought ways to "form a national identity for the hundreds of thousands of people who came to Israel from different countries and cultures." While Ben-Gurion was deeply committed to socialist values, he also had a deep and abiding interest in the Hebrew language and in Jewish culture and history. As prime minister he initiated an effort to microfilm Hebrew manuscripts all over the world so they could be archived at Hebrew University. This developing civil-religious nationalism anticipated the values of a majority of Jews living in Israel decades later, who were neither enamored of the left-wing secular nationalism of the socialists nor moved by the religious nationalism of the religiously observant. As Liebman and Don-Yehiya note (1983:11), most Jewish citizens of Israel support democratic practices and the cultural Jewish symbols of the state.

Echoes of a civil-religious or cultural nationalism emerge clearly in a 1949 Knesset debate on a United Nations proposal to internationalize the city of Jerusalem. In presenting the government's opposition to such a plan, Ben-Gurion noted that "Jewish Jerusalem is an organic, inseparable part of the state of Israel, just as it is an integral part of Jewish history and belief" (quoted in Lorch 1993:549). Menachem Begin argued that "justice, history, emotions, faith favor undivided Jerusalem as the capital of Israel," and he warned that "any attempt to impose alien rule on Jerusalem will be smashed on the rock of resistance of the entire nation" (quoted in Lorch 1993:551–2). Idov Cohen of the socially liberal Progressive Party contended that "the sanctity of Jerusalem derives from the depths of Jewish history" (quoted in Lorch 1993:553). The key elements of this emerging civil-religious nationalism were Jewish history, shared culture, and common experiences, rather than Jewish law or socialist values.

Ben-Gurion's compromise did not, however, solve the underlying conflict among the various groups about the religious character of the state, and it has meant that religion, rather than a unifying factor in nationalist sentiment, has often been a divisive one. In terms of solidifying the religion–nationalism link, conditions put in place at the moment of regime formation are of crucial significance. Once solidified in institutional arrangements, both the initial structure of the state and its ideological orientation can remain quite resilient (Rubin 2013:498). Precisely because Israel accommodates religion and is a self-described Jewish and democratic state, the state's legitimacy can be challenged from the political right if the state is not Jewish enough and the political left if the state is insufficiently democratic. Attitudes toward the state, in short, are conditioned in part by the state's religious policies. The religiously observant challenge any deviation from Jewish religious law; secular, nonreligious Jews question the monopoly enjoyed by the orthodox camp in the realm of religion; and Arab citizens of Israel chafe at what they perceive to be the state's Jewish rather than democratic character.

CHALLENGES TO ISRAEL'S CIVIL-RELIGIOUS NATIONALISM

Developments early in Israel's history further challenged the religious-nationalism nexus in the country. The first of those changes was the immigration of large numbers of Jews from North Africa, Eastern Europe, and the Middle East after the War of Independence. Between 1948 and 1960, Israel more than doubled its Jewish population from 650,000 to 1.4 million. In terms of religion, these Jews were more traditional than the majority of the pre-state Jewish population (Yakobson 2008:13). While these immigrants were not uniformly Haredi or orthodox, they were more committed to the symbols of Jewish culture and practice than they were to the socialist values of Labor Zionism (Liebman and Don-Yehiya 1983:125). In fact, it was a dispute between Ben-Gurion's Mapai and the religious parties over the education of immigrant children (whether or not they would automatically be enrolled in religious schools) that led the dissolution of the coalition government and the election of the Second Knesset. The resulting election was inconclusive, and Mapai once again formed a coalition with various religious parties. In return for their support, the government passed legislation that formalized the system of religious education and gave more control to Orthodox leaders in the running of those schools (Sachar 1996:376–82). Ben-Gurion might have anticipated the eventual triumph of socialism, in short, but the immigration of more traditional Jews meant that the religious and cultural values of Judaism became more important for Israel's nationalism over time while socialist ones were on the decline.

This political compromise on the education issue mirrored Ben-Gurion's previous decision to maintain the millet system in the newly created state of Israel. Political pragmatism drove that choice, but the result was to reinforce the religious identities of various confessional communities. By defining persons in terms of their religious affiliation, the millet system undermined any nationalist frame that minimized those ascriptive identities.

Equally significant has been the fact that orthodox Judaism did not disappear as Ben-Gurion likely thought that it would, and that religious Zionism has been theologically and politically transformed in the past several decades. As we noted above, Orthodox Jews were and are divided into Zionist and non-Zionist camps. For the latter, Zionism has no religious meaning. What matters for this group that is often referred to as ultra-orthodox is public policy based on the Halacha. On the other hand, a messianic nationalism had always been strong among religious Zionists who provided a spiritual rationale for Jewish nationalism. Symptomatic of this view was an Independence Day speech given by Rabbi Zvi Yehuda Kook, the son of Rabbi Abraham Isaac Kook, three weeks prior the 1967 Six-Day War. In that speech, Kook described the agony he felt when he learned about the partition of Palestine.

I could not accept that indeed 'they have divided My land' (Joel 4:2)! – Yes [and now nineteen years later] Where is our Shechem, our Jericho, where?! And all that lies beyond the Jordan – each and every clod of earth, every region, hill, valley, every plot of land that is part of Eretz Israel – have we the right to give up even one grain of the land of God?

(Kook 1967)

Many of Kook's followers, and other religious Zionists, interpreted Israel's subsequent military victory in the 1967 War as a revelation of God's intentions and a fulfillment of God's messianic promises. Particularly significant for this group, sometimes called modern orthodox, was the conquest of territory viewed as part of God's sacred promise to the Jewish people (Levinson and Ettinger 2012; Liebman and Don-Yehiya 1983:201; Rubin 2013:68). They embraced what Ken Wald (2002:117) describes as "territorial maximalism" for religious reasons, i.e., what God has given to God's people cannot rightfully be returned. Kook also

encouraged his followers to settle the territories won during the conflict. The rise to prominence of religious Zionism confirmed for some a
necessary link between Judaism and the state. All of this has meant that
religion plays an increasingly divisive role in contemporary arguments
about Israeli nationalism.

In terms of numbers, Jewish citizens of Israel are divided into three
large groups. Approximately 20 percent of the population is religiously
orthodox, though they are evenly divided between ultra-orthodox and
modern orthodox camps. A smaller percentage, around 10 percent, comprises secular Jews who are either indifferent or hostile to the Jewish tradition and reject any linking of religion and the state. Finally, a majority
of Jewish citizens of Israel are neither orthodox nor anti-religious, but are
instead traditional in the sense that they selectively practice some of the
rituals and customs of the Jewish faith (Liebman and Susser 1997:213–
14; Wald 2002:100).

The other significant demographic change that threatens Israel's
nationalist model has been the growth of the Arab, non-Jewish population in Israel. The Arab population of Israel currently comprises 20
percent of the country's population, similar to its proportion in 1949
(excluding the population in the West Bank). The fraction of the Arab
population decreased to as low as 11 percent with large-scale Jewish
immigration to Israel in the years after independence, but with waning
Jewish immigration and higher fertility rates for Arabs it is expected
to grow to a quarter of the population by 2020 (Statistical Abstract of
Israel 2016). Socialist values might have united secular Jews and Arabs
under the umbrella of secular nationalism, but that nationalist vision has
become far less prominent in Israel in recent decades. A joint statement
put together by prominent Arab citizens of Israel in 2006 promoted a
secular nationalism based on shared liberal democratic values, but it also
called for Israel to abandon its Jewish identity that was seen as a for-
tified ideological barrier in the face of the possibility of obtaining full
equality for Palestinian Arab citizens of Israel (The Future Vision of the
Palestinian Arabs in Israel 2006:13). Because they did not "share collective values or a historical memory with the dominant Jewish community"
(Oded 2011:5) Arab citizens of Israel found little meaning in a civil religion based on Jewish customs and traditions. They were even less enamored, to put it mildly, with the messianic nationalism of religious Zionists.
The rise of both forms of Jewish nationalism (civil-religious and religious
nationalism) has, perhaps not surprisingly, coincided with the resurgence
of Palestinian identity among Israeli Arabs (Lowrance 2005:496). Rightly

or wrongly, Arab citizens of Israel perceive Jewish nationalism in ethno-religious terms, and as a minority within the state their attachment to the country is compromised (Jamal 2004:436).

Political variables have further challenged Israel's nationalist model. Not only has religious orthodoxy not disappeared at the social level, it has similarly not faded away as a party-political factor. The 120 members of Israel's legislative body, the Knesset, are elected under a system of proportional representation. Orthodox religious parties have won a small, but steady percentage of the seats in each of the twenty Knesset elections. A coalition of orthodox parties, the United Religious Front, won sixteen seats in the First Knesset in 1949. Over the course of the next nineteen Knesset elections, the number of seats won by various orthodox religious parties fluctuated between thirteen (1951 and 1981) and thirty (2013). Religious parties won twenty-one seats in the most recent Knesset elections in 2015. While the parties are divided on a host of issues, they nonetheless promote a nationalism that cleaves more closely to religious than secular values.

Because the balance of power in any given Knesset has often been razor thin, these religious parties have often been able to exert considerable influence on the government of the day. The National Religious Party, for example, served in every Labor government. These parties were initially willing to accept what Mirsky (2014:150) describes as "secondary status within the Zionist movement." They traded their political support for control over education and social-welfare policies. Even ultra-orthodox groups that ostensibly rejected the Zionist project participated in this political quid pro quo.

In recent years, however, a number of religious parties have mobilized voters on more contentious issues related to the settlement of the occupied territories and the place of religion in Israeli life. The growing mobilization of these religious voters provided an electoral incentive for the newly formed right-wing Likud Party to appeal to that constituency. In a concession to Orthodox parties in his coalition, as an example, the country's first Likud prime minister, Menachem Begin, agreed to revise the Basic Law to make it easier for women to get exemptions on religious grounds from mandatory military service. A similar dynamic has been at work on issues related to the occupied territories. While secular in orientation and focused mainly on Israeli security concerns, the Likud focus on expanding the settlements in the territories for security purposes dovetailed with the religious arguments of religious Zionists about the sacredness of the land (Sachar 1996:740–2). The transformation of religious

Zionism and its political link to the Likud Party has thus strengthened arguments for a model of religious nationalism in Israel.

A final factor that has helped to destabilize Israel's civil religion has been ongoing conflict between Israel and her various neighbors. In its nearly seventy-year history, Israel has gone to war with one or several Arab nations on almost a dozen occasions. For decades, not a single Arab state was willing to accept the existence of Israel, nor did they seek to stop terrorist incursions across Israel's borders. External threats to the nation can reinforce nationalist sentiment. When that conflict is rooted at least in part in religious differences, or can be presented in that way, religious nationalism is often promoted while the values of civic, secular nationalism can be diminished. Even Ben-Gurion, who was deeply committed to the values of Labor Zionism, nonetheless made decisions as prime minister for political and security reasons that undermined some of his socialist values. Chief among them was his decision to acquiesce to the advice of his military advisors after the War of Independence and impose martial law on the Arabs living in Israel. This status remained in place until after Ben-Gurion left office (Shapira 2014:181). In a debate on that policy, Ya'akov Hazan, the cofounder of the pro-Soviet Communist Party, asserted that "a national movement which discriminates against others today is doomed. A nation which restricts the rights of the minority jeopardizes its own future. The concern for the security of our country obliges us to do our utmost to make the Arab minority loyal to the state ... This cannot be achieved through the Military Government" (quoted in Lorch 1993:868). The wisdom of Ben-Gurion's decision is arguable, but the result of it was implicitly to advance an ethnic or religious nationalism that only reinforced those divisions within Israeli society.

The contingent variables since Israeli independence (demographic, political, and security) have changed over time, and so too has the content of Israeli nationalism. In his study on Jewish nationalism, Shelef (2010) demonstrates that Labor, religious, and revisionist Zionists have evolved their understanding of such key issues as what is included in the homeland, who we are as a people, and what is it that we are to do. Those changes have further undermined the capacity for the state to forge a unifying nationalist vision.

The civil religion described by Liebman and Don-Yehiya might work to unify a majority of Israelis who are "traditional," in short, but it does not play the same unifying role that it does in the United States. Instead, Israel's civil religion faces challenges from the left, from both Jewish secular and Arabs, who would prefer a thoroughly secular nationalism shorn of any relationship with the Jewish religion per se, and from the right who want a more decidedly religious nationalism, either in terms of state adherence to religious law or an unapologetically Jewish state.

PUBLIC OPINION AND NATIONALISM

We have argued that relations between religious groups and the new State of Israel were contentious. Questions about the state's religious self-understanding divided secular and religious Jews, and they pitted Jewish and Arab citizens of the new state against each other. Political elites tried to minimize religion as a contentious issue by adopting the Status Quo Agreement, which cemented an institutional role for religious groups, and by embracing a conception of the state as both Jewish and democratic, hoping in that way to placate the competing religious and secular visions for the new state. Those choices initially minimized conflict around religion, but they did not solve the underlying dilemma, and as a consequence competing models of religion and nationalism developed. For many religious and for most nonreligious Jews, a civil religion developed that embraced Zionism, or that united the cause of the nation with the cause of the religious tradition (Liebman and Don-Yehiya 1983). Yet, this civil religion is not necessarily unifying for orthodox Jews, post-Zionist secular Jews, and to Arab citizens of Israel, all of whom had specific reasons to reject linking the cause of the state with that of a particular faith. In contrast with a country like the United States where the bonds between national and religious loyalties are uniformly strong, Israel evidences noticeable differences in nationalism according to one's religious identification.

The data for this claim, however, have come primarily from religious and political elites. Elite cues are important, of course, but if our argument is sound we should be able to show a similar set of attitudes among the mass public. We therefore next turn our attention to an empirical analysis of how the general public fuses nationalistic and religious values. Very few empirical analyses of religion and Israeli national identity exist. Arad and Alon (2006) commissioned a survey on patriotism in 2006. The authors conclude that when compared to respondents from other developed countries, citizens of Israel score high on some measures of patriotism (willingness to fight for the country and a desire to remain planted in its soil) and relatively low on others (pride in the country). Moreover, these scholars find that Arab respondents are far less patriotic than are

Jewish respondents, and that levels of patriotism also vary among Jewish respondents, with orthodox Jews generally less patriotic than religious, traditional, and secular Jews. This report does not appear to use multi-variate methods, however, so we cannot know whether religious or ethnic identity has independent causal effects on nationalism.

Works by Sorek and Ceobanu (2009) and Staerkle et al. (2010) make use of one of the same databases that we analyze in our research: the International Social Science Programme (ISSP) survey on national identity. Sorek and Ceobanu conclude that secular Jewish Israelis are significantly less proud on almost all dimensions of national pride than any other Jewish Israeli group. However, this article did not include responses from Arab citizens of Israel. Staerkle et al., on the other hand, focus exclusively on ethnic and religious minorities in Israel (Arabs and Christians), and they find that those citizens are less nationalistic than are Jewish respond-ents. One liability of the ISSP, however, is that the only religious questions asked are frequency of attendance at religious services and religious iden-tification. In the case of Israel, what this misses are the various streams within Judaism (ultra-orthodox, religious, traditional, and secular) that are not easily captured by a measure of attendance at religious services.

Our work in this chapter attempts to respond to these limitations of the existing literature. First, using Israeli data from the 2003 ISSP National Identity II module,[1] we created a nationalism scale consisting of six items ($\alpha = 0.650$). The questions asked the respondents about how close they felt to Israel, how proud they were to be Israeli, and whether Israelis' way of life should be adopted by other countries. The final three ques-tions gauged how much respondents agreed with statements on whether they would rather be a citizen of Israel than any other country, whether there were some things about Israel that made them feel ashamed, and if they were often less proud of Israel than they would like to be. When all the items were added together, they formed a scale ranging from six to twenty-eight. While this poll asked dozens of potentially valid indicators of nationalism, we selected these items because they were the most rele-vant to civic nationalism and because some were worded positively and others negatively. This sample included Hebrew-, Arabic-, or Russian-speaking citizens of the state of Israel. It did not survey Arabic-speaking individuals from the West Bank or Golan Heights.

One disadvantage of the ISSP is that it has relatively few country-specific questions. Religious identity measures, for example, are limited to the broad categories of Catholic, Protestant, Jewish, etc., which are not ideal for examining differences among Jewish respondents. Another drawback for our purposes is that the ISSP lacks any items on a specific nationalistic project. We therefore also rely on data from the 2013 Israel Democracy Index.[2] This survey includes questions about generic nationalism, support for a specific nationalistic issue (i.e., settlements), and more nuanced probes about different forms of Jewish identity. The sampling frame paralleled that for the ISSP, with respondents being selected out of the population of Israeli citizens. Generic Israeli nationalism came from an item about one's pride in being an Israeli. We measured attitudes toward settlements using a question about whether "the government of Israel should encourage only Jews to establish new communities."

As Table 3.1 suggests, Israelis' level of nationalism varies greatly by religious tradition. This quantitative result thus confirms our early historical argument. In both surveys, nationalism is lowest among non-Jewish respondents.[3] Perhaps not surprisingly, the most disaffected respondents are Muslims and Christians (many of whom are Arabs). As non-Jews in a predominantly Jewish country, these religious minorities perceive the nation-state to be Jewish and are therefore less likely to embrace the nationalistic mission. Table 3.1 also confirms that even Jewish interviewees exhibit varying levels of national identity based on their religious orientation. The least nationalistic are the non-Zionist Haredi and the

TABLE 3.1. *Nationalism by religious tradition*

Tradition	Mean (ISSP)	Mean (IDI)
Muslim	17.23	2.07
Druze	19.66	2.92
Other religion	17.09	3.24
Jewish	18.86	3.47
Haredi	3.21	
Haredi Leumi	3.68	
National religious	3.58	
Practicing traditional	3.69	
Non-practicing traditional	3.63	
Secular	3.37	
Catholic	16.76	
Christian		2.74
All respondents	18.63	3.24

Sources: 2003–2004 International Social Survey Programme (ISSP), National Identity II, Israeli subsamples; 2013 Israel Democracy Index (IDI).

secular Jews, although their average scores still rank somewhere between "quite" and "very" proud. Nonetheless, their lower averages might reflect some of the historical tensions that these groups experienced during the founding period.

To investigate further the sources of Israelis' national identity, we performed a multivariate regression interpreting these nationalism measures. In general, Table 3.2 suggests that the most salient cleavage in levels of nationalism is between Jewish and non-Jewish respondents. In both surveys, Muslim and Christian respondents are much less emotionally tied to the state of Israel than are their Jewish co-citizens. Jewish Israelis, however, are also divided. Relative to secular (Hiloni) and strictly orthodox (Haredi and Haredi Leumi) Jews, Jewish interviewees who embrace some form of civil religion (National Religious, practicing Traditional, and non-practicing Traditional) are more nationalistic after one controls for other socioeconomic variables (e.g., ethnicity, income, education, age, gender, and urbanicity). In short, Israel's civil religion creates strong bonds to the state for the majority of Israelis who are not secular, orthodox, or Arab. In the ISSP survey, religious attendance appears to have boosted nationalistic sentiments, but this poll did not distinguish between different Jewish respondents the way the IDI study did.[4] These findings reinforce our earlier argument about the deep-seated tensions in Israel over its national identity. The principal nationalist struggle at the state's founding pitted Jewish and non-Jewish citizens against each other but also divided orthodox and secular Jews.

Most of the remaining regressors in Table 3.2 follow the standard hypotheses elaborated in previous works on public support for nationalism. Higher education and (sometimes) income are associated with lower degrees of national identity. Advanced age, on the other hand, correlates positively with elevated nationalism. Although gender and urbanicity produced no statistically significant results, Russian-origin and Arabic-speaking Israelis tended to be disproportionately opposed to the state.

SUPPORT FOR JEWISH SETTLEMENTS

In addition to measuring general nationalism in Israel, we wished to look at attitudes on a very specific nationalistic question. We therefore settled on attitudes toward Jewish settlements, one of the most important nationalistic projects of the past thirty years. This question gets at the tension between the state's commitment to being both Jewish and democratic

TABLE 3.2. *Religious and other determinants of nationalism*

Variable	Coefficient (ISSP)	Standard error	Coefficient (IDI)	Standard error
Muslim	−2.072*	1.047	−1.209*	0.483
Druze	1.972	1.213		
Other religion	−0.807	0.885	0.032	0.510
Jewish Haredi	0.910	0.617		
Jewish Haredi Leumi	−0.184	0.273		
Jewish national religious	0.623*	0.325		
Jewish practicing traditional	0.695*	0.273		
Jewish non-practicing traditional	0.518*	0.268		
Jewish other	−0.538	0.588		
Catholic	−1.888	1.157		
Christian	−0.863*	0.453		
Religious attendance	0.265*	0.051		
Education	−0.276*	0.100	−0.189*	0.045
Income	−7.456*	0.000	0.068	0.059
Woman	0.344	0.238	0.024	0.148
Age	0.023*	0.007	0.153*	0.048
Arabic	0.645	0.968	−1.412*	0.472
Russian	−0.694	0.410	−0.465*	0.204
Urbanicity	0.041	0.099	−0.283	0.154
Constant 1	18.218*	0.859	−3.248*	0.379
Constant 2	−2.154*	0.363		
Constant 3	−0.897*	0.355		
N	925		803	
R²/Nagelkerke R²	0.116		0.283	

*Denotes an effect that is significantly different from 0 at the 5 percent level for Ordinary Least Square (in ISSP) or ordered Logit (in IDI) model.

Notes: All regressors are dummy variables except for Religious Attendance (range = 0–7 [ISSP]), Income (2,250–22,000 [ISSP]; 1–5 [IDI]), Age (18–96 [ISSP]; 1–6 [IDI]), and Education (0–5 [ISSP]; 1–7 [IDI]). Omitted categories for religious identification are Jewish (ISSP) and Secular Jewish (IDI).

Source: 2003 International Social Survey Programme, National Identity I, Israeli subsample; 2013 Israel Democracy Index (IDI).

TABLE 3.3. *Support for Jewish settlements by religious tradition*

Tradition	Mean
Muslim	1.84
Other religion	2.63
Jewish	2.65
Haredi	3.15
Haredi Leumi	3.59
National religious	3.16
Practicing traditional	2.92
Non-practicing traditional	2.64
Secular	2.30
Christian	2.14
All respondents	2.63

Notes: Sample size of Druze too small for valid comparisons.
Source: 2013 Israel Democracy Index.

(Oldmixon and Samaniego 2014). The relevant IDI item asked respondents how much they agreed with the statement "The government of Israel should encourage only Jews to establish new communities."

The average levels of support for mandating only Jewish new communities roughly parallel mean scores for generic nationalism in Table 3.1. Table 3.3 clearly reveals similar religious cleavages between Jews and non-Jews and between secular and orthodox Jews. Not surprisingly, Muslims and Christians almost universally reject this policy, which received weak support among all Jewish respondents. Jews themselves split into the long-standing divisions. Secular Jews, who are generally proud to be Israeli (see Table 3.1) mildly oppose state aid to only Jewish new communities, while the various orthodox streams enthusiastically endorse such an arrangement. Thus, a prominent nationalist issue divides religious respondents in Israel.

As Table 3.4 documents, non-Jewish respondents are predictably hostile to expanding only Jewish settlements. Even when controlling for a host of significant demographic variables, being Muslim still boosts opposition to this policy. Presumably, these citizens perceive the expansion of Jewish communities as a nationalistic project for Jews only and as competition for scarce land. Divisions among Jewish respondents, interestingly, are not as stark as for abstract nationalism. Relative to secular Jews, all other Jewish groups (i.e., Haredi, Hardi Leumi, National

TABLE 3.4. *Religious and other determinants of support for Jewish settlements*

Variable	Coefficient	Standard error
Muslim	−1.469*	0.729
Other religion	−0.184	0.589
Jewish Haredi	1.183*	0.266
Jewish Haredi Leumi	2.467*	0.655
Jewish national religious	1.375*	0.281
Jewish practicing traditional	0.981*	0.222
Jewish non-practicing traditional	0.532*	0.231
Jewish other	0.544	0.643
Christian	−0.619	0.522
Education	−0.096*	0.042
Income	−0.041	0.060
Woman	0.362*	0.148
Age	−0.160*	0.046
Russian	0.628*	0.200
Urbanicity	−0.157	0.155
Constant 1	−1.366*	0.341
Constant 2	−0.625	0.338
Constant 3	0.207	0.338
N	665	
Nagelkerke R²	0.157	

*Denotes an effect that is significantly different from 0 at the 5 percent level for ordered Logit model.
Notes: All regressors are dummy variables except for Income (1–5), Age (1–6), and Education (1–7). Omitted category for religious identification is Secular Jewish.
Source: 2013 Israel Democracy Index.

Religion, and practicing and non-practicing Traditional) strongly endorse this preference policy toward Jews. This situation might represent a case where a civil-religious understanding of the Jewish nature of the state unites almost all religious Jews.[5]

RELIGION AND NATIONALISM IN RELIGIOUS PUBLICATIONS AND PRIME MINISTERS' SPEECHES

Our public opinion findings reinforce our argument about the divisive nature of Israel's civil-religious nationalism. In the United States, the links between religion and nationalism are uniformly strong for all religious traditions. In Israel, by contrast, religion divides Jewish and non-Jewish citizens of the state of Israel on whether they understand the nationalist project in religious or secular terms. In order to determine if schisms also prevail at the elite level, we conducted a content analysis of religious periodicals and official statements for the country's main religious traditions: Modern Orthodox Judaism (Haredi Leumi), Ultra-Orthodox Judaism (Haredi), National Religious, secular Jewish, Muslim, Druze, and Greek Orthodox Christian. For each group we identified a publication that was representative for the tradition as a whole, which was easier for some faith communities than for others. Ultra- and Modern-Orthodox Judaism comprise a broad spectrum of movements which draw on distinct philosophies. Each is united, however, in how they understand the relationship between Jewish values and the modern, secular world. Modern Orthodox Jews work to synthesize Jewish and secular values, while Ultra-Orthodox Jews reject modern secular culture. Implicit within these groups are divergent positions on the Zionist project. For the most part, Modern Orthodox Jews are religious Zionists, while Ultra-Orthodox Jews reject religious Zionism. National Religious is an even broader category that includes individuals who identify themselves in surveys as "traditional religious" or "traditional nonreligious," and even secular or Haredi but say that they belong to the National-Religious camp.

We selected Mercaz HaRav Kook (the Rav Kook Center) for Modern Orthodox Judaism. Mercaz HaRav is one of the leading yeshivas in Jerusalem, a number of prominent religious Zionists have studied there, and the center broadly reflects the views of Modern Orthodoxy. For the Ultra-Orthodox we chose Neturei Karta because it is one of the oldest and largest anti-Zionist orthodox groups in Israel. Describing its mission as "leading the revolution for an ethical, inclusive & inspiring Jewish Israel" (Tzohar 2016), Tzohar is our National Religious representative group. Tzohar is a Zionist group which seeks to bring Israelis closer to their Jewish heritage. The BINA Center for Jewish Identity and Culture is our representative group for secular Judaism. Trying to "bridge the gap of alienation between secular Israelis and their own Jewish heritage," BINA (2016), BINA is the largest secular Zionist organization in Israel.

The overwhelming majority of Christians in Israel are Eastern Orthodox. We used the publications of the Greek Orthodox Patriarch of Jerusalem, who is the head bishop of the Orthodox Church of Jerusalem, as the representative spokesperson for Orthodox Christians. Identifying a single Arab organization is problematic for a number of reasons. First, there is an important cultural and political division between Palestinians and Druze. The Israeli government recognizes the Druze as a distinct religious minority, and they serve in the Israeli Defense Forces. The Bedouins, like the Druze, have the option to serve. Israeli Arabs, on the other hand, are exempt from military service. To get a sufficient number of relevant articles for the Druze community, we used publications from both bladna.co.il and al-amama.com, websites that cater to the Druze community. For similar reasons, we identified three sources for relevant articles from the Israeli Arab community: the Mossawa Advocacy Center for Arab Citizens in Israel, the Legal Center for Arab Minority Rights in Israel, and the Arab Association for Human Rights. These three do not represent all opinions within the Arab Muslim community in Israel. In 2015, the Israeli government outlawed more than a dozen organizations that it viewed as Islamic extremists (Rubin 2015).

An advantage of the groups we selected is that each has an online searchable archive of editorials, articles, and commentaries. We located the relevant texts within each webpage using a search for at least the words or phrases "Zionism," "Israel," "nation," and "Jewish identity" in all issues for as long a time frame as possible. The searches were done in English, Hebrew, or Arabic based on the language of the relevant documents. The specific time frames were: Mercaz HaRav Kook (2007–15); Neturei Karta (2011–15); Tzohar (2005–15); BINA (2011–15); Greek Orthodox (2008–15); Muslim (2000–16); and Druze (2015–16). We read each of the appropriate documents and coded them on at least two dimensions: (1) the degree of nationalism and (2) the religiousness of the nationalism. For example, our Muslim articles universally opposed Zionism. A sizeable percentage of them favored secular nationalism, while a minority advocated a Palestinian or pan-Arab state on religious grounds. Our Ultra-Orthodox group also opposed Zionism using both secular and religious arguments.

Figure 3.1 summarizes the results of our content analysis of the various publications. The results confirm the deeply contested nature of Israeli nationalism among Jewish groups and between Jewish and non-Jewish citizens of the state of Israel. Not surprisingly, not a single editorial, commentary, statement, or article by the Greek Orthodox Patriarch promoted religious Zionism. A few of the articles took no particular stance on Israeli nationalism, but the overwhelming majority of these statements advocate a multicultural, multireligious nationalism that promotes the secular values of tolerance, diversity, and human rights. In his 2015 New Year Address, His Beatitude Theopholis III (2015), Patriarch

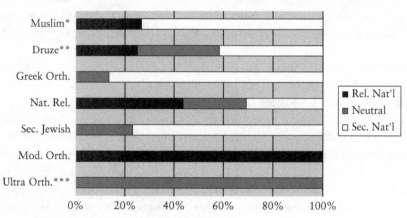

*The form of nationalism is anti-Zionist.
**The form of nationalism could be Zionist or anti-Zionist.
***Ultra Orthodox are generally anti-Zionist on both religious and secular grounds.

FIGURE 3.1. *Abstract nationalism in religious periodicals*

of Jerusalem, asserted that "the identity of Jerusalem is founded not on one tradition or religious group alone. The integrity of Jerusalem, both historically and religiously, depends on the well-being of Jew, Christian, and Muslim here in our midst. Jerusalem is home to all, and depends on all." In a 2013 address to Israel's President, His Beatitude similarly noted that "we who live here are privileged to be part and parcel of this unique multi-cultural and multi-ethnic heritage ... we must deepen our commitment to the democratic value of freedom of worship" (2013).

The arguments of our Muslim organizations are largely secular and are generally harsh in their critique of religious Zionism. The author of an article on Jewish settlements in the West Bank, for example, complains that "the Israeli government confiscates Arab lands and it justifies this by saying it does so for the 'public good.' However, those same lands that are supposedly used for the public good are only benefiting Jewish citizens of Israel" (Halabi 2000). This position is implicitly evoking a secular framework for the national project. In a similar way, another Muslim author suggests that while Arab Palestinians have "become Israeli citizens," they "live under an oppressive military rule that violates their basic freedom and human rights" (Dkoor 2000). The statements of the Druze publications are more nuanced. Most promote secular nationalism, but a few indicate support among the community for Zionism. One article, for example, notes that former Defense Minister Moshe Arens said that on a recent visit to the Golan Heights he saw members of the Druze community proudly waving the Israeli flag (Bladna 2016).

There is greater diversity among the four Jewish organizations but near uniformity within a particular group. On issues of religion and nationalism, Israel is arguably *sui generis* in that groups self-define in terms of their understanding of Zionism. It is to be expected, therefore, that each of the documents we identified for the pro-Zionist Modern Orthodox Rav Kook Center promotes religious Zionism, while the same unanimous percentage of the statements for the secular BINA Center advocates secular Zionism. The same is true for the Ultra-Orthodox Neturei Karta, which exists in part to oppose religious Zionism. Finally, because Tzohar seeks to bridge the gap between religious and secular Zionism, its documents show a more bifurcated pattern, with a nearly even split in those advancing religious versus secular Zionism.

The comments of these groups reflect just how divided Jewish elites are on the central question of religion and nationalism. At one end of the spectrum is Rav Kook. Each year, the group posts a document on Jerusalem Day, which commemorates the reunification and the establishment of Israeli control over the Old City after the 1967 Six-Day War. The holiday is increasingly controversial as are debates about its historical meaning. In its 2008 Jerusalem Day document, the group posted these comments: "We all pray ... for a full return of our nation to its Jewish roots and to a smart and strong government which is faithful to our God and who will build the State of Israel to be the Seat of the Lord of the world" (Kook 2008). The group also weighed in on the exceptionally contentious question of whether or not Jewish soldiers could participate in the expulsion of Jews from the occupied territories. On this issue, the group quoted Rabbi Avraham Shapira, onetime head of the rabbinical court of Jerusalem. Shapira wrote: "According to Torah law, there is an absolute prohibition in giving land in Israel to a gentile ... any order that contradicts Halacha and forces one to violate Torah law has no validity, must not be obeyed and no person has any authority to issue such an order" (Av 2009). What is consistent in these comments is a nationalism that is intimately tied to Jewish religious practices and law. The State of Israel is supposed to be "the Seat of the Lord of the world," and its laws must follow the Torah. A more nuanced understanding of Jerusalem Day and of the nexus between Jewish religion and nationalism comes from Tzohar. One of this organization's commentary's supports religious nationalism: "Jerusalem is the city of the Holy Temple, the place of Divine Inspiration, the seat of the Sanhedrin, the source of Torah for the entire Jewish Nation" (Arye 2013). Yet a separate essay affirms a more inclusive vision for the city: "Jerusalem is a city that is open in all directions and tries to integrate all contradictory religions and opinions, tastes and customs" (Orbach 2013).

At the other and of the spectrum on the nexus between religion and nationalism is the BINA Center. For this group, a commitment to secular values is the defining characteristic of its Zionism. Symptomatic of this view is a 2013 document which argues that "Zionism and the establishment of the State of Israel as a Jewish and democratic state brought about a new possibility – an Israeli, Jewish and secular identity, based on values of human respect and cultural freedom" (Naim 2013). BINA has also been instrumental in promoting the Independence Tractate, an educational program that concerns Israel's Declaration of Independence. In promoting that program, a 2015 document affirms that "we hope to bring the Israeli society closer to pluralistic and democratic values that are inherent in Judaism and Zionism" (Elbaum 2015). What is most important for BINA are the cultural, democratic values that emanate from Jewish tradition and Israel's history.

Arguably in a category entirely of its own is the Ultra-orthodox, anti-Zionist Neterui Kartei. At first glance it seems strange to place this group's statements in the neutral camp when each of the group's documents is replete with theological terms and reflection. An interview with Hirsch (2014), a long-time leader of the group, demonstrates the group's religious interpretation. Hirsch fully rejects the Zionist project, which it describes as a "tragedy" and whose advocates he calls "murderers and war criminals." According to Hirsch, Zionism is a human project that rejects the biblical mandate for Jews to wait for God's redemption of the world. To the extent that Hirsch has a "positive" political project and a corresponding nationalist commitment, it is to "return the government to the Palestinian people." His hope is that this new government will "be gracious and just toward us, as they have treated us during the days of the Diaspora." In short, the current state of Israel has absolutely no positive meaning for Hirsch and those of his Ultra-Orthodox persuasion.

In addition to a measure of generic nationalism, we also analyzed all the relevant articles from the various groups on the specific nationalist issue of Jewish settlements in the occupied territories (Figure 3.2). We coded each article as supportive of Jewish settlement of the occupied territories, opposed to those settlements, or neutral on this very controversial question. Not surprisingly, there is a good deal of agreement within the various organizations, but divergent positions among them. Articles

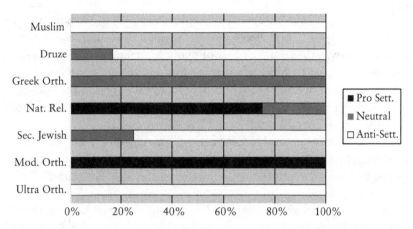

FIGURE 3.2. *Attitudes toward settlements in religious periodicals*

from the Muslim, Druze, Ultra-Orthodox Jewish, and secular Jewish were nearly uniform in their opposition to Jewish settlements in these contested areas. An article from BINA, the secular Jewish group, talks about a sense of "doom" surrounding the "facts on the ground (roads built, settlements expanded, lands confiscated)" (Dow 2016). The titles of one of the articles from Muslim publications make clear their opposition to settlements: "Israeli Confiscation of Palestinian Land: Law and Policy of Settlements" (Halabi 2000). As we noted above, the Ultra-orthodox Neterui Kartie rejects Zionism, so it stands to reason that they also reject the expansion of Jewish communities in the West Bank. At the other end of the spectrum are the publications by the Modern Orthodox, which are entirely supportive of the settlements, and those of the National Religious, which are mostly supportive. An article from the Rav Kook Center, for example, suggests that the Biblical commandment to Canaan "pertains to all areas of the Land of Israel, including Judea and Samaria, and the Golan Heights" (Shapira 2009). The author's use of the biblical terms "Judea and Samaria" rather than "the occupied territories" is meant to reinforce his claim on the legitimacy of Jewish expansion.

There is no searchable database of prime ministers' speeches or official proclamations, so it is not possible for us to replicate the quantitative analysis that we performed in the American chapter. Thus, we chose to do a content analysis of representative speeches by selected Israeli prime ministers. Specifically, we looked at the speeches of Ben-Gurion

(1948–54; 1955–63), Menachem Begin (1977–83), Yitzhak Shamir (1983–4; 1986–92), and Benjamin Netanyahu(1996–9; 2009–present). Ben-Gurion was the country's first of many Mapai or Labor party prime ministers, Begin and Shamir were the first elected from an alternative party, the Likud, while Netanyahu, also from the Likud, is the country's current prime minister. In reading the speeches, we tried to see how each described Israeli nationalism.

Both civil-religious and secular nationalism emerges from David Ben-Gurion's copious speeches. In his 1950 commentary before the Knesset on the proposed Law of Return, for example, he contends that:

the revival of the Jewish state [cannot] be understood without knowing the history of the Jewish people during the Frist and Second Temples, the history of Jewish prophecy, spirit and vision, the history of the Jewish diaspora and the concept of messianism ... the incessant attempts of the wandering nation throughout the generations to return to its land.

(Quoted in Lorch 1993:612)

In a speech six years later in 1956, Ben-Gurion similarly intoned that the establishment of the state of Israel was a "process involving redemption ... as well as the ingathering of the exiles, the imparting of our ancient cultural and moral values" (quoted in Lorch 1993:951). Israeli nationalism, in these words, was part and parcel of the history and culture of the Jewish people. By the same token, however, Ben-Gurion frequently advanced universal political values as the basis for the state of Israel and by implication its nationalism. In the same 1956 speech as that quoted above, Ben-Gurion defined Israel's "messianic" mission as "the removal of ethnic barriers, establishing a regime of social justice and civil liberty" (quoted in Lorch 1993:951). In his comments at the opening session of the Sixth Knesset in 1965, Ben-Gurion noted that it would be "our ability to mold a new, free and progressive society based on mutual help, brotherly love, justice and peace without discrimination" that would allow Israel to become a "light unto the nations" (quoted in Lorch 1993:1472).

Nor did Ben-Gurion waver in his opposition to language or policies that presupposed a notion of religious nationalism. Ben-Gurion rejected a private members' bill that sought to impose a nationwide ban on pig rearing because it would "give the State of Israel the wrong character" (quoted in Lorch 1993:919) by which he presumably meant a religious character. In his presentation of his government and its policies at the opening of the Third Knesset in 1955, Ben-Gurion urged that the "unification of the nation and proper national life require us to cultivate and maintain mutual tolerance and freedom of conscience and religion in Israel" and to "guarantee freedom of religion and conscience to all the non-Jewish communities in Israel" (quoted in Lorch 1993:853).

Not surprisingly, Ben-Gurion's Likud successors devoted a good deal of their rhetorical energy to advancing muscular ideas about Israel's defense and security needs. In his first speech as prime minister in the Knesset in 1977, Begin presented his government's position that "the Jewish people has an eternal, historic, and inalienable right to the land of Israel, the land of our forefathers" (quoted in Lorch 1993:2085). His 1979 statement to the Herut Convention similarly argued that there "has never been a more legal act than the settlement of Jews throughout Eretz Israel, sacred to the Jewish people, given by God and liberated and rebuilt by valiant men. Jewish settlement in Eretz Israel is a right and duty" (Begin 1979).

By comparison to Ben-Gurion, Begin more frequently used religious language in his speeches. He repeatedly referred to the contested territories of the West Bank using the biblical terms Judea and Samaria. That phrase was rarely used by government officials before Begin became prime minister in 1977, but it would be commonplace among subsequent Likud prime ministers. In his 1982 Independence Day Address, Begin used more specifically religious motifs when he noted that

we will be joyous on Independence Day ... We have reason to be grateful to our Father in heaven. Thirty-four years ago, we were only 600,000 Jews in the Land of Israel, a minority. And within that minority was an even smaller minority that fought for our independence and liberty. And with the help of God we were able to overcome all our enemies.

(Begin 1982)

Civil religious and secular nationalist rhetoric does not disappear in the discourse of Likud prime ministers. In a 1987 address Shamir argued that "to survive as a people we must adhere to our history, our culture, our traditions, our values and our heritage" (Shamir 1993:289). He described that history, culture, traditions, values and heritage as "Jewish," but generic phrases like these could be the basis for unity building at least among the Jewish citizens of the state. Shamir invoked secular nationalism when he noted that "Israeli citizens – Jews, Moslems, Druze and Christians – are equal before the law" (Shamir 1993:22). He used that observation, however, to contrast Israel with her Arab neighbors: "Arab citizens of Israel are the only Arabs in the Middle East who can vote freely for a representative democratic government and who enjoy freedom of speech, assembly, and movement" (Shamir 1993:22–3).

Non-Jewish citizens of Israel might have felt less included, however, by his nationalist language that invoked "Jewish unity, Jewish strength, and Jewish commitments to this city [Jerusalem] and to the Land of Israel" (Shamir 1993:82).

Benjamin Netanyahu invoked a famous American term when he suggested that "I think that we have proven in the sixty-five years of Israel's existence that we are exceptional, but we must continue to be so by preserving our spiritual foundations" (Netanyahu 2013). As we noted at the opening of his chapter, Netanyahu brought a new focus in his language to formalizing Israel's status as the nation-state of the Jewish people. In a 2015 address, he said that "foundation for peace" between Israel and the Palestinians would require "first and foremost recognition of the nation-state of the Jewish people, recognition of the Jewish state" (Netanyahu 2015). Moreover, Netanyahu cemented his link to religious nationalism by presenting comments on Jerusalem Day at the Mercaz HaRav Yeshiva, the spiritual home of modern Orthodox Judaism. In his 2015 speech, he noted that "Rabbi Kook believed that Zionism must not disengage from Judaism as he believed that nationalism alone, disconnected from the eternal sources of the people of Israel, has neither justification nor validity" (Netanyahu 2014). At a minimum, each of these statements suggest a nationalism more closely aligned to the religious traditions of Israel's of Jewish majority.

CONCLUSION

Our empirical findings reinforce our arguments about the historical roots of nationalism in Israel. Each of the three factors that we highlighted as being important in determining the link between religion and nationalism has led Israel to an unstable form of civil religion. At the point of state formation, a majority of Jewish citizens of Israel supported the new state and its civil-religious nationalism, but a not insubstantial minority challenged it. The new state of Israel adopted policies to placate both secular and religious groups, declaring Israel to be both a democratic and a Jewish state. However, formal institutional links between religion and the state remained, which kept religious issues at the forefront and made it difficult for religion to be a unifying factor in national identity. Finally, the groups that have grown the most rapidly in recent decades (religious Zionists and Arab citizens of Israel) are the ones most likely to challenge Israel's civil religious model.

Debates on the meaning of Israeli nationalism are virtually built into the country's history and DNA. In this regard, however, Israel is hardly alone. What nationalism means, to whom it applies, and what are its core values are often contested concepts within a state. The United States, for example, has had its fair share of nationalism related controversies. Where the United States differs from Israel, however, is that American civil-religious nationalism has largely united religious groups in support of the nationalist project, and that model has thereby proved to be a stable basis on which to build national identity. Israel's civil religion has not played a similarly unifying role. Instead, civil-religious nationalism in Israel has proved to be unstable as it has been pulled by the opposing poles of religious and secular nationalism.

Endnotes

1. While the authors are grateful to the producers and distributors of this survey, we are solely responsible for the analysis and interpretation of these data.

2. These data were produced and provided by the Israel Democracy Institute and used with their permission. The authors are solely responsible for the analysis and interpretation of this survey, however.

3. The major exception is high levels of nationalism among Druze respondents in the ISSP. However, the IDI survey did not indicate a particularly elevated degree of national feeling among this group.

4. We also ran parallel regressions for only Jewish respondents and only Muslim interviewees. The variable for religious attendance failed to achieve statistical significance among the Muslims, but it was significant and just slightly more positive than in Table 3.2 for Jews.

5. Because IDI researchers primarily asked this question of Jewish respondents and since the poll contained no measure of religiosity, we were unable to examine the effect of religious practice on distinct religious groups' support for settlements.

4

Greece: Stable Religious Nationalism

INTRODUCTION

There are few countries in the world where the links between national and religious identity are as strong as in Greece. The Constitution is presented "in the name of the Holy and Consubstantial and Indivisible Trinity," the Eastern Orthodox Church of Christ is recognized as the "prevailing religion" in Greece, there is a constitutional prohibition on proselytizing, which presumably benefits the nation's largest religious community, and the Orthodox Church has a prominent place in required religious education classes. The history textbooks required in all public schools reinforce the connection between religion and nation by promoting the idea that Orthodox priests and bishops played a leading role in the country's independence movement. Ninety percent of the Greek population identify as Greek Orthodox, and more than three-quarters of the respondents (78 percent) in a 2016 survey indicated that being a Christian was somewhat or very important to being considered truly Greek (Pew Research Center 2016).

Even the election of the openly atheist Alexis Tsipras as the country's Prime Minister in 2015 has not fundamentally changed the nature of these connections. The platform of his Syzira Party promised constitutional reforms to guarantee the separation of church and state, and Tsipras' Education Minister, Nikos Filis, introduced legislation that would have reduced the role of Orthodox teaching in required religious education courses. Archbishop Ieronymos II, the Archbishop of Athens and All of Greece, and de facto head of the Church in Greece, led the opposition to the proposed change. Describing the Orthodox Church as the "mother of our people," the Archbishop suggested that in Greece "the state can never really separate from the church" (National Herald 2017). A few months later, Tsipras removed Filis from office and replaced him with a minister who was more sympathetic to the role of the Orthodox Church in Greece.

For historical, institutional, and demographic reasons Greece fits our model of religious nationalism. As we will note in the pages below, secular nationalism competed with this religious alternative in the country's earliest years. For various reasons, however, religious nationalism prevailed, and institutional and symbolic links between Orthodoxy and the Greek nation were formed that established a strong and persistent pattern going forward. Like the other countries in our study, there have been external challenges to the Greek nation over time, but in each case those threats have reinforced rather than undermined Greece's religious nationalism. Most notably, the frequent conflicts between Greece and Turkey were framed as a religious clash between Orthodox and Muslim communities. Moreover, demographic changes in the country's nearly 200-year history have solidified those divisions as the Orthodox percentage of the population has gradually increased, at the expense of the country's Muslim minority. In contrast with countries like the United States and India, Greece is less religiously pluralistic in 2017 than it was at the point of state formation in 1821. The dominant status of the church in the Greek Constitution has reinforced the close identification between Greek identity and Orthodoxy, a link that has persisted since the earliest years of Greek independence.

RELIGIOUS ELITES AND NATIONALISM AT THE FOUNDING

While a close historical connection eventually developed between Greek and Orthodox identity, the nascent Greek nationalism that emerged among the diasporic Greek community in the late eighteenth century owed more to Greek cultural values, the Enlightenment, and the French Revolution than it did to religious Orthodoxy. In crafting their nationalist vision, leading figures like Adamantios Koraïs and Rigas Feraios combined a passion for the Greek language and classical Greek culture with an adulation for the republican and secular values of the West. For them, the Church specifically, and Orthodoxy more generally, were impediments to their new nationalist vision (Clogg 2013:2; Grigoriadis 2011:167; Bien 2005:224; Frazee 1967:10). Nowhere was this position more clearly articulated than in the highly influential 1806 nationalist tract "Hellenic Nomarchy." Authored by an "anonymous Greek," the

Hellenic Nomarchy presented the Orthodox clergy as a barrier to the nationalist aspirations of the Greek people: "Having a purpose altogether different from other citizens, the clergy always tried, by using God as a means, to dominate their countrymen ... They cover with the mantle of holiness the most evident falsehoods and they fill the weak minds of the people with superstitions" (quoted in Kitromilides 2006:54).

Not only was the clergy "ignorant," in this reading, but the church hierarchy was complicit in supporting a political system that frustrated nationalist efforts. The Orthodox Church was in a critically difficult position vis-à-vis the Greek independence movement. As part of the Ottoman Empire since the fall of Constantinople in 1453, Greece was under the political control of the Ottoman Turks. Having to rule a vast empire of disparate ethnic, linguistic, and religious groups, the Ottomans grouped populations into *millets* based on religious confession. Under the *millet* system, religious communities, including the Orthodox, enjoyed some institutional and cultural autonomy. All Orthodox Christians in the Empire were part of a single *millet*, but it included multiple ethnic groups, including Greeks, Serbs, Bulgarians, Romanians, and Albanians. It was called the Greek *millet* because the Orthodox Church remained under Greek control, led by the Patriarch of Constantinople who was both the spiritual leader of the Orthodox community and its secular representative before the Sultan (Stavrakakis 2002:164). One impediment to a religious frame for Greek nationalism, therefore, was ideological: the church understood itself as a transnational institution, rather than as an ethno-religious one. While the patriarch for the Orthodox community was always Greek, allying himself to a nationalist movement threatened to undermine the universal vision of the church. The rise of nationalism in the nineteenth century thus challenged the self-understanding of the multiethnic Orthodox community (Bien 2005:227).

A second impediment to the formation of Greek religious nationalism was pragmatic: the Ottoman Empire expected the Orthodox hierarchy to oppose separatist movements among its religious communities. As Clogg (2013:11) notes, "the quid quo pro for granting such a high degree of communal autonomy was that the Patriarch and the church hierarchy were expected to act as a guarantor of the loyalty of the orthodox faithful to the Ottoman state." For the most part, the Church leadership in Constantinople acquiesced to this arrangement. The Patriarch at the time, Gregorious V, issued various encyclicals denouncing the insurgents who coordinated the beginning of the Greek War of Independence against the Ottoman Empire in 1821. His successor, Agathangelos, similarly wrote a letter in 1827 during the conflict which reminded his Greek audience of their scriptural obligations to obey their legitimate ruler (Frazee 1967:29 and 67; Clogg 2013:36).

While the origins of Greek nationalism were secular, and there were various factors that worked against the development of a religiously based nationalism, by the early decades of Greek independence the link between Orthodox and Greek identity had been firmly established (Triandafyllidou and Gropas 2009:959). The reasons for this were many. First, the *millet* system made religion the central focus of political and social identity. The main criterion for being Greek under Ottoman rule was the Orthodox faith. By defining persons in terms of their religious identity and institutionalizing those arrangements in an administrative system, the *millet* system reinforced the importance of Orthodoxy for the Greeks. To the extent that national identity is constructed by drawing lines between insiders and outsiders, religion proved to be a powerful mechanism for distinguishing Orthodox Greeks from Muslim Turks. In this way, Greek nationalism became identified with religion during the independence movement (Chrysoloras 2004:53–4).

The Orthodox hierarchy in Constantinople opposed the War of Independence, but this was not the case for a majority of the clergy and Church leadership living in what would become independent Greece. The Greek monasteries supported the revolution, many bishops participated in the war, and an estimated 7,000 priests were killed during the conflict. The Orthodox Bishop of Patras, Germanos III, blessed the Greek flag and offered the liturgy to the assembled army (Frazee 1967:20–1; 45; 101). Thus, leaders of the Orthodox Church in Greece adapted their faith to emphasize resistance to the Ottoman Turks (Loizides 2009:210). Even the Patriarch Gregorious V, who had urged Greeks to oppose the revolution, became a symbol of Greek defiance to Ottoman Turks. Dismayed by the Greek uprising and the apparent failure of Gregorious to tamp down the revolutionary fervor, the Sultan ordered the Patriarch's execution. Gregorious was taken into custody on Easter Sunday while he was officiating the Divine Liturgy and hung by his robes at the gates of the Patriarchate compound. Almost overnight he became a martyr for the Greek cause, and his martyrdom reinforced Orthodoxy as a nationalist symbol against the Ottoman Empire.

While the role of the clergy in the Revolution is debated among Greek historians, the idea that the Greek church "saved" the Greek nation remains the prevailing interpretation in school books and in public opinion (Fokas 2009:357–8). The existence of some debate, nonetheless, helps to explain the release of a comminiqué in 2014 by a Special Synodical Committee on Cultural Identity of the Holy Synod of the Church of Greece. Titled "A reply to the unhistorical views regarding the part of the Orthodox Church in the 1821 Greek War of Independence," the document reminds its readers that "the 1821 Revolution is drenched in the blood of Patriarch Gregory V" and that Bishop Germanos "blessed the standard of the revolution." The document affirms that "had it not been for the Orthodox clergy, the great national uprising would not have been successful" (Holy Synod of the Church of Greece 2014). The point is that the Church, and much of the nation, accepts the historical narrative of the Church's role in the independence movement, and by implication the close links between Orthodox and Greek identity.

Secular nationalism also failed to take root in Greece because the civic values of the early nationalist figures never penetrated at the mass level. As diasporic and highly educated Greeks, Koraïs and Feraios were deeply influenced by the values of the Enlightenment and the French Revolution. This was much less true, however, for the Greek masses who had remained under Ottoman rule for four centuries and did not directly experience those intellectual currents. For them, ethno-religious identity proved to be much more powerful than civic ideals in forging a national identity (Moloktos-Liederman 2007:188; Grigoriadis 2011:168). Perhaps it is the recognition of this close link between religious and national identity that helps to explain the letter sent in 1828 by Ioannis Kapodistrias, a leader of the Independence movement and the country's first head of state, to the Patriarch in Constantinople. He urged the Patriarch to "give us your blessing" for the War of Independence, and he told his interlocutor that "this [Greek] people exists, and it only exists because God has given it the grace to find in the Christian faith the strength to fight, the courage to suffer with perseverance, and the determination to perish rather than submit to the yoke which subjected its fathers ... The fate of Greece is the work of Providence" (quoted in Frazee 1967:77–8).

Secular and civic ideals provided the intellectual foundation for the early advocates of Greek nationalism, and the unique political status of the Orthodox Church within the Ottoman Empire initially prevented the development of a fully formed religiously based nationalism. However, by the time that independence was fully won in 1832 religious orthodoxy and Greek national identity were closely fused. The *millet* system solidified religion as the primary basis of identity formation, religious leaders within what would become independent Greece largely supported the revolution, the hierarchy in Constantinople unwittingly became symbols of religious resentment against the Ottomans with the assassination of Gregorious V, and religion became a mark of opposition against the Empire.

RELIGIOUS DEMOGRAPHICS AND EMERGENT NATIONALISM

As we have noted in various chapters, religious nationalism can more easily be constructed in a religiously monolithic environment. In terms of overall population, Greece was sparsely populated at the point of independence and for decades beyond. According to a very early census, Greece had an estimated population of 752,007 in 1838 (Clogg 2013:286). By 1907, the population had grown to 2.6 million and to 5.5 million by 1920. It is nearly impossible to determine with precision what percentage of the population was Greek Orthodox at the point of independence, but it is reasonable to assume that they constituted a healthy majority. There was, however, a sizeable Muslim minority living in Greece, an estimated 640,000 prior to the start of World War I (Küçükcan 1999:59). Given an overall population of Greece at that time of 5.5 million, more than 10 percent of the population of Greece was Muslim. From our theoretical standpoint, religious orthodoxy was dominant enough during the nation's first century to allow for the development of religious nationalism, though the large Muslim population might have posed a challenge to it going forward.

What is even more noteworthy in the Greek case, however, is that the percentage of the Orthodox population has *increased* over time, and those demographic changes have reinforced the logic of the country's religious nationalism. As we will note in the pages ahead, there has been persistent tension and periodic conflict between Greece and Turkey. One of the more notable was the Greek–Turkish War after World War I. At the end of that conflict, the countries signed the Lausanne Convention Concerning the Exchange of Greek and Turkish Populations. The agreement called for the compulsory movement of Orthodox Christians from Turkey to Greece and of Muslims from Greece to Turkey. The only exceptions were for Greeks settled in Constantinople and Muslims living in Western Thrace. An estimated 500,000 Muslims moved from Greece to Turkey, while 1.5 million Orthodox transferred from Turkey to Greece (Kolluoğlu 2013:533–9). The population exchange was based on the logic of the *millet* system; religion was the sole basis for the mandatory transfer of persons.

For the purposes of nationalism, the result of the population exchange was twofold. First, Greece became even more religiously monolithic, as an overwhelming percentage of its Muslim population was sent away. According to the 1951 Census, 98 percent of the Greek population was Orthodox, and Greece became "one of the most ethnically homogenous countries in the Balkans" (Clogg 2013:104). Purely from a numbers standpoint, demographic changes in Greek history have reinforced the logic of the country's religious nationalism. The exchange also solidified the ideological basis for religious nationalism as it underlined the idea that Greek and Orthodoxy identity were one and the same.

Greece is more religiously diverse now than it was in 1951, but it remains overwhelmingly Orthodox. A 2017a Pew Survey found that 90 percent of the population identify as Orthodox, 4 percent are unaffiliated, 2 percent are Muslim, and the remaining 4 percent are some other religion. Greece is the least religiously diverse of the six countries in our study.

RELIGION IN THE CONSTITUTION

Another variable in the construction of a nationalist frame is how religion is addressed in the country's Constitution. While Greece has had numerous Constitutions in its 185-year history, one thing that has not changed much is the status accorded to the Greek Orthodox Church. The first of three revolutionary constitutions was drafted in 1821–2. The preamble to that Constitution, repeated almost verbatim in all that have followed, are the words "in the name of the holy and indivisible trinity." The Constitution affirmed that the "ruling religion in the Greek state is that of the Eastern Orthodox Church of Christ," while simultaneously affirming that Greece "tolerates every other religion, and the ceremonies and sacred customs of each of them are allowed unhindered" (Provisorische Verfassung Griechenlands). The Constitution established eight ministries, one of which was to be the Ministry of Religion (Frazee 1967:47). Later constitutions would flesh various policy issues out more fully, but the pattern of a close institutional link between the Orthodox Church and the state was fully established in this initial constitution. Further symbolizing the link between religion and the new state was that Bishsop Neophytos of Talantios offered the liturgy to the assembled delegates at the opening session of the Convention (Frazee 1967:47).

Even more significant was that the Constitution conflated Christian (Orthodox) identity with Greek citizenship: "Those native inhabitants of the state of Greece who believe in Christ are Greeks, and enjoy without any distinction all civil rights." While the claim of national homogeneity ignored the reality of Greece's large Muslim minority, Koumandaraki (2002:41–2) rightly notes that the clause "provided the basic material for the construction of Greek national identity" along religious lines. In numerous ways, in short, Greece's first Constitution confirmed the institutional status of the Orthodox Church, and thereby symbolically affirmed religious nationalism as the basis for Greek nationalism. It is also important to note that while it accorded a special status to the Orthodox Church, this first Constitution also guaranteed religious free exercise rights for "every other religion," promoted "equality before the law," and established a representative form of government.

As we noted above, subsequent constitutions have largely confirmed that pattern, both in terms of recognizing the special place of the Orthodox Church and in advancing democratic political values. The current Constitution, drafted in 1975 after a ten-year period of military rule, established Greece as a parliamentary democracy. An early draft of that Constitution moved the country toward a system of Church–State separation, a development opposed by the Orthodox Church. The Constitution that was ratified dropped many of the provisions that concerned the church (Basdekis 1977:57–8). The Constitution opens with the same preamble as the revolutionary Constitution and similarly recognizes the Orthodox Church as the prevailing religion of Greece. The Constitution prohibits proselytism (Article 13), though this provision presumably protects all religions. Members of Parliament and the President of the Greek Republic are inaugurated into office with a religious oath in which they swear "in the name of the Holy and consubstantial and Indivisible Trinity to safeguard the Constitution and the laws." In practice, this oath of office is done in the presence of the Archbishop of Athens and all of Greece, the senior cleric in the Greek Church, who is also an honorary guest at all official government celebrations (Chrysoloras 2004:49).

Religious education is also accorded a privileged status in the Constitution. Article 16 affirms that a basic mission for the State is the "development of national and religious consciousness."

What this means in practice is that religious education is a mandatory subject in the schools and those courses are dominated by the dogma and traditions of the Eastern Orthodox Church (Papastathis 2005:128; Liagkis 2014:155–6). As we noted previously, the religious education classes and the history curriculum present the Orthodox Church as vitally important in the preservation of the Greek nation during the period of Ottoman rule.

By the same token, the Constitution affirms core democratic norms. Article 1 describes the Greek form of government as a "parliamentary republic" and affirms that "popular sovereignty is the foundation of government." The Constitution guarantees equality before the law, equal rights for men and women, and freedom of religion for all "known religions." The Greek Orthodox Church, the Jewish community, and the Muslim minority of Thrace have long been recognized as official religious legal entities. Finally, non-Orthodox Christian Members of Parliament are allowed to take the oath of office "according to the form of their own religion or creed." In 2015, one Muslim MP was sworn-in taking an oath in the name of Allah.

The church has also been granted various legal prerogatives; one of the most symbolically significant was a law passed during the Metaxas dictatorship (1936–41) which stipulated that the local Orthodox bishop had to approve the building of a new place of worship (Papastathis 2015:365). From the time of Greek independence in the middle of the nineteenth century until the end of the twentieth century, not a single formal mosque was in operation in Athens (Triandayfllidou and Gropas 2009:963). Conservative politicians and religious leaders opposed various attempts to get a purpose-built mosque approved in Athens to serve the growing Muslim immigrant population, though the Tsipras government has now formally approved one (Farooq 2016).

There are also numerous symbolic links between Orthodoxy and the Greek State. Official state functions invariably involve clerics from the church. We noted above the presence of leading Orthodox ministers at the oath of office ceremonies for political officials. While he did not take a religious oath of office, Alexis Tsipras nonetheless followed the precedent of prime ministers before him and met with the Archbishop of Athens and All of Greece, Ieronymos II, shortly after taking office. In describing the 2006 celebration of Independence Day, the website for the Greek Orthodox Church noted that the Prime Minister, the President, leaders of the major political parties, and the country's military leadership celebrated a Doxology in the Athens Metropolitan Cathedral led by Archbishop Christodoulos of Athens and All Greece (Holy Synod of the Church of Greece 2006).

Political leaders are also deeply involved in ceremonial Orthodox religious celebrations. The Prime Minister and the Leader of the Opposition in Parliament attended the ceremony for the enthronement for Ieronymos

II in 2008, while the President of the Parliament, the Mayor of Athens, and the Minister of Education and Religious Affairs spoke at the religious event (Holy Synod of the Church of Greece 2008). Political leaders attend various Orthodox holidays throughout the year, including Christmas, Epiphany, and Assumption Day. A press account of the 2015 Epiphany Day celebrations noted where the Prime Minister and the leaders of the opposition parties had attended the sacred event, including the openly Atheist Tsipras who said in brief remarks at the religious ceremony that "today is an important day for the Orthodoxy [and] a bright celebration for the Greek people" (Makris 2015). When he conferred the "Order of the Savior" on Patriarch Theophilos of Jerusalem in 2016, President Prokopis Pavlopoulos noted that "the Order of the Savior is hierarchically the first Order of Excellence. The name and form of the medal were chosen to remind everyone that the National Regeneration was made possible owing to the divine support of the Savior" (Jerusalem Patriarchate 2016). Finally, more than half of the country's national public holidays in Greece are Orthodox religious holy days, including Epiphany, Orthodox Shrove Monday, Orthodox Good Friday, Orthodox Easter Monday, Holy Spirit Monday, and Christmas.

These constitutional features, legal provisions, and symbolic gestures establish a close alliance between the state and the Orthodox Church, leading two analysts to conclude that the Greek Orthodox Church is "effectively an institution of the state" (Halikiopoulou and Vasilopoulou 2013:3). Not only are they institutionally linked, the state and Orthodoxy are ideologically fused as well. The hegemonic role of the Orthodox Church reinforces the idea that Greek national identity is one and the same with religious orthodoxy. This is accomplished with a Greek Constitution and legal regime that simultaneously promotes Orthodox *and* democratic values. Religious nationalism and political democracy can, in short, coexist, though the points of tension between them can become avenues for political dispute.

REINFORCING THE RELIGIOUS–NATIONAL CONSENSUS

A potential challenge to the religious nationalism that emerged in revolutionary Greece was the political, constitutional, and theological status of the Orthodox Church. At the point of independence, the Church in Greece remained institutionally connected to the Orthodox Patriarchate in Constantinople. The revolutionary Constitution affirmed Eastern

Orthodoxy as the prevailing religion of the state, but it said nothing about the status of the Church in independent Greece vis-à-vis the
larger Orthodox community. At a minimum, political independence for
Greece did not initially alter the religious control that the Patriarchate
in Constantinople had over the bishops and religious life within the new
state. The connection to a religious infrastructure beyond the borders of
the Greek state, and to an ecumenical religious community that included
more than just Greeks could have undermined religious nationalism
as the dominant nationalist frame. However, within decades of independence, the Greek Church became institutionally independent from
Constantinople, which in turn reinforced the foundation of Greek religious nationalism.

From the standpoint of secular leaders like Adamantios Koraïs, national
liberation for the country of Greece from Ottoman control had to include
religious independence for the church in Greece from Constantinople
(Kitromilides 2006:165). In 1833, a local synod of Greek bishops
affirmed this position by unilaterally proclaiming the independence of
the Church in Greece (Frazee 1967:112–13). Bowing to political reality if
not so much theological conviction, in 1850 the Ecumenical Patriarchate
in Constantinople formally granted autocephaly to the Church in Greece.
This standing meant that the head of the Church in Greece no longer
reported to the Patriarchate in Constantinople. Subsequent constitutions
(including the current one) reinforced this status by outlining relations
between the Churches in Greece with the Patriarchate in Constantinople.
The Constitution affirms that the Orthodox Church in Greece is "autocephalous" at the same time that it notes the Church is "inseparably
united in doctrine with the Great Church of Christ in Constantinople
and with every other Church of Christ of the same doctrine."

The autocephalous status of the Church in Greece had the paradoxical
effect of weakening the transnational ideological power of Orthodoxy
at the same time that it strengthened the religious–nationalist link in
Greece. On the one hand, autocephaly modernized a church by "separat-
ing it from the pre-modern ecumenicity of the Patriarchate" (Stavrakakis
2003:165). This separation served the secular needs of the state by defining *Greek* Orthodoxy as opposed to *religious* Orthodoxy as a means of
national self-identification. It thereby removed Orthodoxy as a potential
opponent of Greek nationalism, as the Ecumenical Patriarchate had been
in the early years of the War of Independence. In this sense, religious
nationalism destroyed the ecumenical vision of the Orthodox Church.
Yet, an autocephalous church also solidified the ethno-religious character

of Greek nationalism. A newly independent church became "a symbol of national identity" (Fokas 2009:358) and a means by which to bolster the unity of the new nation. Rather than an impediment to nationalism, Orthodoxy, at least in its Greek form, became its champion (Grigoriadis 2011:169; Mavrogordatos 2003:128).

The nationalism that emerged from this process consolidated religious and national identification; to be Greek was to be Orthodox, and to be Orthodox was to be Greek (Papastathis 2012:214). In contrast with many European states where civic ideals gradually replaced religious ones as the basis for national solidarity in the nineteenth and twentieth centuries, religion remained the primary factor in Greek nationalism throughout this period. The consolidation of Greek nationalism along religious lines shaped Greek national aspirations for the next century. The so-called "Great Idea" imagined the reconstitution of a Greek nation that would include all Greek inhabited areas, particularly the large Greek population still living under Ottoman rule (Clogg 2013:46–8; Willert 2012:194). This visionary nationalist idea dominated Greek foreign and domestic politics for much of the next century. The country's borders gradually expanded and more Greeks came to live within the Greek state. The primary example of this process was the population exchange with Turkey following the Greco-Turkish War (1919–22). While Greece decisively lost the war, as we noted above the treaty that concluded the conflict led to a population exchange between the two combatants. Religion was the sole basis for defining who was to move from one country to the other, thus solidifying Orthodoxy as a primary factor in Greek national identity. A result of the population exchange was that Greece became even more religiously monolithic, thus making it easier to promote religious nationalism as the vast majority of the population identified with the Orthodox Church.

Another factor that we have highlighted in several country chapters as crucial in challenging or reinforcing the nationalist model are external threats. As Halikiopoulou notes (2008:306) "as national identity is a means of demarcating the community from outsiders, conflict can foster ethnic cohesion by exacerbating the need to secure this demarcation." In the case of Greece, ongoing conflicts first with the Ottoman Empire and then with Turkey have underpinned the idea of demarcating Greek national identity on religious grounds. Greek independence came as a result of a war with the Ottoman Empire. In that conflict, Greece defined itself as an Orthodox country in opposition to a Muslim empire. The first official war between independent Greece and the Empire, in 1897, was over the political status of Crete, which had a Greek Orthodox majority but was under Ottoman rule. The previously mentioned Greco-Turkish war was an effort to reshape the nation's borders to take in the diasporic Greek Orthodox community. While Turkish victory in that war marked an end to the "Great Idea" that Greek borders would expand into Constantinople and beyond (Clogg 2013:98), it did not end the struggle between the two countries.

Over the past century, Greece and Turkey have battled over numerous issues, one of which has been the status of Cyprus. A majority of the island's population is Greek and they seek unification with Greece, a position opposed by the minority Turkish Cypriots. Further solidifying the religious nationalist link is that the Church of Cyprus organized a referendum on unification with Greece in 1950 with no Turkish Cypriot participation. While the Church in Cyprus is autocephalous, leaders of the church clearly see themselves as part of the larger Greek nation. Jurisdiction over the island has been a point of profound contention between the two countries, led to violence between Greek and Turkish Cypriots, military coups, the introduction of both the Greek and the Turkish military, and concluded with a partition of the island into a Greek (Orthodox) and Turkish (Muslim) sections (Michael 2009). Tensions between Turkey and Greece over Cyprus remain very high. In short, external threats, in the form of territorial conflicts with Turkey, have consistently been defined on the basis of religion, and in the process the link between Greek Orthodox and Greek national identity has been strengthened.

Mylonas (2013) has convincingly demonstrated the link between a country's foreign policy and how it treats its "non-core" minority population. In the case of Greece, there is a logical connection among the country's foreign policy, its religious nationalism, and its treatment of its Muslim minority population. Relations with Turkey dominate the foreign policy agenda, Greek Muslims can be presented as a "foreign" agents whose primary allegiance is to Turkey, and the result is a strengthening of Greek religious nationalism.

Conflicts with Turkey also created political opportunities to exploit the ties between religion and the state. Religious leaders "spearheaded all nationalist initiatives in the latter part of the 19th and throughout the 20th centuries" (Kitromilides 1989:166), while politicians instrumentally used religious nationalist discourse to appeal to the masses (Papastathis 2012:215). The result was to reinforce the support for and the logic of Greek religious nationalism.

This is not to suggest that there has been no debate over the religious character of Greek nationalism. In recent decades, political leaders have periodically advanced policies that weaken the Church–State link. Most notable was a bill proposed and eventually adopted by Prime Minister Costas Simitis in 2000–1 to remove the category of religious identification from citizen ID cards (Moloktos-Liederman 2007). For Simitis, the bill was an attempt to modernize the Greek state by bringing it to up Western European standards on the protection of personal data. For our purposes, it marked a movement toward a more secular political arrangement, and by implication closer to the values of secular nationalism. For many Orthodox religious leaders, the bill not only diminished the political power of the Church, but more importantly it symbolically severed the strong Church–State link in Greece.

Archbishop Christodoulos led a campaign against the proposed law. In a little over a year, he gathered more than three million signatures, or nearly one-third of the country's overall population, asking for a referendum on the voluntary declaration of religion on ID cards (Stavrakakis 2002:32). The bill eventually passed, the President and the Council of State upheld the government's decision, and no referendum was called to challenge the new law. However, the controversy demonstrated the political reach of the Archbishop and the populist appeal of religious nationalism. Throughout his tenure (1998–2008), the Archbishop vigorously defended the political interests of the Church and promoted the idea that Orthodoxy was central to Greek identity. In a 2006 homily to newly ordained members of the clergy, for example, Christodoulos affirmed that the Church is "to achieve the coherence and unity of the Greek people" because "the Church, religion, Orthodoxy, are bonds that unite [our] people." The role of the church, urged the Primate of the Greek Church to the newly ordained, "is the preservation of our national and spiritual identity" (Christodoulos, Archbishop of Athens and All Greece 2006).

Religious nationalism is more likely to prevail when a majority of a country's population is from a single religious tradition. Religious pluralism is one threat to that religious monopoly, as is a secular retreat from religion. As we have previously noted, there is very little religious diversity in Greece, but there is some indication that the country is secularizing. Merely 17 percent of respondents in the 2017 survey indicated that they attend church weekly, less than one-third (29 percent) said that they pray daily, and 62 percent believe that government and religious policies should be kept separate (Pew Research Center 2017a). The ID card controversy and the election of Alexis Tsipras, an atheist who had called for the separation of religion and state in Greece, seemed to indicate fractures in Greek religious nationalism. However, there is ample evidence that Greeks by and large accept the logic behind the country's religious nationalism. An overwhelming majority (89 percent) affirm that Greek culture (which presumably includes Orthodoxy) is superior to others, more than half indicate that being part of the Orthodox Church is "very important to being part of the nation," and they are twice as likely to support funding for the Orthodox Church as opposed to other religious groups (Pew Research Center 2017a).

The threat of a more secular political culture in Greece has been used by the country's religious leaders to juxtapose Greek values from those of Western Europe. Christodoulos in particular reinforced Greek religious nationalism by contrasting what he portrayed as a spiritually bankrupt Western Europe from a religiously vigorous Greece (Chrysoloras 2004:46–7). In a 2006 homily, he argued that Europe had "betrayed Christianity" and abandoned its "spiritual identity." "Our nation," by contrast, "truly knows its identity and we ought to cultivate it in order to ensure the continuation of Hellenism" (Christodoulos, Archbishop of Athens and All Greece 2006). Even the country's contemporary economic crisis has reinforced divisions between Greece and the rest of Europe, and in the process helped to solidify Greek religious nationalism. In the midst of negotiations over a possible European bailout for Greece, Archbishop Ieronymos II said that "it was not possible for us to become a colony ruled by others," and that Greece would avoid that fate when "we reach manhood as a nation and begin to think as Greeks and Orthodox" (Ieronymos II, Archbishop of Athens and All Greece 2012). Even more telling was a 2011 letter from the Holy Synod of the Church of Greece (2011) to the President of the European Commission that contrasted European market values from Greek religious ones:

It would be a scandal if European leaders did not take the cries of simple citizens into account and if these very citizens of Europe were threatened like expendable products. The result of all this is the increase of agony, of despair, of the shrinking of national sovereignty, and eventually the creation of a society with no moral rules. As a Church, we cannot accept this social model.

Perhaps it is not surprising that 70 percent of the Greek respondents in the 2017a Pew Survey completely or mostly agreed with the statement that "there is a conflict between our country's traditional values and those of the West." As we previously noted, the government has worked out an arrangement to build the country's first all-purpose mosque in Athens, but this agreement remains on shaky grounds. While he is widely viewed as more moderate than his clerical predecessor, Ieronymos II nonetheless questions the wisdom of moving forward with the proposed construction. In a 2016 interview, he mused that "it is my opinion that it [mosque] can be postponed for a while, until the issue of Muslims gets sorted out" (Ieronymos II, Archbishop of Athens and All Greece 2016).

There are a handful of Greek Orthodox theologians who have a promoted a "new" theology which seeks to return the church to its ancient roots, and in the process decouple the ethos of the church from Greek nationalism (Willert 2012:184–6). Those voices are not, however, prominent within the church hierarchy, and they are not representative of the views of believers in the pews.

Religious nationalism became the dominant nationalist motif early in the country's independence movement, and historical factors have reinforced that model over time. In that sense, Greece's model of religious nationalism has been relatively stable.

PUBLIC OPINION AND NATIONALISM

As in the other country chapters, we look at popular support for both abstract and issue-related nationalism. Our historical analysis shows the significant role of Orthodox Christianity in the development and promotion of Greek nationalism. In order to measure mass-level nationalism, we used data from the relevant subsample of the 2008 European Values Study. We derived our dependent variable from a four-point item asking respondents how proud they were to be Greek.

As Table 4.1 shows, Greeks are very nationalistic, and religion identification seems related to Greek identity. Those who are Orthodox demonstrated the highest levels of Greek pride, but non-Orthodox believers and the nonreligious were only slightly less nationalistic. The results from the regression in Table 4.2 present a slightly more nuanced portrait of the connection between religion and nationalism. Religious attendance was strongly associated with higher degrees of nationalism, suggesting that religiously practicing Orthodox Greeks are the most nationalistic. While we would have expected non-Orthodox believers to exhibit lower measures of national pride, the very small number of such respondents ($N = 11$) bars us from more detailed analysis of this group. For the nonreligious, meanwhile, the statistical effect of their lack of church attendance overwhelms any direct influence of their religious identity per se. In reality, we suspect that these "nonreligious" are in fact culturally Orthodox.

TABLE 4.1. *Nationalism by religious tradition*

Tradition	Mean
Orthodox	3.59
Other religion	3.36
Not religious	3.31
All respondents	3.59

Source: 2008 European Values Study, Greece subsample.

TABLE 4.2. *Religious and other determinants of nationalism*

Variable	Coefficient	Standard error
Other religion	−0.745	0.659
Not religious	−0.085	0.211
Religious attendance	0.332*	0.065
Education	−0.095*	0.039
Income	−0.041	0.043
Woman	0.139	0.147
Age	0.014*	0.005
Urbanicity	−0.087*	0.030
Constant 1	−3.423*	0.524
Constant 2	−1.678*	0.457
Constant 3	0.558	0.449
N	856	
Nagelkerke R^2	0.127	

*Denotes an effect that is significantly different from 0 at the 5 percent level for ordered Logit model.
Notes: All regressors are dummy variables except for Religious Attendance (range = 1–7), Education (0–9), Income (1–12), Age (18–94), and Urbanicity (1–8).
Source: 2008 European Values Study, Greece subsample.

PUBLIC HOSTILITY TO TURKEY

As we have noted several times in this chapter, conflict with Turkey has been a constant theme in Greek history. We therefore selected mass attitudes toward this country as an indicator of a specific nationalist issue. The item asked interviewees if they have a very favorable, somewhat favorable, somewhat unfavorable, or very unfavorable "opinion of Turkey." Given Greece's religious nationalism, we would therefore predict that

TABLE 4.3. *Hostility to Turkey by religious tradition*

Tradition	Mean percent
Orthodox	3.10
Other religion	2.80
Not religious	2.77
All respondents	3.09

Source: 2013 Spring Pew Global Attitudes Survey, Greece subsample.

TABLE 4.4. *Religious and other determinants of hostility to Turkey*

Variable	Coefficient	Standard error
Other religion	0.354	0.844
Not religious	−0.462	0.471
Religious attendance	−0.017	0.069
Education	−0.050	0.042
Income	−0.118	0.086
Woman	−0.026	0.144
Age	0.001	0.004
Urban	−0.324	0.166
Constant 1	−4.636*	0.482
Constant 2	−1.830*	0.406
Constant 3	−0.108	0.399
N	709	
Nagelkerke R^2	0.019	

*Denotes an effect that is significantly different from 0 at the 5 percent level for dichotomous Logit model.

Notes: All regressors are dummy variables except for Religious Attendance (range = 1–6), Income (1–5), Age (18–91), and Education (1–10).

Source: 2013 Spring Pew Global Attitudes Survey, Greece subsample.

Orthodox Greeks would be more hostile toward the majority-Muslim Turkey than would be nonreligious citizens or those who profess other faiths. As Table 4.3 indicates, levels of opposition to Turkey are high overall, but they are more pronounced among the Orthodox.

As Table 4.4 documents, neither religious affiliation nor practice has a statistically significant effect on anti-Turkish sentiment. The pervasiveness of hostility to Turkey among all respondents reinforces the importance of an "enemy" in defining national boundaries. The conflictual history between Greece and Turkey solidifies this national distinction as does the difference in majority religion. So while Greeks do not appear to be learning attitudes toward Turkey in their churches, the society as a whole promotes such values.

RELIGION AND NATIONALISM IN RELIGIOUS PUBLICATIONS AND POLITICAL LEADER SPEECHES

To analyze elite attitudes, we conducted a content analysis of leading religious periodicals for three religious traditions in Greece: Orthodox Christianity, Judaism, and Islam. For each group, we identified a related organization and their most conspicuous (or only) online presence. For the Orthodox, this source was the official website of the Church of Greece for years 2004–17. For Judaism we selected the online publications of the Central Board of Jewish Communities in Greece for 2012–17. And for Islam, it was the Facebook page of the Muslim Association of Greece for 2012–17. We would ideally have preferred a publication for a Muslim association in Thrace, since Muslims in this part of the country are citizens of Greece. The Facebook page, by contrast, focuses primarily on the Muslim population in Athens, which consists in large part of recent immigrants who are less likely to be citizens of Greece. However, the Facebook page was the only online source available to us. Among the Orthodox and Jewish texts, we searched for the terms "nation," "country," and "nationalism" and read over each document that contained one or more of these terms. For the Muslim group, the available materials were limited, forcing us to review all publications on the relevant website during the given time period. We coded each document as supportive of the existing link between religion and nationalism, as opposed to this arrangement, or as neutral.

Overall, Figure 4.1 confirms our hypothesis about Greeks' religious nationalism. The data reflect the close identification of the nation with Greek Orthodoxy, as elites from this tradition overwhelmingly affirm this connection. In fact, not a single document from the official church website questions the fundamental connection between Greek and Orthodox identity. Symptomatic of the views of Orthodox leaders are the comments from a 2016 interview with Archbishop Ieronymos II (Ieronymos II, Archbishop of Athens and All Greece 2016). When asked if he was "ready" for a separation of Church and State, Ieronymos juxtaposed a possible institutional relationship (which he nonetheless

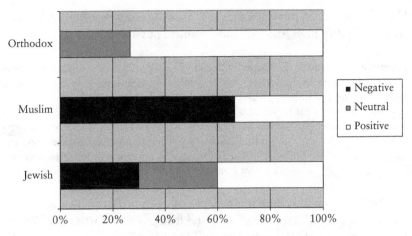

FIGURE 4.1. *Abstract nationalism in religious publications*

would likely oppose) from an ideological one which he suggested was inconceivable:

In our Church, in our Orthodoxy, the term separation does not exist ... Separate from whom? My child? There is a maternal relation between the church and our people? Who will separate us? Therefore, we do not mind at all about the relationship with the state. If they tell us that they want us to separate from the people [however] they won't succeed in that, it is not possible.

The picture is more nuanced for the few religious minorities in Greece. Most publications from the Muslim Association of Greece questioned some aspects of the institutional relations between church and state in Greece. In particular, they tend to question the exclusive benefits that flow to the Orthodox religion. A 2012 post on the group's Facebook page noted that it was "unfair" that Christian Orthodoxy was taught in the schools but Islam was not. There were numerous posts on the webpage that decried opposition to building a mosque in Athens. The Chairman of the organization, Naim Elghandour, said that the opposition of the Prime Minister at the time, Antonis Samaras, was "rooted in racism" (Dabilis 2012). While not specifically a rejection of Greece's religious nationalism, these comments at a minimum imply a hope for a more even-handed public policy.

Greek Jews are less critical, though some documents question some part of the status quo narrative. In particular, the Board is quick to highlight anti-Semitism in Greek society, Greek politics, and in the Greek

Church. The Board put out a press release on a 2016 Pew Research Study that found very high levels of anti-Semitism in Greece:

Regarding our country, the results are highly worrisome ... Greece holds the highest score in Europe regarding society's negative attitudes towards the Jews. These results must not come as a surprise to us. For a long time diffused anti-Semitism is common in Greece, as this recent survey came to confirm. Anti-Semitic incidents increase more and more. Intolerance seems to have put roots in the very heart of society. The rhetoric of stereotypes and conspiracy theories, as well as prejudice against the Jews, and secondly against the Muslims, is widely tolerated by a major part of Greek society.

(Central Board of Jewish Communities in Greece 2016)

The Board has also been quick to call out anti-Semitism by members of the right-wing Golden Dawn Party, and leaders of the Orthodox Church who have similarly trafficked in anti-Semitic tropes. In particular, the Board has highlighted the rhetoric of The Metropolitan Bishop of Piraeus, Seraphim, who has at different points in his career blamed the country's financial problems on a conspiracy of Jewish bankers and claimed that the Holocaust was orchestrated by Zionists. In their press release, the board concluded that Piraeus' various anti-Semitic statements "are not compatible with the status of an official of the Greek Orthodox Church, a Church that evokes love and solidarity, neither with the status of a state official who is obliged to remain loyal to the Constitution and the laws of the Greek state" (Central Board of Jewish Communities in Greece 2017).

But, there are also several documents on the website of the Board that tacitly affirm the role of religion in Greek nationalism and draw a parallel between the role of Orthodoxy in Greece and Judaism in Israel. A 2015 document reports on a Christian–Jewish colloquium "in recognition of the special place of Orthodox Christianity in the Greek tradition and the special place of Judaism in the life of the people of Israel" (Central Board of Jewish Communities in Greece 2015).

We did a similar search for speeches or public comments made by Greek prime ministers and presidents about Orthodoxy and nationalism. Given his periodic conflict with the church, it is perhaps not unexpected that Alexis Tsipras has not used explicitly religious language in describing the Greek nation. What is perhaps more surprising is that there is very little rhetoric from other prime ministers and presidents explicitly linking the nation with Orthodoxy. It is possible that the absence of that language is a proverbial case of the dog that did not bark. The place of Orthodoxy in the Greek nation has been so widely accepted among political leaders of all political stripes that they have simply not needed to point it out. Now that Tsipras has questioned the political role of the Orthodox Church, rhetoric linking nation and Orthodoxy might increase. In the 2015 electoral campaign, as an example, Prime Minister Antonis Samaras pledged that religious icons would "not come down from walls in public areas because the Greek people believe" (Press Project 2015).

What is much more common in Greek political life, as we noted earlier in the chapter, is for politicians of all political persuasions to join in religious ceremonies. Even Tsipras has followed the lead of his predecessors and attended public celebrations of Epiphany and Assumption Day. In 2016, he joined Archbishop Ieronymos II for a celebration commemorating Greek resistance in WWII (BHMA 2016). While Tsipras has been a rather passive participant at these religious events, others have been more actively engaged. Not only did he attend the 2016 Holy and Great Council of the Orthodox Churches held in Crete, Greek President Prokopis Pavlopoulos read the Lord's Prayer before Communion was offered during the Divine Liturgy (Sotiropoulos 2017). Participation in these events by political and religious leaders reinforces the symbiotic relationship between Orthodoxy and the Greek nation.

To measure the attitudes of religious elites toward a specific nationalist issue, we selected publications that mentioned the Greek–Turkish conflict in Cyprus. We coded the texts as siding with the Greeks ("positive"), the Turks ("negative"), or neither ("neutral"). The Facebook page of the Muslim group contained not a single reference to this conflict. Figure 4.2 shows that the overwhelming majority of Orthodox and Jewish elites support the Greek position. Very few documents were even neutral.

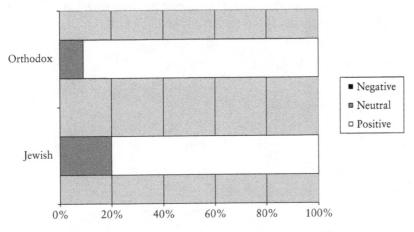

FIGURE 4.2. *Support for Greek Cyprus in religious publications*

Characteristic of this attitude was homily by Ieronymos II which declared that "nor should we forget or underestimate historic phenomenon such as those of the Asia Minor disaster or of the occupation of *our* [emphasis added] Cyprus" (Ieronymos II, Archbishop of Athens and All Greece 2016). There was no need for the Archbishop of Athens and all of Greece to remind his audience what he meant by the term "our Cyprus."

CONCLUSION

Our historical and quantitative findings reinforce our argument about the importance and stability of Greek religious nationalism. Historical factors established religious nationalism as the dominant model at the point of state formation, and a semi-path-dependent process, linked to both institutional and demographic factors, has taken hold over time to underpin the importance of that initial framework. Religious nationalism has been further reinforced through the definition of "the other" largely in religious terms, thus strengthening the cultural role of Orthodoxy in Greek nationalism. The greatest challenge to the model going forward is likely to be demographic. The groups that are the least likely to express strong nationalist sentiment are those with no religion and those who are religious but are not Orthodox. By some measures both groups are growing as a proportion of the Greek population. It is possible that the link between religion and nationalism will be broken by political leaders like Alexis Tsipras who wish to move away from a close link between religion and nation. What seems just as likely, however, is that the recent immigration of large numbers of Muslims to Greece will reinforce the political incentives to mobilize voters along cultural and religious lines, thus strengthening the country's identification with its Orthodox traditions.

5

Malaysia: Unstable Religious Nationalism

INTRODUCTION

In the midst of graft accusations and a competitive reelection campaign, Malaysian Prime Minister Najib Razak's governing United Malays National Organisation (UMNO) decided to appeal to the base of its Islamist rival for votes, the Malaysian Islamic Party (PAS). In the overwhelmingly Muslim city of Kuala Terengganu, for example, authorities condoned infrared surveillance cameras inside the screening rooms of the only local cinema to ensure that young couples keep their attention on the movie and not on each other. Such sharia-esque measures gratify local Muslim clerics, but the large minority of non-Muslim Chinese and Indians in Malaysia and its governing coalition view the growing Islamization of their country with alarm. As one opposition legislator put it, "If UMNO and PAS continue to mix religion with politics we will end up as two Malaysias" (*South China Morning Post* 2017).

In Malaysia, the country's founders established Islam as the nominal state religion despite an ethnically diverse, multireligious population. The result of this perhaps suboptimal arrangement is the constant threat of ethno-religious conflict and sporadic episodes of actual interreligious and interracial violence. Malaysia's model of religious nationalism has become highly unstable, threatening to destroy any unified national identity and to force individuals' primary allegiances back to the ethnically and religiously segregated groupings in which most Malaysians live much of their day-to-day lives.

We believe that the relationship between religion and nationalism within a nation state stems from the role and status of religion at the country's formation. Thus, we look at three interrelated aspects of religion as a new state is created: the function of religion in the ideology of the emerging political leadership, the constitutional status of religion in the new regime, and the nation's demographic composition when the state is created. In Malaysia, each factor tended to undermine the stability of the religious–nationalist approach set out in the country's founding documents.

This chapter summarizes relations between religion and nationalism in Malaysia. We offer an historical overview of this process and an analysis of modern attitudinal data on their interaction on a prominent nationalistic issue in the twenty-first century: its rivalry with China. A shorter section summarizes our parallel content analysis of religious publications and prime ministers' speeches. As in earlier parts of this book, we find that the arrangement set up at the country's founding and similar constitutionally critical moments remains highly important for comprehending today's relationship between religion and nationalism.

RELIGIOUS ELITES AND NATIONALISM AT INDEPENDENCE

The precolonial history of what is today Malaysia dates back to the first centuries of the Christian era, when Malay and foreign traders passed through the various straits of the region in their pursuit of wealth via international commerce. By the 1500s and 1600s, European naval powers such as the Portuguese and Dutch began establishing colonies in the region. But it was primarily the British who gave modern Malaysia its colonial imprint. In 1786, the British East India Company set up a port on Penang which gradually led to London's domination of the area until the middle of the twentieth century. By about 1900, the British had established an export-led economy based on tin and rubber and spurred the immigration of thousands of Chinese and Indians to work in the mines and on the plantations. Politically, colonial control varied from direct rule in Singapore to a loose proxy arrangement in parts of Borneo (Bunge and Vreeland 1984:1–4). This relatively tranquil political situation continued until the beginning of World War II.

With Japanese conquest and occupation of the British protectorate between 1942 and 1945, Malays began to question the legitimacy of colonial rule even from London. Chinese in the region, meanwhile, suffered terribly under Japanese authoritarianism, losing thousands of community members to massacres and military casualties. Although the British had tried at least half-heartedly to maintain a modicum of interethnic peace, the Japanese overtly tried to play the allegedly "friendly" Malays against the "hateful" Chinese. In response, many left-wing Chinese went underground to fight the Japanese invaders and Malay "collaborators" as part of the British-aided Malayan People's Anti-Japanese Army (Bunge and Vreeland 1984:4; Andaya and Andaya 2001:257–64).

At war's end, one of the main reasons for Britain to grant Malaya statehood was what was referred to as the "Malayan Emergency" (Short 1975; von Vorys 1975:87–8), or an ethnically Chinese-based Communist insurgency that lasted from a little after the departure of the Japanese army to a couple years after formal independence. Led by the Malayan Communist Party (MCP) and its Malayan People's Liberation Army (MPLA), this guerrilla campaign against British colonial rule and the economic exploitation of peasants and workers pressured London to hand political power over to non-Communists such as the increasingly well-organized Malay Muslims. Though British authorities had coordinated with the MCP when both were fighting the Japanese during World War II, in 1948 London blamed the Communists for a series of killings of European plantation owners and managers. After labor unions called for strikes and the county descended into general unrest, the colonial government banned the MCP, arrested or deported hundreds of its members, and declared a martial-law-style "Emergency." In response, the remaining MCP and affiliated operatives went underground and began a protracted low-level war against the British that would lead to perhaps 11,000 deaths on all sides. To counter this threat to its survival, the UK government set up an often-brutal authoritarian regime, dispensed with most civil liberties, and engaged in scorched-earth-like "starvation" and ethnic "resettlement" campaigns against the MPLA and its (alleged) Chinese and aboriginal supporters. By the end of the 1950s, these tactics and the new lure of Malayan independence were proving "successful" in weakening the insurgency and turning mainstream political leaders against it (Bunge and Vreeland 1984:244–5; Andaya and Andaya 2001:269–74; Cheah 2009; Hale 2013).

Of course, it was not hard to convince most Malays to sign up to a new state where Islam was the official religion and their ethnic group received special, constitutionally guaranteed privileges. The only real challenge to what became known as the Alliance government was an Islamist party calling for even more pro-Malay and pro-Islamic policies than those already enacted (Andaya and Andaya 2001:278). No Malay Muslims who maintained the support of their community argued for equal treatment of Malays and minorities at all levels of government;

those Malay leaders such as Onn bin Jaafar (Soh 2010), who opposed excessive Malay communalism, soon found themselves pushed aside. Instead, as Malaysia's founder Tunku Abdul Rahman put it, the Malays (i.e., Muslims) should be the masters of their own house and decide the country's power structure (Healy 1982:10):

This is a Malay country, and privileges should be given to the Malays ... What will become of the Malays if we concede every time to the insatiable demands of the other races? ... Some people say independence should be handed to "Malayans." Who are these Malayans? The Malays will decide who the "Malayans" should be.

As a descendent of traditional Malay royalty (Healy 1982:1), Tunku himself symbolically represented – as did his ancestors – both political and religious authority and thus helped cement the centuries-old bond between religion and state. Then and now, the most important Muslim religious authorities were the state-level sultans (Lapidus 1988:776–8; Roff 1994:67–74), who received special deference in the federal constitution and thus had little reason to object to the new state or to the establishment of Islam once they were assured that the federal government would not impinge upon their state-level religious rights (Ibrahim 1979; Fernando 2006). And even Tunku had to be careful not to alienate his soft-Islamist base by promoting ethno-religious equality or suggesting that certain indigenous non-Muslims who were ethnic cousins of the Malays also belonged to the core, founding group of first-class citizens (Barr and Govindasamy 2010).

The overwhelmingly non-Muslim, Chinese and Indian minorities, in contrast, seemed more skeptical about the new arrangement. Some condemned it outright as a combination of "British imperialism and Malay feudalism" (Neo 2006). Chinese Christian politicians such as Tan Chee Khoon (1984) complained about unfair religious double-standards such as the law forbidding the proselytizing of Muslims but not of Christians, Buddhists, or Hindus. Non-Muslims likewise worried about whether the new government would pressure them to convert to Islam or otherwise abandon their Chinese or Indian culture. During preliminary talks on the constitution, for example, some Malay and British representatives suggested to a Chinese delegate that in exchange for full citizenship, the Chinese should "give up some of their culture." In response, Chinese delegate Khoo Teik Ee asked, "Cannot a [Chinese person] identify ... with the country [of Malaysia] unless he [or she] adopts its religion [i.e., Islam]?" Colonial official Roland Braddell replied that such an individual "can feel a Malayan – I quite agree, but not to the same extent as a Malay" (von Vorys 1975:101–3; Lee Kam 2007). Braddell's answer thus hardly comforted non-Muslims in their fear of being coercively converted to Islam or forcibly assimilated into traditional Malay society. Partly because it was smaller and probably more divided by regional, class, and caste differences, the Indian community seems to have offered less effective resistance to Malay domination, but this fact does not necessarily imply that Indians were any happier than Chinese were about their second-class citizenship in the Malaysian Federation (Kent 2007:24–32).

At independence in 1957, most Malay Muslims supported the new, Malay-dominant government, but only some Western-educated elites among the Chinese (Buddhist) and Indian (Hindu) communities fully joined this nationalist venture (Bunge and Vreeland 1984:53–4). From the very beginning of modern Malaysian history, many religious and ethnic minorities distrusted the new state. Little wonder, then, that postindependence history has turned into a continuous struggle to keep the twin centrifugal forces of religion and ethnicity from tearing the country apart and that most ethnic Chinese and Indians (read religious Buddhists, Christians, and Hindus) exhibit much less enthusiasm for the Malaysian national project.

Finally, one should note two important geographical changes in 1963 and 1965 that further altered the religious and ethnic calculus. First, in 1963 Singapore, Sarawak and Sabah (a.k.a. North Borneo) joined what is now peninsular Malaysia to form the new "Federation of Malaysia" (Andaya and Andaya 2001:282–7). The addition of all three territories arguably tended to undermine the societal and political stability of the expanded country since these new areas contained disproportionately large non-Muslim populations. Singapore was majority Chinese ethnically and hence overwhelmingly non-Muslim, while the other two regions were home to massive numbers of Christians.

Second, perhaps partly out of fears of non-Muslim, Chinese dominance in the Federation, the Malaysian government expelled Singapore two years later. From the Singapore side, conversely, Chinese were afraid of being controlled by Muslims. The dominant ethnic group in Singapore opposed "affirmative action" in favor of Malays, which the Chinese claimed was being implemented at their expense (Healy 1982:21–4; Bunge and Vreeland 1984:59–60). Moreover, the original borders of this region had been drawn by various European colonial powers who did not necessarily take ethnic divisions into account. As we will show in Chapter 7, a similar postcolonial dynamic occurred in south Asia with the partition of India and Pakistan, although the tensions between Singapore and Malaysia are not as great. After 1965, the borders of Malaysia have thus included marginally fewer Buddhists and Christians but not as few as in 1957.

RELIGIOUS DEMOGRAPHICS AND EMERGENT NATIONALISM

The religious, ethnic, and economic demographics of Malaysia lie at the root of its unstable form of religious nationalism. In Malaysia, a religious division typically also correlates strongly with an ethnic divide and an economic cleavage (von Vorys 1975:21–52). In particular, economic differences among the three major ethnic groups – Malays, Chinese, and Indians – often exacerbate debates over religion. Malays are by definition all Muslims, but they are also disproportionately rural and poor. Chinese Malaysians are typically Christian, Buddhist, and/or Confucian but more likely to be urban and affluent, at least in peninsular Malaysia. Ethnic Tamils could be Hindu or perhaps Christian, but they also tend to live in cities and enjoy better-than-average incomes. Analyzing official statistics, Saari, Dietzenbacher, and Los (2014) found that the per capita income of ethnic Chinese was 74 percent higher than that of ethnic Malays, and that the per-person income of Indians was also 36 percent greater than for Malays. Malays tended to earn little because they worked disproportionately in poorly paid, low-skilled jobs in rural farming communities. Chinese enjoyed the highest salaries since they more often occupied more highly skilled positions in cities. And Indians fell somewhere between the two first ethnicities in income for similar occupation-related reasons (see also Willford 2005).

Next, religion closely maps onto ethnicity. According to the 2010 Census, 63 percent of Malaysian citizens are Muslims, 20 percent Buddhists, 9 percent Christians, 6 percent Hindus, and about 1 percent each practitioners of Chinese folk religions or secularists. Ethnicity and religious identification are closely linked. About 67 percent of Malaysians belong to the "Bumiputera" group (Malay or related ethnicities native to the region), 25 percent are Chinese, and 7 percent Indian (Department of Statistics Malaysia 2011:5; 9). Thus, ethnic Malays are overwhelmingly Muslims (officially 100 percent), Chinese Malaysians predominately Buddhists, Confucianists, and/or folk religionists (87 percent) or perhaps Christians (11 percent), and Indian ethnics primarily Hindus (86 percent) with a Christian minority (6 percent). Geographically, the heartland of Islam lies in Peninsular Malaysia, while in Sarawak somewhere between

43 percent and the majority of the population embraces Christianity (Bunge and Vreeland 1984:110; Department of Statistics Malaysia 2011:82–98; Hoffstaedter 2011:17; Liow 2016:139).

The origins of this diversity lie mainly in Malaysia's colonial history. Ethnic Malays make up the majority of the population and descend from the original inhabitants of the region before European exploration (Bunge and Vreeland 1984:3). Their conversion to Islam came through interaction with Arab, Chinese, and especially Indian Muslim traders who traveled through and sometimes settled in the area beginning in the tenth century of the current era (Andaya and Andaya 2001:53–4). Many Chinese Buddhists and Indian Hindus immigrated to what is today Malaysia during the 1800s under British rule. Along with Europeans, they came to dominate the modern part of the economy such as tin mining and the export of rubber while ordinary Malays and their local, traditional rulers remained in semifeudal conditions in the countryside (Bunge and Vreeland 1984:4). Christianity mainly arrived with the Portuguese, Dutch, and British colonial powers, but Christians from South Asia and Hakka-speaking communities in China also carried the Gospel with them when they migrated to the region (Liow 2016:140).

In today's Malaysia, the country's ethnically segregated party system further inflames ethno-religious tensions. By far, the most politically powerful political party is the UMNO, the leading component of the coalition that has governed Malaysia since its founding. Founded in 1946 to advance the interests of Malays, the UMNO allied itself with the Malaysian Chinese Association (MCA) and Malaysian Indian Congress (MIC) and has governed the country continuously since independence. The UMNO's Malay leaders arguably tempered the party's original ethnic chauvinism and now rule with the aid of some sympathetic Chinese and Indian politicians from the related parties and claim to adopt policies that benefit all Malaysians regardless of background. Mass support has been growing, however, for opposition groups such as the Islamist-oriented PAS, increasingly popular among poorer Malays, and the "non-communal," democratic-socialist Democratic Action Party (DAP), whose voting base is disproportionately Chinese urbanites (Bunge and Vreeland 1984:187–8, 219–26; Hoffstaedter 2011:17–27). Even an outsider to Malaysia, then, would have a reasonably good chance of guessing a person's party affiliation, ethnicity, and perhaps even class simply from his or her religion. Obviously, such extreme fractionalization does not make for a stable society or polity.

RELIGIOUS ELITES AND NATIONALISM AT THE ESTABLISHMENT
OF RUKUN NEGARA

In what became known as the 13 May Incident (a.k.a. the Kuala Lumpur Riots), the relative ethnic truce established at the country's founding broke down in 1969 in a series of bloody racial riots. Of course, independent Malaya and then Malaysia had experienced intercommunal violence before (Horowitz 2001:254–6, 75; Turnbull 2009:291), but never with such deadly results. Medium-term causes of the bloodletting centered on Malay perceptions that the government was not doing enough to lift them out of rural poverty and Chinese and Indian complaints that the administration was instead favoring Malays for aid and status and in any event not helping the more urban non-Malays who also suffered from economic privations. These grievances in turn created fissures in the party system that were exploited by disproportionately Chinese, ostensibly "non-communal" or "pro-equality" opposition leaders campaigning for their group's preferred position on education and language policy (Andaya and Andaya 2001:295–7). After the results of the May 10, 1969 federal election in Peninsular Malaysia showed much less support for the pro-Malay, Alliance government (a drop from 58 to 49 percent of the total vote compared to the previous election) and much more enthusiasm for the opposition parties, many Chinese and some Indian residents of Kuala Lumpur took to the streets to celebrate their victory. Some marchers allegedly also ridiculed the Malays "losers" in racial terms, provoking Malays into attacking Chinese and Indians physically. At least two weeks of South-Asian-style, communal rioting followed (Bunge and Vreeland 1984:60–1). In the end, somewhere between two and eight hundred (or even more) largely Chinese citizens were shot, slashed, drowned, or burned to death (von Vorys 1975:363–8), and thousands of Chinese living in the capital became homeless (Andaya and Andaya 2001:298).

After authorities suppressed the worst of the violence, they moved on to suspend the constitution, postpone elections in Sabah and Sarawak, dissolve parliament, and set up a "National Operations Council" (NOC) that ruled by decree (Bunge and Vreeland 1984:61; Andaya and Andaya 2001:298). Supposedly to prevent future outbreaks of such ethnic conflict, the "emergency" government likewise adopted several new policies to address Malays' feelings of disadvantage. One of these, referred to in the national language as Rukun Negara (national pillars or principles), remains the foundation of Malaysia's religion–state relations.

The first medium-term policy change the NOC administration made was to ban public discourse that might incite ethnic conflict. Amending the Sedition Act of 1948, the authorities criminalized speech that openly challenged Malays' special privileges, the primacy of their language, the position of their traditional rulers, and their advantages in citizenship law. Violating individuals faced exclusion from public office for five years, and offending organizations risked being disbanded (Bunge and Vreeland 1984:61).[1] Likewise suppressed were certain ethnically tinged publications, such as one Mahathir Mohamad's critical book *The Malay Dilemma* (Andaya and Andaya 2001:299), certain newspapers, media from political parties, and even particular issues of *Time* and *Newsweek* (von Vorys 1975:354; Lee 1990).

The NOC took a more material approach to reducing Malay unrest in its New Economic Policy (NEP), which amounted to a kind of affirmative action policy for Malays. Overall, the NEP aimed both to foster overall economic growth and to ensure that Malays possessed a greater share of the country's wealth. In theory, such an approach was not to be a zero-sum game in which Malays benefited at the expense of Chinese and Indians. Rather, the government asserted that indigenous Malaysians would gain from a nationwide economic boom, not via government-administered redistributive policies. Specific programs included development projects in the largely Malay countryside as well as payments to rural commodities producers. In a parallel policy track, the state transitioned most secondary education from English- to Malay-language instruction, expanded the number of universities, and used racial quotas to make it much easier for Malays to be admitted instead of Chinese or Tamils. These and related NEP initiatives continued through 1990 (Salim 1983; Andaya and Andaya 2001:301–16).

But the most relevant policy change for our purposes was the establishment of Rukun Negara as a kind of official ideology that is now "catechized amongst school children" and recited publicly "on every Merdeka [National] Day" (Shafie 1985:69). Aiming to foster a sense of national unity among all Malaysians regardless of ethnic background, the five bedrock principles state that all citizens should: (1) believe in God, (2) stay loyal to the King and country, (3) uphold the constitution, (4) maintain the rule of law, and (5) practice good behavior and morality (Salim 1983). According to the NOC-affiliated Department of National Unity that formulated it, Rukun Negara would help ensure "a democratic way of life[,] a just society in which the wealth of the nation shall be equitably shared[,] a liberal approach" to Malaysia's "rich and diverse cultural traditions," and a "progressive society" based on "science and technology" (Andaya and Andaya 2001:298–9).

In the abstract, most of these ideals seem hardly objectionable, yet the different ethno-religious groups and their leaders have showed themselves more or less supportive, perhaps based on how they believed the Malay-dominated government would implement Rukun Negara. One has difficulty finding reliable, direct measures of opposition to Rukun Negara since the government increasingly censored the press and outlawed most public criticism of the regime in response to 13 May. We might nonetheless presume that citizens who were not Malay or Muslim might have felt less comfortable pledging loyalty to the Muslim and ethnically Malay king, known in Bahasa as the Yang di-Pertuan Agong (Bunge and Vreeland 1984:61). Indian Hindus and Chinese Buddhists conceivably might have viewed an emphasis on monotheism as an attack on their religions. Few Malaysians would have opposed "morality" per se, but Indian and Chinese Christians and Indian Hindus might have felt uneasy about specifically Islamic interpretations of virtue that a Muslim-majority government might want to promote in the future. Muslim leaders in the NOC administration who helped formulate the language of Rukun Negara, such as Shafie (1985:36–45), of course advocated strenuously for its adoption and presented it as a solution to the "crisis of values" that had allegedly caused the violence of 13 May. Yet some of the stricter groups of Sunni Muslims (e.g., followers of the "Dakwah" movement) were presumably uncomfortable with the more pan-religious guarantees in the constitution, such as the right to freedom of religious practice for non-Muslims (Bunge and Vreeland 1984:110–8). Over time, religious minorities and even some more fundamentalist Muslims have come to show much less willingness to embrace the ruling government's interpretation of Rukun Negara, which is supposedly a unifying set of nationalist principles. In other words, Malaysia's religious nationalist model has become increasingly unstable because the country's distinct religious and ethnic groups now disagree about the validity of its foundational nationalist ideology, or at least about how the state currently implements Rukun Negara.

RELIGION IN THE CONSTITUTION

Indeed, this discord about the country's nationalist project predates the establishment of Rukun Negara, reaching all the way back to debates over the new state's form of government. Here again, Malay Muslims enjoyed special status in the original 1957 Constitution, while citizens from other ethnic or religious backgrounds received fewer privileges. In religious terms, the founding document essentially set up a system of first- and second-class citizenship in which Malay Muslims occupied the dominant legal position.

According to the plain text of Article 3, Part I, of the 1957 Constitution, "Islam is the religion of the Federation" (CommonLII 2017). As in Greece, one religion alone receives official endorsement from the state; believers in other faiths can only hope that the politically empowered Muslims will wield their influence benevolently. At least some of the framers appear to have had similar expectations since the next clause reads that "other religions may be practised in peace and harmony in any part of the Federation." The religiously relevant Article 3 concludes with a discussion of the rights and duties of the Malaysian king (Yang di-Pertuan Agong), including his role as "Head of the religion of Islam" and parliament's right to set up a religious council to advise him. In western terms, the equivalent arrangement might be if the Pope established Roman Catholicism as the state religion of Vatican City but then graciously allowed any hypothetical non-Catholic residents to worship there too so long as they did not create a public disturbance. Like Greece's, Malaysia's constitution thus combines nominal establishment of one faith with (at least de jure) protection of certain democratic rights.

Of course, unfair actions against religious minorities may very well cause civil unrest. Article 8 (CommonLII 2017) therefore assures citizens that

Except as expressly authorized by this Constitution, there shall be no discrimination against citizens on the ground only of religion, race, descent or place of birth in any law relating to the acquisition, holding or disposition of property or the establishing or carrying on of any trade, business, profession, vocation or employment.

The same article nonetheless specifies that the Constitution permits Islamic "personal law" and allows religious institutions to hire only "persons professing that religion." Article 12 further asserts that

there shall be no discrimination against any citizen on the grounds only of religion, race, descent or place of birth in the administration of any educational institution maintained by a public authority, and, in particular, the admission of pupils or students or the payment of fees.

An important provision in Article 8 nevertheless appears to undermine these antidiscriminatory guarantees, approving of "any provision for the protection, wellbeing or advancement of the aboriginal peoples of the Malay Peninsula (including the reservation of land) or the reservation to aborigines of a reasonable proportion of suitable positions in the public service." In the minds of many non-Muslims, then, such language probably suggested a two-tiered system of constitutional rights: a privileged one for the Muslim-Malay majority and a second, lesser one for religious and ethnic minorities. Should Malay Islamists choose to manipulate this explicit constitutional provision, moreover, it could conceivably form the rhetorical foundation for governmental support of Sharia-based policies.

Finally, Article 11 (CommonLII 2017) affirms that "Every person has the right to profess and practice his religion and, subject to Clause (4), to propagate it." Clause 4, however, limits the import of this provision by admitting that the "law may control or restrict the propagation of any religious doctrine or belief among persons professing the religion of Islam." Christians, for example, may evangelize members of the Hindu and Buddhist minorities but have no constitutional right to try to convert believers in the majority religion, Islam. Muslims, in contrast, presumably have the right to try to proselytize anyone they wish. One can once again see how religious minorities might feel slighted by this supposedly universal declaration of citizens' rights.

During constitutional debates preceding Malaya's independence, everyone did not agree on such two-track arrangements, however. In fact, the official British report summarizing these discussions, known as the Reid Commission paper, did not call for Islam to be the state religion. On the contrary, the commissioners themselves, the traditional Malay rulers, and many non-Muslim organizations argued for a secular federal government that would treat all religions equally. The politically powerful, Malay-dominant Alliance party, however, urged the nominal establishment of Islam – but did not support an Islamic state – and claimed that having an official religion would not harm followers of other faiths (Fernando 2006). In paragraph 169 of the Reid Commission (1957) report, the delegates stated:

The majority of us think that it is best to leave the matter on this basis [i.e., possible Islam establishment at the state level but not at the federal one], looking to the fact that Counsel for the [state-level, traditional Muslim] Rulers[who feared religious interference by federal authorities,] said to us – "It is Their Highnesses considered view that it would not be desirable to insert some declaration such as has been suggested that the Muslim Faith or Islamic Faith be the established religion of the Federation ..."

The authors of the report noted, however, that the Alliance Party and commissioner Abdul Hamid, a judge from Pakistan, desired establishment. According to Hamid's dissenting opinion in the paper, "a declaration [establishing Islam] will not impose any disability on non-Muslim citizens in professing, propagating and practising their religions, and will not prevent the State from being a secular State." As the justice saw it, many majority-Christian countries such as Norway and Denmark have similar clauses in their constitutions without the provisions "caus[ing] hardships to anybody."

Once the Reid Commission issued its recommendations, however, a later "Working Party" reviewed them. This committee included the High Commissioner Donald MacGillivray, Alliance delegates such as Tunku Abdul Rahman, and representatives of the traditional (Muslim) Malay rulers. During the first meeting of this group on February 22, 1957, Tunku insisted that Islam be declared the established religion. He claimed that the government would nonetheless remain secular and that the federal administration would not try to undermine the religious authority of the traditional Malay rulers in their particular states. Although two Alliance delegates to the Working Party were not Malays, they did not object to this proposal because their Malay counterparts in the Alliance had assured them that the establishment of Islam would be merely symbolic, not affecting the rights of non-Muslims. Even as late as the nineteenth meeting, however, the Malay rulers still seemed uneasy about the new provision and how it might be misinterpreted. Tunku then repeated his assertion that "the whole Constitution was framed on the basis that the Federation would be a secular State." Tunku's Muslim-centric position eventually prevailed, and he and his Alliance Party colleagues were able to persuade members of the later London Constitutional committee as well as the British Parliament that they "had no intention of creating a Muslim theocracy and that Malaya would be a secular state." In the end, the British Colonial Office did "not consider that there can be any reasonable fear of discrimination against non-Moslems" and signed off on establishment. Some modernist Muslims, secularists, and Christians in the Malayan legislature as well as a few similarly minded members of the British House of Commons and House of Lords criticized the revised language on religion during debate, but they lacked the votes to block approval of Malaya's founding document (Fernando 2006; Ibrahim 1978).

Thus, from the very beginning of modern Malaysia, some minorities contested the religious–nationalist model established by the 1957 Constitution. If religious outsiders had constituted simply a few percentage points of the population as they do in Greece, such dissent would hardly have mattered. Because the proportion of country- and regional-level religious minorities is much higher in Malaysia, however, this model has shown its relative instability time and again since 1957 and arguably helped provoke the bloody racial riots of 1969 and later governmental suppression of any further criticism of the country's ethnic (read: religious) arrangements.

RENEWED RACIAL TENSIONS AND CONTINUING CHALLENGES TO RELIGIOUS NATIONALISM

After the institution of Rukun Negara, Malaysia has nonetheless experienced a number of crises related to "race" or religion and to this day remains profoundly divided along twinned ethnic and religious lines. Some of these episodes reflected not simply the underlying tension among the major groups but also suggested that the model itself was at risk of being modified or even abolished in favor of something more like civic or secular nationalism. At the outset of this book we hypothesized that some of the most important threats to a country's model of religion and nationalism stem from external threats. From 1969 until about 1990, Malaysia continued to experience low-level domestic violence partly sponsored by foreign powers, and since then the ethno-religious pot has never ceased to boil or at least simmer. Even if the country's religious nationalism appears more stable today than it did during the race riots of 1969, we believe changes in the ethnically linked political coalitions could still lead to the model's breakdown under suitable conditions.

Especially during the Cold War, domestic guerrilla movements partly supported by Communist China and other sympathetic foreign states challenged the central government or at least its regional affiliates. Had these ethnic Chinese-led rebellions succeeded in overthrowing the Malay-Muslim administration, the new rulers would have probably lost little time in disestablishing Islam and adopting secular nationalism à la the People's Republic of China (PRC). (Conversely, of course, the Chinese threat could have also reinforced Malays' Muslim identity over against that of the "godless" Chinese Communists.) The first significant offensive, known as the Communist insurgency in Sarawak, lasted from late 1962 to 1990 and was rooted in the near-feudal rural poverty of many of Borneo's ethnic Chinese (Andaya and Andaya 2001:306–7). Aided by anti-British rebels from Brunei and members of the Indonesian army, the predominantly Chinese Sarawak Communist Organization (SCO) began military operations in Sarawak at the end of 1962 (Cheah 2009). By the beginning of the 1970s, the SCO and its allies were widely feared for their attacks on "hostile" civilians and members of the Malaysian police and army. The government responded with military counterattacks, mass arrests of suspected Communists (Andaya and Andaya 2001:307), and the forcible relocation of many ethnic Chinese into concentration-camp-like "New Villages." Violence declined somewhat after SCO leader Bong Kee Chok surrendered along with three-quarters of the rebel forces in 1974. Hostilities did not completely end until the cessation of the Cold War in 1990, however, when the remaining Sarawak guerrillas signed a peace treaty with Kuala Lumpur (Porritt 2004; Cheah 2009).

During the parallel "Second Malayan Emergency" from 1968 to 1989, ethnically Chinese, Communist rebels attacked government positions in Kinta district and along other parts of Peninsular Malaysia's border with Thailand (Andaya and Andaya 2001:305). Supported initially by Mao's China and directed from Beijing by the Chinese-Malaysian leader Chin Peng (Chin 2003; Cheah 2009; Ng 2011:100–1), the insurgents also benefited from the pro-Communist sympathies of many poor Chinese in local "New Villages" and similarly depressed communities in southern Thailand (Andaya and Andaya 2001:305). In some of their more successful operations, the local Communists killed Malaysia's Inspector-General of Police and the security chief of Perak state (Cheah 2009). Violence peaked in the mid-1970s before ending with a peace treaty between the Malaysian government and the MCP in 1989 (Central Intelligence Agency 1976:8; Andaya and Andaya 2001:305). By then, the PRC had tapered off its support for the MCP after Malaysia switched recognition from Taipei to Beijing and Prime Minister Mahathir lobbied Deng Xiaoping's government to cut off aid (Cheah 2009).

Even with the return to relative ethnic peace in the 1990s, changing electoral coalitions and the increased Islamization of Malay Muslims (Milne and Mauzy 1999:80–9; Barr and Govindasamy 2010; Andaya and Andaya 2017:357–73), despite grave warnings by the country's founder against "fanaticism" (Tunku 1983:69–72), pose persistent risks to Rukun Negara and the religious-nationalism model as a whole. On the one hand, the UMNO and its coalition partners have moved further and further in an Islamist direction (Lee 1988; Liow 2016:150; Andaya and Andaya 2017:371) in order to maintain popular support among the also ever-more-Islamist rank-and-file voters. So far, this strategy has allowed the ruling alliance to hold onto the reins of government and win the UMNO votes from Malay Muslims who might have otherwise been tempted to cast their ballots for the explicitly Islamist Parti Islam Se-Malaysia, or PAS (Liow 2004, 2009). And so long as the ruling party remains in power, Malaysia's model of religious nationalism if not necessarily the original version of Rukun Negara will likely survive. On the other hand, the Muslim-dominated government has increasingly provoked non-Muslims by siding with the advocates of an Islamic state instead of a nominal, English-style established-religion model that is fundamentally secular. If ethnically Chinese or Indian Malaysians who practice Buddhism, Christianity, or Hinduism decide that the Malay-run administration is intent on further restricting or eliminating non-Muslims' freedom of religious practice in favor of a more Saudi or Iranian approach, these minorities might revolt forcefully or even violently, threatening the entire state structure. In such a situation, one can even imagine some moderate and/or opportunistic Malay Muslims joining religious minorities in reforming or overthrowing the ever-more-extreme system and replacing it with a secular or at least neutral model (cf. the Indian Bharatiya Janata Party's similar potential effects on moderate Hindus in Chapter 7).

Of course, such a scenario remains speculative if not a little fanciful. But a pessimist could project current trends out into the future and arrive at just such a result. And the 2008 general election, which did not go well for the governing coalition, contained hints of such developments (Liow 2009:195–203). Some of the more worrying incidents in recent Malaysian politics include a 2013 Court of Appeal ruling forbidding Malay-language, non-Muslim publications from using the word "Allah" to refer to God (Shah 2015; Leong 2016; Matchen and Carnahan 2016); during related police "enforcement" actions, customs officials seized Malay-language Bibles (Liow 2009:197), and in 2010 Islamists fire-bombed three churches in Kuala Lumpur in protest at Christians' use of the Arabic word for God. The year before, Muslims upset at the establishment of a Hindu temple in their neighborhood reacted by kicking around the decapitated head of a cow – an animal which is holy to Hindus (Kuppusamy 2010). In political developments during the 2013 election, meanwhile, the relatively moderate Malay-Muslim opposition leader Anwar Ibrahim and his coalition won the popular vote but failed to gain a majority of the parliamentary seats because of Malaysia's arcane and arguably unfair electoral system (Lim 2013). Ibrahim (2006) himself believes that Islam and "constitutional democracy" are compatible and that the Koran teaches "freedom of conscience, freedom of expression, and the sanctity of life and property" are "moral imperatives." At least one party in the current opposition coalition, moreover, explicitly calls for secularism (Democratic Action Party 2017). Unfortunately for Anwar, after the 2013 polls the UNMO government once again jailed him for "sodomy" after highly suspect and widely criticized "legal" proceedings (Ives 2016; Amnesty International 2017). The officially victorious 2013 candidate for Prime Minister, Najib Razak, turned out once in office to be so corrupt that even the relatively conservative former Prime Minister Mahathir (Ismail 2002) joined a new political alliance with Anwar to fight for Razak's ouster (Blakkarly 2016). Feeling targeted for restrictions on their religious freedom, Christian pastors and other community leaders have begun politically mobilizing laity by preaching the virtues of voting – and "voting wisely" (i.e., for the opposition) – and opening up their churches for registration drives (Liow 2016:157). In the streets of Kuala Lumpur, meanwhile, ethnically and religiously tinged protests and violence make some observers fear a reprise of the 1969 riots (*Guardian* 2016). In the ever-more-repressive policies toward religious minorities and the ever-more-troubling electoral and governmental turmoil, one can imagine several ways in which a new group of more secularly oriented leaders would gain power and seek to abolish or minimize the special status of Islam.

PUBLIC OPINION AND NATIONALISM

As in the other country chapters, we wanted to examine mass-level support for both abstract and specific nationalism. For abstract nationalism, we used data from the Malaysian subsample of the 2011 World Values Survey. As for Greece, we used the Pew 2013 Global Attitudes Survey and selected views of a historically opposing neighbor to measure concrete nationalism. The relevant question asked respondents to rate their hostility to China on a scale from one to four.

Overall, levels of generic nationalism among Malaysians are high and follow the patterns that we would expect in a religiously nationalistic state (see Table 5.1). The major exception is Hindus, whose average levels of national pride are slightly more elevated than even for the Muslim

TABLE 5.1. *Nationalism by religious tradition*

Tradition	Mean
Muslim	3.70
Buddhist	3.28
Hindu	3.76
Christian	3.58
Confucian	3.36
Not religious	3.22
All respondents	3.61

Source: 2011 World Values Survey, Malaysia subsample.

majority. We can only speculate about the causes of this anomaly, but the few Hindus could perhaps feel economic solidarity with the Muslim majority against the more-affluent ethnic Chinese. Alternatively, Hindus might appreciate the Muslim-dominated government's opposition to at least some religious proselytizing (officially of Muslims only) by Christians. The results from our regression in Table 5.2, however, more clearly match our theory. Here, the Buddhist, Christian, Confucian, and nonreligious minorities are substantially less nationalistic even after controlling for major demographic factors. Religious attendance appears to boost national pride, as we would expect it to do among the religious majority. Our attempts to dive deeper into this relationship for minority groups, however, foundered on the shoals of a lack of relevant demographic data.

HOSTILITY TO CHINA

Our second dependent variable is Malaysians' views of the PRC. While relations between Malaysia and China have not been nearly as frosty as those between Japan and the Middle Kingdom, PRC-backed Communist rebels did menace the Malaysian government for decades (see Bunge and Vreeland 1984:230), and the Malay majority probably has greater apprehension about ethnic Chinese than about any other domestic minority. Finally, several of our other country chapters measure popular nationalism via attitudes toward a politically powerful neighboring state.

Overall, Malaysians are not stridently anti-Chinese (see Table 5.3). The most friendly to the PRC are the Buddhists, who might envision a sacred

TABLE 5.2. *Religious and other determinants of nationalism*

Variable	Coefficient	Standard Error
Buddhist	−1.394[*]	0.167
Hindu	0.433	0.262
Christian	−0.811[*]	0.262
Confucian	−1.157[*]	0.319
Not religious	−1.132[*]	0.496
Religious attendance	0.170[*]	0.034
Education	−0.060	0.037
Income	0.196[*]	0.035
Woman	0.082	0.126
Age	0.002	0.005
Sarawak and Sabah	0.768[*]	0.203
Johor	0.089	0.206
Selangor	−0.304	0.166
Federal territories	0.456	0.270
Constant 1	−4.575[*]	0.644
Constant 2	−2.182[*]	0.433
Constant 3	−0.949[*]	0.412
N	1288	
Nagelkerke R^2	0.193	

*Denotes an effect that is significantly different from 0 at the 5 percent level for ordered Logit model.
Notes: All regressors are dummy variables except for Religious Attendance (range = 1–7), Education (1–9), Income (1–10), and Age (18–80).
Source: 2011 World Values Survey, Malaysia subsample.

TABLE 5.3. *Hostility to China by religious tradition*

Tradition	Mean percent
Muslim	1.99
Buddhist	1.76
Hindu	1.99
Christian	2.42
All respondents	1.97

Source: 2013 Spring Pew Global Attitudes survey, Malaysia subsample.

connection to the historically Buddhist nation. In Table 5.4, no other religious affiliations showed any significant effect on views of China, however, and religious importance also failed to yield any substantive results,
even in a series of unreported regressions for each religious group in turn.
Malaysians therefore do not appear to be politically mobilized against
China in religious settings.

RELIGION AND NATIONALISM IN RELIGIOUS PUBLICATIONS AND PRIME MINISTERS' AND OPPOSITION LEADER'S STATEMENTS

To analyze leaders' opinions, we conducted content analysis of major
online religious periodicals for five main religious traditions in the country: Islam, Buddhism, Hinduism, Roman Catholicism, and Protestantism.
For each religious group, we found a representative publication or organizational website: Malaysian Muslim Solidarity, Malaysian Buddhist
Association, Malaysia Hindu Sangam, *Herald Malaysia* (Catholic), and
National Evangelical Christian Fellowship of Malaysia. We conducted

TABLE 5.4. *Religious and other determinants of hostility to China*

Variable	Coefficient	Standard error
Buddhist	−0.709[*]	0.216
Hindu	0.027	0.314
Christian	0.589	0.350
Religious importance	−0.212	0.169
Education	−0.123[*]	0.051
Income	0.013	0.035
Woman	0.174	0.145
Age	−0.008	0.005
Sarawak and Sabah	0.724[*]	0.228
Urban	0.274	0.169
Constant 1	−2.182[*]	0.749
Constant 2	−0.122	0.744
N	689	
Nagelkerke R²	0.090	

[*]Denotes an effect that is significantly different from 0 at the 5 percent level for ordered
Logit model.
Notes: All regressors are dummy variables except for Religious Importance (range = 1–4),
Education (1–9), Income (1–12), and Age (18–86).
Source: 2013 Spring Pew Global Attitudes survey, Malaysia subsample.

a search of each outlet for the term "Rukun Negara." As we noted previously in this chapter, this expression is a core yet contested concept in religion–state relations in the country. We then coded each relevant document as understanding this term as including all religions, restricting itself to Islam alone, or taking no position on this question.

Not surprisingly, Figure 5.1 demonstrates that religious minorities do not interpret Rukun Negara in a religiously restrictive way; all articles in their publications took either a multireligious or neutral approach. Although a representative writer in the Catholic *Herald* affirms "our Rukun Negara" and "our Federal Constitution," for example, she nonetheless bemoans "holier-than-thou organisations [telling] us that we [can't] mingle with fellow Malaysians who profess[s] different religions because they [are] a threat to our own faiths" (Rashid 2015). In the same publication, the Archbishop of Kuala Lumpur prays that "all of [Malaysia's] people of diverse races and cultures [will] work selflessly ... to make Malaysia a truly united and harmonious nation, guided by the principles of the Rukun Negara" (Leow 2015). In their own publication (Ng 2010), evangelical Christians similarly accept the first principle of the Rukun Negara (i.e., belief in God) but oppose Muslim extremists' demands that the text of the first rule be revised from "God" to "Allah." The Malaysian Buddhist Association (2009a) cites "Article 4 of Rukun Negara [which] guarantee[s] a liberal approach towards [Malaysia's] rich and varied cultural traditions." According to this Chinese-language essay, all Malaysians "are free to believe in and practice their religion, customs

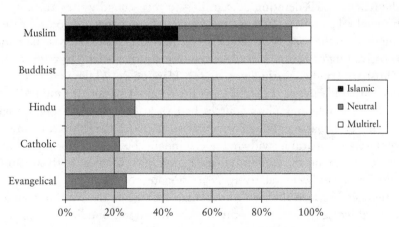

FIGURE 5.1. *Abstract nationalism (meaning of Rukun Negara) in religious publications*

and culture, as long as they do not hinder the national unity." Buddhists desire "a society in which these different characteristics are turned into our assets and power." Hindu media (*Hindu Malaysia Sangam* 2015) do not necessarily explicate Rukun Negara in much detail but do urge readers to "report to the police or Malaysia Hindu Sangam" any person or "group found condemning Hinduism with the intention for conversion." In the view of this official Hindu organization, the Federal government should protect Hindus from being converted to Islam, Buddhism, or Christianity. Not a single document from any of the minority publications interpreted this core principle of Malaysian nationalism to exclude non-Muslims.

Materials from the Muslim organization, on the other hand, are much more likely to advance Muslim nationalism. In particular, less than 10 percent of the Muslim statements interpret the "National Principles" in a multireligious way, while nearly half connect Rukun Negara to an Islamic identity. One article from the Muslim media site Ismaweb (Annuar 2016), for example, suggests that Rukun Negara would allow the banning of a concert by American pop singer Selena Gomez because her songs are "mainly about love and lust; in other words, sex." According to the author, "we are living in an Islamic country" and "adhere to our Rukun Negara." But "this act of hedonism, by bringing her into the country" goes against "our religion of the federation[,] which is Islam." A similar essay criticizes a British-funded conference on liberalism, holding that "In Malaysia, our identity is that, Islam and multiculturalism is made possible by Article 1 [of the Constitution], where Islam is recognized as the religion of Federation." According to this second writer, the constitutional religion–state arrangement permits "some form of control being imposed on the society, including the Sedition Act," and likewise bars the proselytizing of Muslims and the use of the term "Allah" to refer to the Christian Trinity (Nurhidayah 2016). Here again, Malaysia's religious diversity undermines the stability of the religious-nationalist model.

The five religious news sources had very little to say about China. For the two that mentioned anything at all about the subject, the averages were comparable, with an understandable but very minor pro-China tendency among the Buddhists (see Figure 5.2). Overall, both Muslims and Buddhists were relatively dispassionate about China. The largest difference between the two traditions is that while the Muslim sources were universally neutral on the Middle Kingdom, Buddhist statements showed much more variance, with around 28 percent negative about the PRC, roughly 28 percent neutral, and about 43 percent positive.

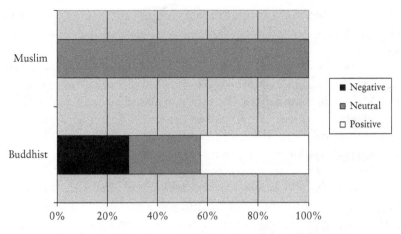

FIGURE 5.2. *Attitudes toward China in religious publications*

A representative Muslim article (Ismaweb 2016) discusses China's work on the Scarborough Shoal and mentions that the Philippines, Vietnam, Malaysia, Brunei, and Taiwan also claim islands in the South China Sea. The author takes no side in this dispute, however. The Buddhist source contains similar essays but also complains about the disrespectful treatment of Buddhist monks in the Hong Kong/PRC production of the film "Shaolin Temple" (Malaysian Buddhist Association 2009b). On the other hand, a Buddhist writer opined that "the opening of Buddhism in China has played a positive role in the development of Buddhism toward the world, especially Malaysia" (Yu 2009). This minimal role for attitudes toward China contrasts markedly with the parallel situation in Greece in the previous chapter. There, hostility toward Turkey tends to go hand-in-hand with animus toward Greek Muslims, which would undermine the stability of the Greek model of religious nationalism if the Muslim population were more substantial.

As for most of the countries in this book, Malaysia appears to lack a centralized, online compilation of the chief executive's speeches. We therefore were forced to conduct a more qualitative analysis of the discourse of several important Malaysian prime ministers as well as of one prominent opposition leader. In particular, we examined the rhetoric of Prime Ministers Tunku Abdul Rahman (1957–1970), Mahathir Mohamad (1981–2003), and Najib Razak (2009–present). We also looked at talks and writings by key opposition leader and former Deputy Prime Minister Anwar Ibrahim. In reviewing these texts, we aimed to see how they employed the words "Rukun Negara" and to understand what this approach suggested about their understanding of Malaysian nationalism and its religion–state arrangements.

Malaysia's founder, known locally as "the Tunku," appears to have advocated a tolerant, relatively trans-religious version of Rukun Negara and Malaysian nationalism. For him, non-Muslims were not necessarily second-class citizens, or at least to the extent that current Malaysian Islamists seem to view religious minorities. During the preamble speech to his "Proclamation of Independence" of August 31, 1957, for example, Tunku (1957) expresses his confidence that his fellow citizens will "with the blessing of God" overcome the challenges that come with "Malaya['s] step[ping] forward to take her rightful place as a free and independent partner in the great community of Nations." The formal proclamation itself, however, does begin with the very Muslim Bismillah: "In the name of God, the compassionate, the merciful." His Malaysia Day speech of September 16, 1963 evokes similarly tolerant themes, expressing gratitude that "10 million people of many races [and therefore religions] in all the States of Malaya, Singapore, Sarawak and Sabah now join hands in freedom and unity." Tunku also showed pride that the Federation of Malaya's "multi-racial [i.e., multireligious] society emerged, endured and survived as a successful and progressive nation, a true democracy and an example to the world of harmony and tolerance." Finally, in a talk to UMNO party leaders (Tunku 1960:8), the founder of the country emphasized that he wanted to

eliminate illiteracy ... [and] teach ... Islamic doctrines very, very clearly in accordance with the true teachings of Islam in order to prevent villagers from being deceived and misguided by irresponsible parties. In the last election we have been able to hear how the Holy Religion has been manipulated for political benefits. In some places the villagers have been told to vote for the PAS (Malaysian Islamic Party) if they want to enter heaven, or that they will become a Kafir [an Arabic term meaning "unbeliever" or "disbeliever"] if they vote for other parties.

While Tunku may have approved of nominal religious establishment along the lines of Anglicanism in England, Malaysia's former colonial master, he clearly opposed the Iran-style Islamic Republic model countenanced or openly advocated by many of his supposed political followers today.

Though ostensibly opposed to "ignorant Islamic fundamentalism," Prime Minister Mahathir Mohamad appeared much more tolerant of such extremism than Tunku was and adopted a much more militant, aggrieved tone than his predecessor. During a lecture at the illustrious Egyptian Islamic institution Al-Azhar University, Mahathir (2003) bemoaned that "there has never been a time when Muslims are so looked down upon, so treated with disrespect, and so oppressed as they are today." The founder of Islam, according to Mahathir, "did not believe that for the Muslims this world is not important ... He not only believed that Muslims have a share of Allah's bounties on earth but that Muslims must be prepared to fight for their earthly share." Scientific education for Muslims is important, he emphasized, because otherwise Muslim countries will not be able to produce their own "guns and rockets, warships and warplanes, armoured cars, etc." in order to "deter and defeat our [infidel] enemies." Like Tunku, Mahathir also complains about the PAS and its claim that "anyone not joining or supporting it is not a Muslim." According to PAS propaganda, simply "voting for this party in elections will guarantee a place for them in heaven." Such electoral abuse of Islam, the Prime Minister asserted, has caused "a deep split among the Muslims of Malaysia." Though he condemned the PAS on the surface, his overall approach makes one wonder whether he was more concerned about his UMNO coalition losing votes or influence to the PAS or about Malaysian Islamists undermining the constitution and violating the civil liberties of religious minorities and moderate Muslims.

Mahathir (2003) contends, for example, that "Muslims were not meant to have countries and to be divided according to race or nation." Yet today, "their loyalty to their state [e.g., Malaysia?] is more than to Islam." Such dicta sound quite close in their fundamental assumptions to those put forward by the Bin Ladens and Ayatollah Khomeinis of the world. Elsewhere Mahathir (2002) noted that among the PAS, "hatred for the so-called secular [UMNO] Government is fostered from the kindergarten onwards. Fighting against this hate campaign absorbs much of the time of [my] Government and hinders development." In actuality, however, "Malaysia is already an Islamic country. The State religion is Islam and Muslims can practise their religion and apply the syariah laws as family laws." The status quo government meets "all the religious needs of Muslims." As for non-Muslims, Mahathir claimed that they "are free to practise their religions" not because of fundamental human rights or the principles of the Malaysia constitution, but rather "because this is permitted by Islam." According to the plain words of the Prime Minister, then, even religious minorities are in some way subject to Islamic teachings and could in theory be deprived of religious free practice if Islam supported such a restriction.

At least rhetorically, our third Prime Minister, Najib Razak, appears much closer to Tunku than Mahathir on religious nationalism; in fact, Najib ostensibly is primarily interested in economic development. He claims to support "Malaysian democracy" and praises his father (also a prime minister) for "willingly re-established parliamentary rule" in 1971 following the post-May 13 authoritarian period (Najib 2016). The son also notes that the elder prime minister "cared for the well-being of all, and was a prime minister for all races, all Malaysians" even if "his innate sense of social justice would not permit him to see the underprivileged, the bumiputra, [economically] lag behind" ethnic and religious minorities. According Najib, both he and his father adopted "Rukun Negara as [our] national philosophy to support our democratic way of life, create a just society, and preserve our rich and diverse cultural traditions." To maintain Malaysia's "national unity," Najib (2017) affirms in a similar speech, the nation must "strengthen the pillars and fabric of a multi-faith and multi-racial society." Besides closely following "the Malaysian Constitution ... [and] the principles of Rukun Negara," he emphasizes, "we have to look for our core values that can cut across all faiths and all communities in the country," especially a spirit of "moderat[ion]." Finally, during a National Day proclamation, Najib (2010) asserts that "the real challenge for Malaysians today is to transform the country [into ...] a developed and high-income nation by the year 2020" and warns Malaysians not to allow racial or religious extremism to "under-min[e]" the country's economic progress; otherwise, he fears, "Everything which we have achieved, everything which we have built, and things which are dear to us, will be destroyed."

Since Malaysia constitutes a "hybrid," or semidemocratic/authoritarian regime rather than a full, liberal democracy (Mauzy 2006), we thought it would be interesting to see what unelected opposition leaders also think about Rukun Negara and related issues. (Presumably, they would be prime ministers themselves if Malaysia's elections were truly free and fair.) Currently, Anwar Ibrahim probably represents the most important dissenting voice in Malaysian politics. And as we will see, Anwar currently claims to espouse a firmly liberal, multicultural, form of Muslim-state relations despite his earlier work in Mahathir's government. According to a talk that Anwar gave at Stanford University (Ibrahim 2014), "Islam and democracy are fully compatible." Islamist terrorist organizations such as ISIS "have no [theological] legitimacy whatsoever, and the term Islam or Islamic state cannot be ascribed to them." He likewise calls on "Muslim clerics, influential Muslim organizations, and all eminent Muslim democrats" to "condemn not just ... extreme and violent groups but also the dictatorships and autocratic regimes in the Muslim world that have persistently denied democratic rights to their citizens." Quoting the Quranic admonition against "compulsion in religion," Anwar believes that "you cannot force a person to become a Muslim. Freedom of faith is allowed." Given Malaysia's "multiracial and multi-religious" society, he continues, good governance and political discussion "can only be realized" if the different "contending parties refrain[n] from cantankerous and open disputes regarding religion and philosophy." In his own country, Anwar laments, "what has been a relatively peaceful and multi-ethnic nation is being fractured by competing voices of intolerance suggesting that citizenship is no longer based on the belief in a nation but rather in the absolute supremacy of a single religious or ethnic group." The root problem, he opines, lies with "religious authorities" who "kow-tow to political masters who cling to power through diabolical tactics of divide-and-rule." For Anwar, then, Rukun Negara would have to mean freedom of religious practice for all Malaysians, even Christians, Hindus, and Buddhists, and the end to second-class citizenship for religious and ethnic minorities. Should he or someone like him eventually come to power in Malaysia, Islamist-style religious nationalism may well face stiff headwinds.

CONCLUSION

For the religious nationalist model, Malaysia represents close to a worst-case scenario. Forcing established Islam and now increasingly an Islamist-oriented state onto Malaysia's numerous and economically powerful religious minorities has proven hazardous even if it has not yet produced ex-Yugoslavia levels of interethnic violence. Yet the rural, conservative Malay base of the ruling party demands more and more pro-Islamic policies instead of satisfying itself with the arguably more symbolic religious victories won at independence. Where this clash of values will end is anyone's guess, but an outside observer can too easily imagine the country descending into more 1969-style ethnic bloodletting or even ethno-religious "cleansing" or partition à la India and Pakistan.

This bleak prospect contrasts greatly with the situation in Greece, where an almost complete lack of religious diversity has produced remarkable stability for its model of religious nationalism. In Greece, religion is rarely linked to ethnicity or partisanship, and both wings of the political spectrum largely acquiesce in a symbolic and political role for

Greek Orthodoxy. And any changes over time have only reinforced the strength of the Greek model, whether one considers demographic shifts or external threats.

Endnotes

1. So great is the fear surrounding this restriction on criticizing the established religion–state arrangements that even many overseas Malaysians appear hesitant to critique them. While out-of-town presenting a chapter of this book at an academic conference, for example, I attended a local Chinese-language church service with my Mandarin-speaking wife and son. After the worship service concluded, members and visitors such as ourselves ate lunch together in the main church building. We ended up eating with the pastor's wife, who happened to be an ethnically Chinese Malaysian. Delighted with the opportunity to discuss the topic of this chapter with an expert, I naively queried her about how most Chinese Christians in Malaysia viewed Rukun Negara. She refused to answer, however, even after I asked in Mandarin whether she spoke Bahasa (she did) and was familiar with the term (the equivalent of asking a native-born American who George Washington was). Eventually, the conversation turned to other topics, but the pastor's spouse still seemed curious about what we were saying about Malaysia in this book. When I told her of our critique of the second-class citizenship of non-Muslims, however, she immediately stood up and walked away from the table, saying nothing. Although I have had similarly awkward encounters with PRC Chinese when discussing their political system, I had naively assumed that the situation for semidemocratic Malaysia would be much more open.

6

Uruguay: Stable Secular Nationalism

INTRODUCTION

In one small, historically Catholic country in Latin America, most citizens prefer the term "republic" to "nation," celebrate "Family Day" instead of Christmas on 25 December, and did not object when the government declined to send an official representative to Pope Francis' inauguration. Here, the most prominent contemporary political leader is a former guerrilla, and the women's movement is so strong that wives received the right to divorce their husbands as early as 1913 (Goñi 2016). Yet this highly secular state is not the officially atheistic, Communist country of Cuba but rather the *laico*, strongly liberal-democratic land of Uruguay. Lacking both religious fervor and pronounced nationalism, Uruguay contrasts markedly with many of its South American neighbors and represents a particularly stable form of the secular nationalism model.

In Uruguay, a low level of religious affiliation and a correspondingly weak Catholic Church meant that little opposition to a nonreligious polity developed, and the nationalism that emerged relied little on religious identity. From the beginning, Uruguay was more secular than elsewhere in Latin America, and the Catholic Church faced enormous impediments to establishing influential religious institutions in the country. Under the relatively late Spanish colonialism, indigenous peoples made up only a small proportion of the population of the region, for example, and these *indígenas* vigorously fought conversion. After independence from Spain in the early 1800s, many prominent Uruguayan thinkers further challenged Catholic teaching by adopting French-style anticlericalism or similarly nontraditional views. Thus, deprived of its typical bases of support,

the Church never functioned as the political power-broker it became elsewhere in the Americas, and to this day, the Catholic hierarchy exerts little
effective political influence in Uruguay.

This chapter outlines relations between religion and nationalism in
Uruguay. We offer an historical overview of this process and an analysis
of contemporary public-opinion data on their interaction on arguably
the country's most salient nationalistic project in the twenty-first century:
its dispute with Argentina over paper-pulp mills on the Uruguay River. A
shorter section summarizes our parallel content analysis of religious publications and presidential speeches. As in previous chapters, we find that
the system established at the country's founding and similar constitutionally crucial moments remains critically important for understanding
today's relationship between religion and nationalism. In Uruguay, each of
the key factors determining the relationship between religion and nationalism tended to promote secular nationalism, as opposed to a nationalism
linked to a particular tradition or to a pan-religious perspective.

RELIGIOUS ELITES AND NATIONALISM AT THE FOUNDING

During Uruguay's founding in 1830, the initiators of the state did not
see themselves as basing their nationality primarily on a Catholic identity, but conversely, they did not hold a grudge against religion per se
either. Political leaders such as Artigas shunned anticlericalism, sometimes because they themselves were, at least privately, practicing believers. Local religious leaders, meanwhile, generally supported Uruguayan
independence even if it was not going to establish the Catholic Church
as an all-powerful political institution. As one scholar sums up the early
situation, "when the Republic of Uruguay was established under the constitution of 1830, the leaders were all sincere Catholics, and until the
death of Father Larrañaga in 1848 there was no occasion for any conflict
between church and state" (Espinosa 1940).

More than any other individual in the early history of Uruguay, José
Gervasio Artigas represents a kind of George-Washington-style founder
of the nation. Successively fighting against the Spanish, Argentines, and
Portuguese in pursuit of Uruguayan autonomy, General Artigas died as
an exile in Paraguay in 1850. His importance for Uruguay's sense of
nationhood and ultimate political independence cannot be overestimated,
however. In 1810 the capital city of the "Banda Oriental" (an early name
for what would become today's Uruguay) maintained nominal allegiance

to Spain. At the time, Captain Artigas was responsible for maintaining order in the Uruguayan countryside, well outside Montevideo. After the colonial capital of Buenos Aires achieved de facto independence from the Spanish throne in 1811, however, he allied with the revolutionaries from across the Río de la Plata and led his troops in defeating the Spanish at Las Piedras (today a suburb of Montevideo) and laying siege to the Uruguayan capital itself. In July 1811, Montevideo's leaders rescued themselves by unifying with the Portuguese, who flooded in from Brazil. A few months thereafter, the city's authorities reached a peace deal under which the Spanish and Portuguese soldiers as well as Artigas and his 16,000 independence-oriented followers all left the country. Two years later, the federalist-oriented Uruguayan commander returned to the Banda Oriental with his troops to direct a second attack on the more unitary-leaning Montevideo. After many setbacks and struggles with Spanish and Argentine forces, Artigas conquered the city in 1815. The Uruguayan hero lost little time in setting up an independent government to administer the new nation and consolidate its power. But in 1816 thousands of Portuguese soldiers invaded from the north, and by 1821 they had forced Artigas into permanent exile in Paraguay and incorporated Uruguay as the "Cisplatine Province" of Brazil (Street 1959; Pendle 1963:18–23; Alisky 1969:18–19; Hudson and Meditz 1992:8–10).

Throughout most of his life, Artigas maintained a strong Christian faith that could hardly form the basis for any kind of anticlerical political movement. Raised in a devout Catholic family and educated at a Franciscan school, he would regularly read the Bible, pray the rosary, and attend mass. Artigas took special care to promote religious education, even teaching the Catechism to young churchgoers himself. He also tried to help convert the region's indigenous people to Christianity and in his old age distributed many of his possessions to the poor of Paraguay. In 1815 he even constructed a church building and attended the first mass there along with his soldiers and Uruguayan followers (Gaudiano 2002:59–81; 91–2; 157–9; 183–99). This personal devotion thus dissuaded him from attacking the church or religion in general and also seems to have motivated him to advocate for religious liberty in such key founding documents as the "Instructions of Year XIII," intended to guide Uruguayan delegates negotiating with Buenos Aires in 1813 over the future form of the new nation's government. Point 3 of these guidelines, for example, tells his representatives to "promote civil and religious liberty to the greatest extent imaginable." On the other hand, this protoconstitution employs little specifically religious rhetoric even in justifying independence for Uruguay. Rather, the first point of the document merely states matter-of-factly that "all political connections between [Uruguay] and the state of Spain are, and should be, totally dissolved" (Artigas 1813a); thus, Uruguay rejected the kind of close church–state arrangement adopted by its former colonial master. Even in Artigas' "Inaugural Address" of the same year, one searches in vain for the words "God," "religion," or "Catholic." Instead, he speaks of Uruguayans' "sacred rights" in an Enlightenment – not theological – sense and asserts that his "authority emanates from you [the people] and … ceases in your sovereign presence" (Artigas 1813b). So while the Uruguayan leader was personally religious and supported freedom of conscience, he framed his founding of the new country in secular or rationalist terms rather than religious ones.

One of the most important intellectual influences on Artigas, moreover, was his distant cousin (Cayota 2010:8) José Benito Monterroso, a Roman Catholic priest who served as the leader's occasional and later permanent secretary from as early as 1813 until 1820 (Cayota 2010:10–11; 2011:137) and who also actively participated in the founding of the Uruguayan nation (Cayota 2011). Artigas dictated his "Instructions of Year XIII" to the Franciscan cleric (Cayota 2011:137), for example, and Monterroso – a former philosophy professor at the University of Córdoba (Cayota 2010:9) – appears to have exerted a profound intellectual influence on the leader of the Banda Oriental (or Eastern Bank [of the Uruguay River]), especially on matters of religion and social justice. The founder of Uruguay trusted Monterroso so much that Artigas had him draft most of his less-weighty correspondence himself (Cayota 2011:137–57). One is hard pressed to argue, therefore, that Artigas was hostile to religion or that his cleric-secretary Monterroso opposed Uruguayan nationalism.

Monterroso's brother-in-law by his sister Ana (Cayota 2010:8), Juan Antonio Lavalleja, represents the next-most-important political leader during the founding. Following on Artigas' heels, Lavalleja rallied his guerrilla fighters (known as the "Thirty-Three Heroes") to resist Portuguese Brazil's attempted annexation of what at the time was called the Banda Oriental. By 1828, Brazil had given up its claim to the region, allowing for formal Uruguayan independence on August 27 (Hudson and Meditz 1992:xxvi). If one examines the proto-country's formal Declaration of Independence of August 25, 1825 (Administración Nacional de Educación Pública 2016), which was formulated under Lavalleja's broad leadership (Abadie 2001), one is hard pressed to argue that this new nation's foundations were mainly religious. The text does contain one passing reference to the "Parish Priest" who is to combine with the local "Notary" or "Secretary" in publicly announcing and formalizing the Declaration. Yet the document remains otherwise secular, relying primarily on the rationalist view that the "peoples of the Eastern Province" possess "inalienable rights" to throw off the "absolute despotism" of Portugal and Brazil. Nonetheless, Lavalleja himself hardly seems anticlerical; according to one version of his landing in Uruguay, for instance, the general immediately has his co-militants kneel and swear "before God and for their country" to liberate the Banda Oriental from "the foreign power or die in the struggle" (Castellanos 1955:64).

Another key religious figure who lent his moral authority to the creation of the new nation was Dámaso Antonio Larrañaga (Favaro 1950). Leader of Montevideo's main cathedral, the Iglesia Matriz, and later appointed Vicar General for the Banda Oriental, Larrañaga supported Artigas' national project and consequentially ended up suffering privations and abuses similar to those of the Uruguayan founder's early lay followers. "I am an [Uruguayan] patriot without being a charlatan," the pro-independence cleric would declare decades after the Revolution. The politically active priest also contributed greatly to intellectual life and national identity in the new country, working as head of the eventual National Library of Uruguay and as senator legislating the establishment of what would become the University of the Republic (Espinosa 1940; Favaro 1950:XI–XII; 37–63; 90–7). Little wonder American historian Espinosa (1940; see also González Demuro and Robilotti 2005; Sansón Corbo 2011) concludes that "in every phase of the struggle for independence – as soldiers, political advisors, chaplains, and as contributors to the war chest – the clergy [such as Larrañaga and Monterroso] were in the forefront."

RELIGIOUS DEMOGRAPHICS AND EMERGENT NATIONALISM

A stable form of secular nationalism emerged naturally from the religious demographics of the new country. From the outset, Uruguay was more secular than its regional neighbors, and the Catholic Church faced enormous impediments to establishing influential religious institutions there. Under Spanish colonialism, indigenous peoples constituted only a small fraction of the population living in the region, and such *indígenas* strenuously opposed conversion (Hudson and Meditz 1992:91; see also

Blanco Acevedo 1936:11–17). The Banda Oriental experienced effective Spanish colonization relatively late, in the 1700s, after much of the missionary impulse of earlier centuries had faded away. Even under nominal Spanish-Catholic control, moreover, the area remained a religious backwater; instead of having their own regular bishop based in a diocese in Montevideo, devout Uruguayans nominally looked to senior Catholic clerics in Buenos Aires for religious guidance until as late as 1878. The scarcity of parish priests hardly helped matters (Fitzgibbon 1953; Walker 1992:42; Sansón 1998:22–3, 37–40). And the scarcity of resources or initiatives to establish monasteries and Catholic educational institutions also impeded effective evangelization of the society (Sansón Corbo 2011).

After independence in 1830, the society continued to secularize. Urbanization and industrialization of parts of the country went hand-in-hand with a "modernization" of society, part of which included the "elimination of religious references in social norms" (Sansón Corbo 2011). Many Uruguayan intellectuals of the era further undermined Catholic authority by adopting French-style anticlericalism (Hudson and Meditz 1992:91; Walker 1992:48), spiritualism, positivism (Sansón Corbo 2011), or materialism (Whitaker 1964). Other Uruguayans – Catholic or not – became Freemasons, who were not known for their theological orthodoxy (Walker 1992:46–8; Sansón 1998:23). Immigration also played a role. By 1830, many English and French colonists had begun arriving on the northern shore of the Río de la Plata, but they tended to be either nominally or not at all Catholic. Poor Italian and Spanish migrants to Uruguay later in the nineteenth century may have retained some Catholic identity but were hardly devout (Fitzgibbon 1953; Whitaker 1964). Some, such as the followers of the violently anticlerical, Italian nationalist hero Giuseppe Garibaldi,[1] loathed Catholicism (Menthol Ferré 1969). In the interior of the country, priests were scarce but nonmarital births were not; a typical rural resident might not have seen the inside of a church building since his or her infant baptism and have only the fuzziest of notions of fundamental Christian doctrine (Vanger 2010:78–9).

Despite the political leadership of many self-identifying Catholics during the founding period, the general Uruguayan populace tended not to practice their faith very fervently or to be especially knowledgeable about the basics of their religion. Part of the problem was material or economic; occasionally priests in some poorer parishes could not perform such rites as baptisms because the necessary liturgical vessel was lacking from the sparsely equipped churches (Sansón 1998:34–7; Sansón Corbo 2011; see also Fitzgibbon 1953). At first, the few local priests railed against the ever-more-prevalent evil of "amancebamiento," or cohabitation (Sansón 1998:36–7). Later, over the last few decades of the nineteenth century, the number of religious as opposed to only civil marriages dropped in some districts by around 40–80 percent (Sansón Corbo 2011). By the turn of the twentieth century, only about 60 percent of the population considered themselves Catholic, a far lower proportion than in the rest of South America (Alisky 1969:83).

To this day, the Catholic Church exerts little effective political influence in Uruguay (Hudson and Meditz 1992:188). What nominal power it used to wield mainly derived from its supposed affiliation with several Christian-Democratic political parties such as the Civic Union (Pérez Antón 1987). The political offspring of this attempted alliance between church and state have essentially merged with more-established groupings on the "Broad Front" (leftist), "Colorado" (moderately left-of-center), or "Blanco" (right-of-center) portions of the country's partisan spectrum (Pérez Antón 1987; Hudson and Meditz 1992:172–83; 188). In recent electoral campaigns, a candidate's claims of explicit support by the Catholic Church seem less likely to gain her or him votes but more apt to invite public ridicule or unfavorable comparisons with the "devoutly Catholic" Spanish dictator Francisco Franco (Caetano 2013a).

In the twenty-first century, religious practice and belief remain exceptionally low by Latin American standards. According to the Latinobarómetro (2015), 35 percent of Catholics in Uruguay consider themselves "non-practicing," as opposed to 25 percent in neighboring Argentina, 13 percent in Brazil, and a mere 9 percent in Paraguay. The equivalent figures for generic Evangelicals ("Evangélica sin especificar") were 21 percent in Uruguay but only 9, 5, or 7 percent for Argentina, Brazil, and Paraguay, respectively. While in Uruguay 42 percent of respondents claimed to be atheists, agnostics, or nonreligious in 2015, in the neighboring three countries this statistic varied between 2 and 12 percent. Meanwhile, the relatively marginal Afro-Brazilian religious tradition poses little challenge to the secular state (Guigou 2008). Small Methodist, Waldensian, and Anglican communities remain, but the country's once-significant Jewish population continues to dwindle because of emigration to Israel and elsewhere (Fitzgibbon 1953; Alisky 1969:83–4; Porzecanski 2009). Contemporary social conditions thus continue to undergird Uruguay's stable form of secular nationalism.

RELIGIOUS ELITES AND NATIONALISM DURING SEPARATION
OF CHURCH AND STATE

The second major event in Uruguay's religion–state history took place in 1918, when political leaders inspired by the separationist thinking of President José Batlle y Ordóñez formally disestablished the Roman Catholic Church but left behind a relatively benign structure that allowed broad freedom for both religious practice and state action. By the latter half of the nineteenth century, the country had become more religiously plural, with more Protestants and Jews having arrived via immigration, and less religiously orthodox, with many Uruguayan elites embracing non-Christian perspectives such as deism, rationalism, and materialism. At the same time, the institutionalized Catholic Church suffered from grave internal weaknesses that made it ill-equipped to fight the ascendant anticlericalism of the era (Menthol Ferré 1969).

Batlle himself was vehemently anticlerical and personally hostile to all traditional religious institutions, especially the Roman Catholic Church. On the one hand, he apparently toyed with the ideas of reincarnation, an afterlife, and communication with spirits, especially after his teenage daughter died of tuberculosis (Arena 1939:252–3; Vanger 2010:18). He likewise believed in some form of intelligent, if malevolent, creator. For all "positive," or traditional religions such as Roman Catholicism, on the other hand, he had nothing but disdain. Apparently following Marx, he held that such belief systems did nothing but "cloud the conscience of the people" by "poisoning them with stupefying prejudices." The Catholic Church gave alms to good Catholics who "get down on their knees before their idols" but withheld aid from needy people who were not believers. The history of the Spanish Inquisition's massacres of "heretics and wizards" made Batlle fly into a rage. He despised even relatively liberal Catholic priests and claimed the Bible justified bloodshed, incest, and other "abominable crimes." Even for the person of Jesus Christ he had no respect; according to Batlle's vision of the founder of Christianity, Jesus had borrowed his major doctrines from others, had encouraged a retrograde theology justifying capitalist exploitation of the poor, and had even engaged in exhibitionist tricks (Arena 1939:253–6; Fitzgibbon 1953; Vanger 2010:80; 100).

Some of Batlle's bitter animus against Catholicism appears rooted in his own personal life. When his cousin's wife, Matilde Pacheco de Michaelsson, was abandoned by her husband Ruperto and thrown out of their house by her mother-in-law, Batlle's father Lorenzo sheltered Sra.

Pacheco and her five children in his own home. The young "Pepe" Batlle, who also lived with his *papá*, found himself tending to his newly arrived relatives and soon enough fell in love with the still-married Matilde. Over the next decade, she bore him three living children even though Batlle did not become her husband in even a civil ceremony until the death of Ruperto and birth of the third child. Presumably incensed at polite "Catholic" Montevideo's shunning of his wife and beloved daughter Ana Amalia during his presidency, Batlle refused to take part in a religious wedding (Vigil 2003; Vanger 2010:17–19).

Even before formal separation of church and state, the government had gradually been chipping away at the prerogatives of the Catholic Church (Edmonds 2013). In 1861 the government seized control of many aspects of the burial of human remains; previously, the Catholic Church had primarily administered cemeteries on its own (Caetano and Geymonat 1997:56–8). In 1885 the General Assembly of Uruguay made civil marriage obligatory even for those couples who formalized their vows in a church. Clergy who conducted religious ceremonies without having received a certificate of civil marriage faced six months to a year in prison (De Aréchaga 1894:37; Ponce de León 1905:28–55). Secularization accelerated at the beginning of the twentieth century, however, as Batlle and his lieutenant Claudio Williman led the anticlerical charge. Crucifixes were banned from state hospitals in 1906 and "God" and "gospels" from oaths in 1907. Religious education was abolished in public schools in 1909, while three divorce laws in 1907, 1910, and 1912, each more liberal than the last, in the end gave women divorce on demand (Carreras de Bastos 1909; Oneto y Viana 1910; Menthol Ferré 1969; Hudson and Meditz 1992:22–4). Though devout Catholics hardly rejoiced in such "reforms," they were powerless to block them. As one lay leader complained in 1909, "we did everything within our power to stop [the divorce law] from being approved." But this "protest fell into the void ... with the same glacial indifference as when leaves fall from the trees and become the playthings of the wind" (Carreras de Bastos 1909:9).

Always weak both institutionally and in public support, the Catholic Church was only able to offer limited effective resistance to most of these changes. In the latter part of the nineteenth century, Montevideo Archbishop Mariano Soler did show organizational genius and worked tirelessly to expand Catholicism among the Uruguayan population and to establish parochial schools to train the next generation of the faithful (Menthol Ferré 1969; Caetano and Geymonat 1997:121–5).

Unfortunately for the interests of his religious community, however, Soler died in 1908 and had not yet been replaced by the time Batlle began to militate very actively for church–state separation. Because of Vatican–government conflicts, the post of archbishop remained unfilled for a decade until Juan Francisco Aragone was installed in 1919. The Uruguayan church's interests were therefore nominally represented during the height of the conflict by the Papal Nuncio in Buenos Aires, the Italian Alberto Vassallo di Torregrossa[2] (Montevideo Archdiocese 1918:3; Caetano and Geymonat 1997:107; Ignasi Saranyana 2002:253; Sansón Corbo 2011). Other significant de facto leaders of the local church included Isasa (1909; Caetano and Geymonat 1997:125–6), the Apostolic Administrator, and José Johannemann, a Vatican envoy designated Apostolic Visitor (Montevideo Archdiocese 1918:3–6; Sansón Corbo 2011; see also Pou Ferrari and Mañé Garzón 2005).

The formation of the pro-Catholic Unión Civica party in 1912 represents perhaps the most coordinated if ultimately fruitless effort to stop the separation of church and state (Pérez Antón 1987). Championing "Religion, Fatherland, Family, and Property" (Fitzgibbon 1953), his new group arose out of two earlier Catholic-defense organizations: the small, elite-based Club Católico de Montevideo of 1878 and the later, pan-national Unión Católica of 1889. Though these previous groups engaged in ideological or "public action" against the various anticlerical initiatives of the late nineteenth century, the new Unión Civica explicitly focused on partisan, political struggle (Secco Illa 1946:27–31). In an early speech in support of the Civic Union, Bishop Isasa reminded listeners of the Vatican's call to fill national legislatures with "Catholic representatives" to "defend the good cause." According to Isasa, "concerning oneself with politics" is a "holy ... duty" (Secco Illa 1946:122). Party founder Joaquín Secco Illa likewise believed the organization was necessary because "the Colorado Party expelled us, [and] the National Party doesn't help us." Some lay, practicing Catholic elites formerly affiliated with the Colorados followed him into the new party as did the church hierarchy, but Uruguay's Catholic masses remained tied to the Blancos. This partisan divide between Catholic elites and ordinary parishioners further inhibited any religious opposition to the political changes of 1918 (Menthol Ferré 1969; see also Secco Illa 1916; Espinosa 1940), and this party never received a substantial number of votes (Hudson and Meditz 1992:92).

During the political battle over separation, the church also received support from some unexpected quarters: esteemed Uruguayan liberal writer, Colorado politician, and nationalist theorist José Enrique Rodó (Antuña 1948:213–27; Albarran Puente 1953). He himself was hardly a practicing, devout Roman Catholic; although Rodó seems to have abandoned the semi-orthodox Catholic faith of his mother once he began his university studies (Benedetti 1966:13), he continued to admire Christ as a heroic figure and developed a kind of poetic, joyful, love-based, and socially relevant form of Christian belief (Lago 1973:15–20). His religious views remained far from what the Uruguayan clergy would have recognized as Catholic, however, and he was at pains to explain publicly that he was not a Catholic priest or anything close. Yet in his 1906 letter to the editor entitled "Liberalism and Jacobism: The Expulsion of the Crucifixes," Rodó supported religious tolerance against what he termed the overweening, anticlerical "Jacobism" common in some government circles. Removing crosses from the walls of public hospitals, Rodó wrote, represented "an act of open intolerance and moral and historical incomprehension, absolutely irreconcilable with the idea of elevated equity and generous breadth that is included in any legitimate meaning of liberalism." Since the idea of altruism is rooted in religious ideals espoused by Christ, the government commission "had expelled from houses of charity [public hospitals] the image of the creator of charity" (Da Silveira and Monreal 2003:113–23). This defense of some role for Christianity in Uruguayan society is especially interesting for our purposes because Rodó is known internationally as perhaps the most important theorist of Latin-American nationalism of his generation (Ardao 1970; Brading 1998). Despite his opposition to the imperialism and crass utilitarianism of the (Christian) United States (Lago 1973:87–97) and his devotion to a countervailing Uruguyan or pan-Latin-American culture, Rodó believed that such Catholic symbols as crucifixes belonged in state hospitals and that Christianity could contribute positively to Uruguayan society (Espinosa 1940).

Indeed, the vision of secular nationalism that developed after separation of church and state was not so much the consensus view of both Catholic and nonreligious Uruguayans as the relatively anticlerical worldview of Batlle, his political and intellectual lieutenants, and the vast majority of Uruguay's secular or only nominally Catholic population. The Catholic Church had tried to defend an alternative religious nationalism, but the clergy simply lacked the social and political resources to get their version adopted. Catholic journalist and Civic Union supporter Antuña (1948), for example, did attempt to promote a more "God-and-country" approach. During a 1916 pilgrimage to Piedra Alta (where

Uruguay's founders declared independence in 1825), Antuña (1948:133–5) expounded on the nobility of the Uruguayan nation:

Noble is this rock on which legendary gentlemen and epic men united the Catholic faith and the love of the homeland and of liberty into a single form of enthusiasm ... [They were founding] a Christian country, great above all for being Christian, great for proclaiming God, great for proclaiming the Gospel, great for respecting in its ever-ascending existence the faultless principles of Christianity.

In the last decades of the nineteenth century, Archbishop Soler similarly promoted "devotion to the fatherland" (culto a la patria), which included religio-patriotic festivals and pilgrimages. Later, Ricardo Isasa argued that defending Catholicism was the same as promoting "true patriotism" and that advocating Batllista "Jacobism" amounted to a false form of nationalism. In his newspaper article of 1914, the priest Juan B. Padrós went even further, claiming that "God is the author of the homeland" and that "without religion, there is no country [patria]." Thus, "because fools exist who don't have any religion, so too do fools exist who don't love their country" (Caetano 2013b:28–34).

Despite such pleas, in the end the Catholic Church and its few allies were no match for Batlle and his anticlerical activists. The Constitution of 1918 formally separated church and state but, at least by today's standards, did so relatively benignly (Hudson and Meditz 1992:25). The government stopped supporting Catholicism and allowed all religious beliefs. The Catholic Church retained ownership of most of its buildings even if they had been partly constructed with state funds. Religious congregations were exempt from taxes. Newly inaugurated presidents no longer needed to swear their oaths of office to a deity. Uruguay cut off formal diplomatic relations with the Vatican (Fitzgibbon 1953). The Batllistas likewise rebaptized Christian national holidays as secular ones: Easter Week became "Tourism Week" and Christmas "Family Day" (Hudson and Meditz 1992:91; Goñi 2016). The government even tried to make Sundays and all formerly Catholic holidays regular workdays, but it was forced to back down in the face of traditionalist opposition (Vanger 2010:46–7). Batlle and his Colorados considered other, even more extreme proposals on church and state, but he decided to omit them from the final draft of the constitution so as to avoid further delays and to prevent rejection of his overall package (Vanger 2010:100; 208–9; 265). For its part, the Catholic Church seems to have accepted separation as inevitable (Caetano and Geymonat 1997:105–11) and therefore advised future priests to avoid "intervene[ing] in political parties" and discussing, "whether inside or outside of the church, issues that are merely political" (Montevideo Archdiocese 1918:36).

RELIGION IN THE CONSTITUTION

Although Uruguay eventually adopted this secular constitutional order, the country's first legal charter established Roman Catholicism as the state religion in 1830 (Parlamento del Uruguay 2016a). For its era, however, the document remained remarkably tolerant and spends little time addressing religion at all; if Catholicism received special honors from the government, believers in other religions remained free to practice as they wished (Bewes 1920). As was typical in Catholic countries, the founding charter opens with the words "In the name of God Almighty, Author, Legislator, and Supreme Guardian of the Universe." Section I, Chapter III, Article 5, likewise reads "the religion of the state is the Roman Apostolic Catholic one," and the President is required to swear "by the holy name of God and these holy gospels to ... protect the religion of the state" (Section VII, Chapter I, Article 76; Rodríguez Araya 1955:158–62). Yet "regular clergy" are forbidden from serving as Representatives in the legislature (Section IV, Chapter II, Article 25, Clause 2), and all humans – presumably regardless of their religious beliefs – "are equal before the law," with no "distinctions recognized among them except those of talents and virtues" (Section XI, Chapter I, Article 132).

Especially for the epoch in a nominally Roman Catholic country, the debates over the wording of the 1830 constitution appear to promote a liberal, universalistic view of religion rather than a narrow and specifically Catholic approach. When delegate Manuel Barreiro recommended opening the document with the particularly Christian invocation "In the name of the Holy Trinity ...," for instance, his colleagues in the constitutional convention refused his request (Asamblea General 1870:14–16). Instead, the more generic, merely theistic formula quoted above eventually prevailed. The same deputy Barreiro, whose mother was Artigas' cousin (Flores Mora 1951) and who as an ordained Catholic priest was obviously a zealous adherent of the Vatican (Rodríguez Araya 1955:201), later proposed language specifying that the Uruguayan government would "accept and protect each and every determination of the Church and its general councils and of its Supreme Pastor the Pontiff of Rome." Barreiro further specified that the new state should never "accept or tolerate [religious] practice by any cult [secto]," by which he probably meant Protestants. Once again, however, his less rabid contemporaries voted his proposed amendment down (Asamblea General 1870:32) and contented themselves in the end with the much more abstract and tolerant version in the previous paragraph. Although he had begun studying for the priesthood as a young man, Assembly Secretary and lawyer José Ellauri (Rodríguez Araya 1955:222–3) came close to arguing against any establishment at all, contending that his conationals had been practicing Catholicism for the previous three centuries and would likely continue to do so regardless of what the constitution stated. A majority of the delegates did not go so far, however (Asamblea General 1870:33–6).

By the 1918 revision of the Constitution (Parlamento del Uruguay 2016a), Uruguayan political leaders were ready to disestablish Catholicism but not prepared to create a truly hostile, anticlerical regime (Bewes 1920). Ironically, the 1918 Constitution spends more time than the original document did in discussing religion even though the institutions of church and state were to be much less intertwined:

All religions are free in Uruguay. The state does not support any religion. It recognizes the Catholic Church's ownership of all of the temples that were totally or partially built with funds from the National Treasury except for the chapels intended for use as asylums, hospitals, jails, or other public establishments. It also declares exempt from all forms of taxation those temples currently used for worship services by the different religions.

(Section I, Chapter III, Article 5)

Also paradoxically, Section IV, Chapter II, lifts the restriction on clerics who wish to serve as Representatives in the legislature, but the President no longer needs to swear a Christian oath to defend the now-nonexistent state religion (cf. Section VII, Chapter II, Article 74).

Most participants in the 1918 constitutional convention seem to have accepted church–state separation as a given. The only question was how draconian the restrictions on religion would be. An initial vote on whether to delete the establishment language of the 1830 constitution (Article V), produce three voices for maintaining an established Catholic Church versus twelve ballots against. More serious disagreement revolved around whether the Church was to keep its properties for which the state had already expended funds and whether the material possessions of religious groups should be tax-exempt. In the end, however, most delegates affirmed language guaranteeing free exercise for all religions, ending any form of religious establishment, allowing Catholic authorities to keep almost all of their real estate, and exempting religious bodies from paying taxes on their places of worship (Convención Constituyente 1918:3–4; 8–9). At the beginning of the debates, the Civic-Union-affiliated delegate Hugo Antuña opposed separation itself, declaring that Catholic establishment was "a most fundamental principle that concerns the gravest rights and social interests and that the Church has taken special care to teach and defend at all historic opportunities both ancient and modern" (Antuña 1948:111). In the end, however, he tended to vote with the majority of his colleagues on the later religion-related measures detailing the new religion-state relationship (Convención Constituyente 1918:3–5; Antuña 1948:87–95; 110–11). The Catholic Church and the Uruguayan state did divorce in 1918, yet the process imputed little fault to either side, and post-separation relations remained amicable.

POST-SEPARATION CHALLENGES TO THE RELIGIOUS–NATIONAL CONSENSUS

Since the formal division of church and state in 1918, the general framework of relatively benign separationism has remained comparatively stable. Perhaps the two most important potential challenges to this mode of governance have been the military dictatorship of the 1970s and the more recent rise of a local form of Christian Democracy. At the height of the dictatorship, during which Uruguay held the dubious world record for the most political prisoners per capita (Weinstein 1988:56), the regime made little effort to reestablish the Roman Catholic Church as the state religion. The greater threat to Uruguay's relatively benign separationist arrangement came from the military's attempt to end free exercise by repressing almost all traditional religions; during this especially dark political era, the dictatorship arrested and tortured priests, forbade religious processions, limited parochial education, closed down Catholic organizations and otherwise violated the religious liberty of many Uruguayan believers. The government likewise coopted parts of the Catholic leadership as a way to undermine the authority of the Archbishop and tried to get them to issue pro-regime statements (Edmonds 2013). In more recent decades, some Christian-Democratic-oriented politicians have attempted to link Catholic belief to Uruguayan nationalism and so push the country's institutions in a more religious-nationalist direction. Lacking a sufficiently devout population, however, such activists have not been able to undo the constitutional changes of 1918 and seem just as likely to provoke an anticlerical backlash among the bulk of secular voters (Caetano 2013a).

TABLE 6.1. *Nationalism by religious tradition*

Tradition	Mean
Evangelical	3.46
Catholic	3.44
Other religion	3.41
Not religious	3.42
All respondents	3.43

Source: 2011 World Values Survey, Uruguay subsample.

In the end, then, Uruguay's model of secular nationalism has remained remarkably durable over the past century.

PUBLIC OPINION AND NATIONALISM

As in the other country chapters, we wanted to examine mass-level support for both abstract and issue-related nationalism. We located no quantitative studies of religion and nationalism in Uruguay. Our historical-constitutional analysis has demonstrated the minimal role of religion in the development of Uruguayan nationalism. In order to measure generic nationalism, we used data from the relevant sub-sample of the 2011 World Values Survey (WVS). Since Uruguay is not included in the International Social Science Programme, we relied on the single item from the WVS on how proud respondents were of their nationality.

As Table 6.1 demonstrates, Uruguayans are highly nationalistic but religion seems not to be a factor in predicting such attitudes. On a four-point scale, interviewees in each category (i.e., evangelical, Catholic, not religion, other religion) on average differed only a trivial amount (range = 3.41–3.46). The results from the regression in Table 6.2 confirm this finding, with neither religious identification nor religious practice achieving statistical significance. The result for religious attendance holds even if we restrict the sample to a single religious tradition. Instead of religion, income and urbanicity predict levels of our dependent variable. Thus, the highest levels of national pride are found among the traditional, landed upper-class in Uruguay's rural heartland instead of among the urban poor in Montevideo. These results substantiate our earlier narrative about the essentially secular quality of Uruguayan national identity. In this small

TABLE 6.2. *Religious and other determinants of nationalism*

Variable	Coefficient	Standard error
Evangelical	0.084	0.369
Catholic	−0.378	0.203
Other religion	0.010	0.317
Religious attendance	0.081	0.051
Education	−0.064	0.040
Income	0.090*	0.045
Woman	−0.010	0.154
Age	0.008	0.005
Ethnic minority (Black or Asian)	0.371	0.315
Urbanicity	−0.135*	0.036
Immigrant origin	−0.368	0.284
Constant 1	−4.953*	0.552
Constant 2	−3.126*	0.431
Constant 3	−0.427	0.404
N	681	
Nagelkerke R^2	0.058	

*Denotes an effect that is significantly different from 0 at the 5 percent level for ordered Logit model.
Notes: All regressors are dummy variables except for Religious Attendance (range = 1–7), Education (1–9), Income (1–10), Age (18–88), and Urbanicity (1–8).
Source: 2011 World Values Survey, Uruguay subsample.

South American country, religion neither boosts nor inhibits a strong allegiance to the nation.

PUBLIC HOSTILITY TO ARGENTINA

For the past century, Uruguay has largely avoided the kinds of major military conflicts or territorial disputes with neighboring countries that might lead to pronounced nationalism. We therefore had to search diligently to find something similar to the Iraq War, settlements in the Occupied Territories, or the Kashmiri dilemma. The closest equivalent nationalistic project upon which Uruguay has embarked in recent years is probably its ultimately successful effort to build a complex of paper pulp mills on the Uruguay River (Carrere 2005; *Clarín* 2006; *Nación* 2006; Junta Nacional de Vida y Misión 2007; Palermo and Reboratti 2007; Toller 2009; Infobae 2010; International Court of Justice 2010; Pintos 2010; Salinas 2010; *Gaceta* 2011), which separates Uruguay from

TABLE 6.3. *Hostility to Argentina by religious tradition*

Tradition	Mean percent
Evangelical	66.1
Catholic	59.0
Nonpracticing Christian	50.8
Other religion	73.0
Not religious	49.5
All respondents	56.3

Notes: Evangelical includes Baptists, Pentecostals, Methodist, Adventists, and not-otherwise-specified Protestants and evangelicals. Other Religion is comprised of Jehovah's Witnesses, Mormons, Jews, "others," and practitioners of African-origin religions.
Source: 2006 Latinobarómetro, Uruguay subsample.

Argentina. These efforts generated tremendous popular, political, and legal opposition in Argentina and intensified national feeling in Uruguay. Unfortunately, no publicly accessible dataset exists which asks specifically about these mills. However, at the height of the controversy in 2006, the Latinobarómetro did ask respondents about which country they considered the "least friendly" to Uruguay, with one option being "Argentina."

Table 6.3 summarizes the results for this question by major religious tradition in Uruguay. Clearly, most Uruguayans considered Argentina to be the number one rival nation, at least under the existing political circumstances. While this outcome held for all citizens, individual religious groups did vary significantly in their hostility to their neighbor to the south. The least religious Uruguayans (i.e., nonreligious individuals and nonpracticing Christians) were correspondingly the least antagonistic to their ethnic cousins across the Río Plata. The most religious Uruguayans (evangelicals, other religious), on the other hand, were the most hostile. Catholics, who exhibited a moderate degree of religious commitment, were between the other groups.

These variations across different religious groups largely disappear, however, when one controls for demographics and pro-environmental attitudes (see Table 6.4). Admittedly, general attitudes toward Argentina do not perfectly capture views on the pulp mills, even when measured at the height of the crisis. Since we needed to use different datasets in Tables 6.2 and 6.4, the demographic items are not perfectly comparable. Nonetheless, the overall results for this concretely nationalistic question do not differ substantially from our findings for abstract nationalism, where religion had no overall impact. The only exception arises from

TABLE 6.4. *Religious and other determinants of hostility to Argentina*

Variable	Coefficient	Standard error
Evangelical	0.680	0.372
Catholic	0.325	0.197
Nonpracticing Christian	0.011	0.275
Other religion	0.976*	0.446
Religious commitment	−0.024	0.116
Education	−0.076	0.058
Class	−0.160	0.097
Woman	0.121	0.153
Age	−0.042	0.079
Urbanicity	−0.044	0.027
Environmentalism	−0.074	0.096
Constant	1.342*	0.481
N	767	
Nagelkerke R^2	0.044	

*Denotes an effect that is significantly different from 0 at the 5 percent level for dichotomous Logit model.
Notes: All regressors are dummy variables except for Religious Commitment (range = 1–4), Class (1–5), Age (18–95), Education (1–17), Urbanicity (1–8), and Environmentalism (1–4).
Source: 2006 Latinobarómetro, Uruguay subsample.

the "Other Religion" category in Table 6.4, but it is so small and miscellaneous that it does not undermine our overall conclusion. This public-opinion analysis thus reinforces our argument from the historical section about Uruguay's stable model of secular nationalism.

RELIGION AND NATIONALISM IN RELIGIOUS PUBLICATIONS AND PRESIDENTIAL STATEMENTS

If religion has little net effect on mass attitudes in Uruguay, are the results the same for religious and political elites? To examine this question for spiritual leaders, we first located representative publications for each of the major traditions in the country: Roman Catholic, evangelical Protestant/pentecostal, and Jewish. Within each media source, we searched for articles containing the Spanish equivalent of "secularism" (laicismo) or "Argentina." Unfortunately for our analysis, no document in our database discussed relations with Argentina or the conflict over the pulp mills. Nor did the evangelical publication *Código Vida* (2016), which is linked to the Pentecostal mega-church Misión Vida para las Naciones of Montevideo, directly cover even secularism. Within the Catholic and Jewish materials, however, we were able to code the various essays according to whether they were positive, negative, or neutral toward Uruguay's religion–state arrangements. As Figure 6.1 demonstrates, both Catholic and Jewish elites overwhelmingly supported secularism; at about 82 percent positive, the minority Jewish clerics were roughly 13 points more enthusiastic than the Catholics. Still, only one article from each community was openly critical of laicismo. All the remaining texts stayed neutral. A typically pro-laicismo article quotes the Roman Catholic Cardinal Gianfranco Ravasi, who noted that even Christ in his dictum to "render unto Caesar what is Caesar's and unto God what is God's" laid the theological foundation for secularism (Conferencia Episcopal del Uruguay 2016). Similarly, an essay published by a prominent Jewish organization, the Comité Central Israelita del Uruguay, affirms that "religious beliefs are private by their very nature. They should not become issues in public life" (Corti 2011).

Our next step in content analysis is to examine how Uruguayan political elites view religion and nationalism. If the country really does feature a stable form of secular nationalism, we would expect little elite rhetoric linking faith with feelings toward the country. To test this hypothesis, we performed a content analysis of all presidential inaugural addresses since the state's founding in 1830. In particular, we searched for the Spanish equivalents of "homeland" (patria) and "God" (Dios) in the official online repository of such speeches (Parlamento del Uruguay 2016b). All

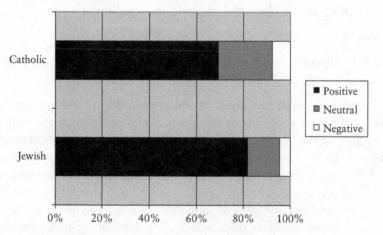

FIGURE 6.1. *Abstract nationalism in religious publications*

addresses that contained both words we coded as three, all with only "God" as two, all with only "homeland" as one, and all without either term as zero.

As Figure 6.2 documents, presidential discourse in Uruguay appears low in nationalism in general since around half of the speeches failed to mention even the word for "homeland," much less "God." Roughly the other half did talk about the country as one's "homeland," but only three inaugural addresses over the close to two centuries of independent Uruguayan history use "God" and "homeland" simultaneously. In 1879 the authoritarian President Lorenzo Latorre spoke of the "public peace that is the basis of ... the progress of our homeland [patria]" and, in a closing sentence, asks "God" to "enlighten" him as he begins his duties as chief executive. A century later, in 1972, the dictatorial Juan María Bordaberry likewise noted that his "homeland has what is necessary" so that everyone can work together for the "happiness of all." He elaborated that "God has blessed our land with such gifts" that "honest labor" and general "harmony" suffice to produce abundant "riches." Finally, in a long discourse in 1990, the neo-liberal National Party candidate Luis Alberto Lacalle took office and delivered what is perhaps the most religiously nationalistic such speech on record. Using "homeland" five times and invoking "God" thrice, Lacalle promised to view each Uruguayan as a "fellow son [hijo] of God," called for "the protection of God, [who is] the beginning and end of all things," and, in a theologically immodest allusion to Saint Francis, implored the "God of our fathers [sic]" to "make me an instrument of your peace." Other sections of the talk laud

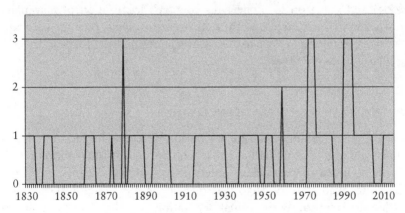

FIGURE 6.2. *Number of references to "God" or "Homeland" in presidential inaugural addresses*

the "Armed Forces'" role in "safeguarding ... the peace and liberty of the Homeland." Another passage proclaimed his "healthy passion" for the National Party and Lacalle's supreme love, his "love for the Homeland." His atypical effort to use religion to inspire nationalist feelings in his fellow Uruguayans ended with the cry "Long live the Homeland!" (Viva la Patria!).

Overall, then, only three presidents since 1830 have ever combined "God" and "homeland" in their public speeches upon assuming office, and two ended up as dictators. The third such political leader, a right-of-center, religious-nationalist wannabe, took power democratically but arguably failed to capture the imagination of ordinary Uruguayans who had already been steeped in 160 years' worth of secularism. When Lacalle ran for re-election in 2009 against the left-of-center former guerrilla José Mujica, Mujica publicly ridiculed Lacalle for claiming to be the "candidate of God" and for asserting that "Providence" had prepared the National Party leader for success in the electoral campaign. Using colorful, colloquial Spanish, Mujica declared (Caetano 2013a),

I don't believe in a political leader elected by God or anything similar. These [elections] are arrangements and agreements among humans. [Such claims] are a step backwards in the history of humanity ... It's the same thing as what [Spanish dictator] Franco said when he ordered that coins be imprinted [with the inscription] "Francisco Franco, Caudillo [authoritarian leader] of Spain by the Grace of God." It pains me that in a republican and democratic country [such as Uruguay] someone is calling attention to these things.

The flamboyant Mujica ended up beating Lacalle handily (Barrionuevo 2009) and going on to pioneer his country's legalization of marijuana and gay marriage (Carrillo 2013; Romero 2013). Thus concluded perhaps the most ambitious effort to fuse Christianity and nationalism in very secular Uruguay.

CONCLUSION

Uruguay's secular nationalism has faced few demographic or political challenges, and the model has proved stable since its final formation in 1918. Founded in particularly infertile ground for Catholic devotion, the Uruguayan state of 1830 was one of the most religiously tolerant in South America. With formal separation of religious and political authority in 1918, the country likewise pioneered a benign form of lay government most conducive to removing any religious underpinnings from the local form of national identity. Uruguayan citizens are not at all likely to embrace the fervent Catholicism typical in Poland or Ireland, and they are equally unlikely to adopt these nations' much closer bond between religion and the state.

Endnotes

1. Garibaldi represented a hero for Uruguayan patriots as well because of his defense of Montevideo during the Civil War in the 1840s (Garibaldi 1888:95–183; Menthol Ferré 1969).

2. Interestingly enough, Vassallo di Torregrossa later also served as Nuncio in Munich, Germany, during the rise of National Socialism. On October 15, 1933, he publicly greeted Hitler and made conciliatory remarks that the Nazis used in a campaign poster to persuade German Catholics to vote for them in the upcoming elections (Wolf 2010:55; 225).

7

India: Unstable Secular Nationalism

INTRODUCTION

One need look no further than the persistent controversy in India around patriotic slogans to prove Marx's dictum that history repeats itself, first as tragedy, and second as farce. In his 1938 presidential address before the All-India Muslim League, Muhammad Ali Jinnah, president of the League for more than thirty years and eventual founder of Pakistan, spoke about the famous nineteenth-century nationalist poem and song *Vande Mataram*. The singing of the song at nationalist gatherings had already been a point of contention between the Congress Party and the Muslim League. Many Muslims objected to the song because it gave the impression of the worship of Mother India, which to them was a form of polytheism. Jinnah warned his audience that once in power the Congress Party "with all of its pretensions of nationalism" would start right away with the singing of the "*Vande Mataram*." Not only is it sung at Congress gatherings, Jinnah mused, "Muslim children in government and munici-pal schools are compelled to sing it. Muslim children must accept *Vande Mataram* as their national song, no matter whether their religious beliefs permit them to do so or not. It is idolatrous and a hymn of hate against Muslims" (Jinnah 1942:70). From the standpoint of Indian nationalists who imagined a unified multireligious postindependent Indian state, the tragedy was that this controversy personified the religious divisions between the Hindu majority and the Muslim minority that led eventually to the formation of the separate countries of India and Pakistan.

Nearly eighty years later, in a 2016 rally of the Indian nationalist Bharatiya Janata Party (BJP), Devendra Fadnaviscurrent, the Chief

Minister of the Maharashtra state in India and a member of the BJP, was quoted as saying, "while residing in this country, some people say they will not chant 'Bharat Mata Ki Kai.' I condemn them. This is a question of India's existence. Those who refuse to say the slogan have no right to stay in India." The Chief Minister and his largely BJP audience well understood that the term Bharat Mata Ki Kai (hail mother India) personifies India as a mother goddess, and in particular the Hindu goddess Durga. Shortly after the speech India's largest Islamic seminary, Darul Uloom Deoband, issued a fatwa stating that Muslims should refrain from chanting the slogan because it implied the worship of a Hindu God, was a form of polytheism, and contradicted the monotheistic tenets of their faith. Fadnaviscurrent subsequently asserted that those who opposed the phrase were "divisive forces who want to create a rift in our country and wish to break our unity" (Deccan Chronicle 2016). The truth, of course, was that Fadnaviscurrent well understood that his words would contribute to the divisiveness that he claimed to be rejecting. The farce is that Fadnaviscurrent and Hindu nationalist parties in India seem intent to replicate the past in their politicization of religious divisions in India.

As we have noted in previous chapters, a key factor in determining the relationship between religion and nationalism within a nation state is the role and status of religion at the point of state formation. In the case of India, religion played a powerful role before, during, and after the country's independence from British rule. India was not simply religiously diverse in the sense that there were multiple spiritual traditions occupying the same space, it was also socially and politically divided on the basis of religion. The most decisive moment in that history, arguably, was the partition of Pakistan from India largely on religious grounds. At the mass level, in short, religion was a very powerful force.

Understanding the potential for the destabilizing effects of religion on the Indian nation, Indian political elites attempted to forge a national consensus on the basis of shared democratic political values. Religious issues could not be ignored in the process of state formation, but a majority of the members of the Constituent Assembly that drafted the country's new Constitution believed that secular political values could unify the nation, while a focus on religion would undermine it. Secularism, variously understood and interpreted, would be the answer to the conundrum of the polarizing history and the contemporary effects of India's religious and communal differences. The Constitution was secular insofar as no religion was officially recognized by the state and religious liberty for all was protected, but it was not a secularism that implied a strict separation between religion and public policies.

The political rise of Hindu nationalism over the past several decades demonstrates the fragility of this original model and the increasingly contested nature of Indian national identity. In particular, Hindu nationalist movements challenge the state's secular nationalist character, and they contend that secularism was imposed from above by political elites who gave insufficient attention to the religious sensibilities of the Hindu masses from below. Exploiting the political opportunities for mobilization along religious lines, Hindu nationalists have underscored the instability of India's secular nationalism. At the same time, the secular constitution prevails, there are features of it which restrain religion, and India as a secular state remains a powerful model to which subsequent movements, even those based on religion, have had to pay attention. In short, India is a model for secular nationalism, but it is an unstable one.

To some extent this instability was baked into Indian nationalism at the time of state formation. A commitment to a democratic, secular constitutional order left unanswered numerous questions about the status of religious groups in India. Would religious groups retain the personal status laws they had under British colonial rule, or would the state establish a uniform code of laws? What references, if any, would there be to the cultural and historical values of the religious majority Hindus in the new Constitution? How could a political democracy avoid having political parties and movements appealing to the voters on the basis of religion? Coupled with a rise in postindependence violence on religious lines, these unanswered questions would later become the basis for the politicization of religious disputes and a challenge to secular basis of Indian nationalism. The roots of the contemporary conflict around religion in India very much have their origin during the process of state formation.

This chapter outlines relations between religion and nationalism in India. We offer an historical overview of this process and an analysis of contemporary public opinion data on questions related to their interaction on the most salient nationalistic issue in India over the past several decades: relations with Pakistan. We contend that patterns established at the time of state formation continue to be of crucial importance to contemporary understandings of religion and nationalism, and that those divisions are reflected in popular attitudes toward the state.

ELITES AND NATIONALISM IN COLONIAL INDIA

Given India's mind-boggling religious, ethnic, regional, and linguistic diversity, it is remarkable that any unified idea of Indian nationalism developed at all. The Indian subcontinent that Britain ruled for nearly 200 years consisted of thousands of ethnic groups, four major families of languages, hundreds of different castes and tribes, and every major religion the world. In a 1942 article written for the *New York Times* titled "Can Indians Get Together," Jawaharlal Nehru contended that the minorities problem in India was "created by foreign authority," and that once this impediment was removed the minorities' problem would "fade away" (Nehru 1979:519–21). Nehru was partially responding to the claim of many British officials that the subcontinent was so internally divided that only a strong British rule could hold India together. Contrary to Nehru's assertion, however, the British did not create communal divisions *ex nihilo*. The most important of those divisions, based on religion, predated the British raj. Under the rule of the precolonial Mughal Empire, as an example, Hindu, Muslim, and Jewish personal law were recognized in such areas as inheritance, marriage, caste, child custody, and divorce. Once in power, the British adapted themselves to the precolonial status of religious groups, which meant implementing a similar policy of non-interference in the personal laws of the local population (Rautenbach 2006:242; Chatterjee 1998:351–2).

Where Nehru is on firmer ground is his implication that both inadvertently and by design British colonial policy codified the divisions among the Indian population in a way that had never been accomplished before. In the area of religious law, for example, court decisions made over decades created a de facto Anglo-Hindu and Anglo-Muslim case law set of precedents. The result was that the courts formalized a personal law tradition that had historically had greater fluidity and awareness of local sensibilities (Galanter and Krishnan 2000:106–7). This institutionalization was part of a larger pattern of colonial rule. As Van der Veer (1994:19) has noted, "the 19th century saw a massive state project undertaken by British officials to enumerate, classify, and thereby control a quarter of a billion Indians." This project included the taking of censuses that included caste, profession, and religion in the data that was collected. Van der Veer and others have argued that a purpose of the policy was to divide and control the native population. At a minimum, the administrative imperatives of the colonial state drove the process. Confronted with the task of governing so vast a territory and so large a population, the British devised a mechanism to simplify their rule (Baber 2000:64). The result might not have been the creation of communal divisions, but it certainly helped to consolidate those identities among Indians and would eventually contribute to the politicization of religious cleavages.

Nowhere was this more evident than in the Morley-Minto Reforms of 1909 that provided for separate electorates for Muslims to various legislative councils in India. Leaders of the Muslim League pressed for the reforms while the Congress Party opposed them. Under the provisions of the act, Muslims could only vote for Muslim candidates in designated Muslim constituencies. The act was later expanded to include designated seats for Sikhs, Christians, and Scheduled castes. Seen in its most positive light, the reforms were an attempt by the British to introduce a limited form of political representation for Indians in the governance of British India, and to do so on the basis of an accurate representation of the country's primary religious communities. Less charitably, the reforms formalized the concept of separate electorates by religion into Indian politics. Either by design or accident, the reforms further divided Indians on the basis of religion, which in turn contributed to more communalism in Indian politics (Tejani 2013:712–16; Hibbard 2010:120).

Much like pre-independence Israel, Indian political elites proposed three nationalist models during their independence movement: secular nationalism, religious nationalism (both Hindu and Muslim), and civil-religious nationalism. The divergence of views was most evident in the development of the separate anticolonial organizations, the Indian National Congress, the All-India Muslim League, and the All India Hindu Mahasabha. The groups offered different conceptions for the relationship between religion and nationalism in a postcolonial India, and underscored the degree to which religion was a divisive force among political elites.

Founded in 1885 among the educated Indian elite, the Indian National Congress, or Congress, began as a reform movement, but it would eventually embrace self-rule and political independence from Britain (McLeod 2002:93–7). Many of the leaders of the Congress were western-educated, many were inspired by civic notions of nationalism, and they were vigorous advocates for social and economic reform. Nothing signified this perspective better than the passage of a resolution at the 1931 meeting of the Congress in Karachi. The Karachi Resolution, a precursor to the Indian Constitution, laid out a framework for what self-rule in India would mean. It combined economic socialism and political liberalism. The resolution called for state ownership or control of key industries and services and guaranteed to all a decent standard of living. The document also provided for basic civil liberties including universal adult franchise, freedom of speech, press, assembly and association. It also promised the neutrality of the state in regard to all religions, and equality before the law "irrespective of caste, creed or sex." Implicit in this latter assertion, which became a popular slogan in Congress circles, was that ascriptive identities had no place in Indian nationalism (Bajpai 2002:184).

For Nehru, and many others in the Congress, religious identities, what they pejoratively called "communalism," could never be the basis for Indian nationalism. Given India's religious heterogeneity, Nehru's concern was hardly manufactured. Prior to the partition, about 70 percent of the Indian population were Hindu, 24 percent were Muslim, and 2 percent were Christian (Joshi, Srinivas, and Bajaj 2003:13). The remaining 4 percent were Sikh, Jain, Buddhist, and a variety of other religions.

Nehru juxtaposed what he called "medievalism and modernism." He associated a "medieval outlook" with both the Muslim League and various Hindu nationalist organizations; he argued that medievalism was "wholly inconsistent with both democracy and any modern conception of politics or economics." "The Congress," on the other hand, "represents the modern outlook, politically, economically, nationally, and internationally" (Nehru 1981:41). Medievalism had no place in the development of Indian nationalism because it defined membership in the political community on the basis of religious, ethnic, and linguistic ties. The pillars of modern Indian nationalism, by contrast, were to be "independence, democracy, and unity" (Nehru 1979:520). As an organization committed to those shared, secular goals, only the Congress could claim to represent all Indians and provide the necessary antidote to the dangers of sectarianism (Ludden 1996:13; Brasted and Khan 2007:433; Tejani 2013:705).

Working both within and outside of the Congress, Hindu nationalists offered a strong challenge to this secular vision. Politically, organizations like the Rashtriya Swayamsevak Sangh (RSS) and the Hindu Sabha, later renamed the All India Hindu Mahasabha, opposed what they saw as the capitulation of the British and the Congress Party to Muslim demands. In particular, Hindu nationalists opposed the idea of separate electorates for Muslims established under the Morley-Minto reforms, and later reaffirmed under the terms of the 1916 Lucknow Pact between the Indian National Congress and the Muslim League. Ideologically, they offered a nationalism that hewed closely to Hindu identity. In his famous 1909 treatise, *Self-Abnegation in Politics*, Lal Chand contended that "patriotism ought to be communal and not merely geographical"

(Chand 1938:101). The "poison" of the Congress's secular national-ism was that it "makes the Hindu forget that he is a Hindu and tends to swamp his communal individuality into an Indian ideal" (112). The answer to this "suicidal" self-abnegation was to "reverse the idea pro-pounded by the Congress that we are Indians first and Hindus next" (70).

Other religious nationalists followed suit and offered greater clarity on what constituted Hindu identity, and would therefore serve as the basis for Indian nationalism. V. D. Savarkar, president of the Hindu Mahasabha, provided what Christophe Jaffrelot (Jaffrelot 2007:85) describes as a "charter of Hindu nationalism" in his 1923 tract *Essentials of Hindutva*. "The Hindus," Savarkar wrote, "are united not only by the bonds of the love they bear to a common motherland but also by the bonds of a common blood. They are not only a Nation but a race ... All Hindus claim to have in their veins the blood of the mighty race incorporated with and descended from the Vedic fathers, the Sindhus" (Savarkar 1923:30–1). Non-Hindus were inherently suspect in this race-based nationalism. While Indian "Mohammedans" and "Christians" might have inherited with Hindus a "common Fatherland," they could not be recognized as true Hindus because their "outlook smack(s) of a foreign origin. Their love is divided" (42). For Savarkar, India could not be separated from the timeless Hindu culture that the majority commu-nity inherited (Annavarapu 2015:134).

Another ideological and political leader of the Hindu nationalist move-ment was M. S. Golwalker, who was General Secretary of the RSS for more than thirty years. Golwaker argued in his 1938 work, *We or Our Nationhood Defined,* that the "indispensable ingredients" for a nation were a common race, religion, culture, and language. "In this country, Hindusthan," that meant "the Hindu Race with its Hindu Religion, Hindu Culture and Hindu Language complete the Nation concept" (quoted in Jaffrelot 2007:116). Golwalker warned his readers that those "willfully indulging in a course of action detrimental to the Hindu nation are traitors and enemies of the National Cause or to take a more char-itable view mere simpletons, misguided ignorant fools" (116–17). This was a not so veiled reference to leaders of the Congress Party and the secular nationalism that they promoted. The assassination of Mahatma Gandhi in 1948 by Nathuram Godse, a defender of the so-called Hindu motherland and one-time member of the RSS, demonstrated the serious-ness of Golwalker's charge. The Hindu nationalism proffered by Chand, Savarkar, and Golwalker stood in dramatic contrast with the secular nationalism of the Congress.

Many Muslim leaders similarly critiqued the nationalism of the Congress Party, but for them the problem was that it was *too* sympathetic and beholden to Hindu political and ideological interests. Founded in 1906, the Muslim League sought to protect the rights and interests of Indian Muslims (Afzal 2013: Part One). Until the 1930s, most Indian Muslims expected to be part of a unitary Indian nation after independence. The League did not discard secular nationalism as a goal, at least initially, so much as the group and its leaders rejected the assertion of the Congress that it could even-handedly represent the interests of all Indians (Ludden 1996:13). In their view, Indian politics were inherently communal; it was therefore vitally important to have an organization that could effectively represent the minority Muslim community within a larger Hindu polity. In his 1937 Lucknow presidential address before the League, Jinnah contended that "the majority community have clearly shown their hand that Hindustan is for the Hindus; only the Congress masquerades under the name of nationalism, whereas the Hindu Mahasabha does not mince words" (Jinnah 1942:27). "The Congress," he argued in a speech the following year, "is nothing but a Hindu body" which "can afford to assume a non-communal label, but it remains exclusively Hindu in its spirit and actions" (Jinnah 1942:41). In Jinnah's view, the Congress, under the guise of religious neutrality, was in fact offering a Hindu nationalism that differed little from that of the Mahasabha.

Another leader of the League who had a strong influence on Jinnah was Sir Muhammad Iqbal. Iqbal made a political case for a separate nation for Indian Muslims, and he made an ideological argument for Islamic religious nationalism. His book *The Reconstruction of Religious Thought in Islam* provided a framework for how a reconstituted Islam might survive and thrive in the modern world. One of the issues that animated Iqbal in that work and others was the relationship between Islam and nationalism. In his 1930 presidential address before the League, Iqbal rejected the plausibility of a purely secular nationalism which understood the nation to "mean a kind of universal amalgamation in which no community entity ought to retain its private individuality" (Iqbal 1954:12). This kind of nationalism was inconceivable in India where racial and religious identities remained strong and "each group is intensely jealous of its collective existence" (7). Moreover, Iqbal argued that secular nationalism, with its "displacement of the Islamic principle of solidarity," was "simply unthinkable to a Muslim" (13) because it was inconsistent with the unity of state and society implicit in Islamic thought. The only plausible solution was a "communal settlement," a "Muslim Indian within

India" where Indian Muslims could fully develop "on the lines of his own culture and tradition" (8). Ten years later, in 1940, the Muslim League officially endorsed this position for a separate Muslim state in the Lahore Resolution.

In addition to secular nationalism and the competing Hindu and Islamic religious nationalisms, Mahatma Gandhi offered a type of civil-religious nationalism for the emerging Indian state. Like Nehru and other secular leaders of the Congress, Gandhi was deeply committed to religious equality and he repudiated the idea that Hindus and Muslims were separate nations. This did not, however, lead Gandhi to conclude that there should be a strict separation of religion from politics. Instead, he wrote that "a politics bereft of religion are a death-trap because they kill the soul" (Gandhi 1939:16). Far from political sectarianism, however, Gandhi's religiously inspired politics was capacious, pluralistic, and consistent with what he saw as the best of all religious traditions. It was, in his words, a "religion that transcends Hinduism, Islam, Christianity, etc. It does not supersede them ... It harmonizes them and gives them reality." (Gandhi 1958:59). While very much inspired by his own Hinduism, as Jaffrelot notes (2007:4) "[Gandhi] promoted a syncretistic and spiritual brand of the Hindu religion in which all creeds were bound to merge or converge." This commitment to interreligious harmony also had political implications, as Gandhi took up the rather quixotic cause of Indian Muslims to save the Caliphate after the defeat of the Ottoman Empire after World War I (Lelyveld 2011:156–62).

Nandy (1998:343) has provocatively argued that Gandhi's religious tolerance "came from his anti-secularism," and this is true to the extent that it was a tolerance born out of traditional religious concepts. In contrast with many in the Congress Party who inevitably saw religion as a divisive rather than as a unifying force, Gandhi knew that religion formed a major element in Indian life, and he believed that it would have to form a major element in its nationalism as well. "Indian nationalism," he assured his readers, "is not exclusive, nor aggressive, nor destructive. It is health-giving, religious and therefore humanitarian" (Gandhi 1958:121–2). Because it promoted religion as a fundamental feature of Indian identity, Gandhi's nationalism parted company with Nehru's secular ideal, at least insofar as Nehru's secularism implied a strict separation of religion from politics (Van der Veer 1994:23).

For our purposes, Gandhi's ideal functioned as a type of civil-religious nationalism. Religion was meant to be a supportive element that united Indians of disparate spiritual traditions in the nationalist cause. It was not an effort to usurp or privatize the role of religion, as with secular nationalism, but neither was it simply the marrying of nationalism with a religious tradition, as was the case with Hindu and Muslim religious nationalisms. Instead, Gandhi's model intended to stress the points of spiritually commonality among a very diverse population, and a policy commitment to an equal respect for all religions (Bajpai 2002:189).

Political developments leading up to independence further intensified the religious divisions among the Indian population. The political success of Congress Party candidates in the 1937 provisional elections, the first election in which a large number of Indians could vote, created additional fissures between the Congress and the Muslim League. Congress party candidates won more than half of the 1,500 seats contested, and the Congress formed governments in seven provinces (Metcalf and Metcalf 2006:196). The political victories of the Congress helped to accelerate the Muslim League demand for the partition of India, a position the League formally adopted in the 1940 Lahore Resolution.

Even more dramatic was the partition of British India at independence along communal lines. The creation of a Muslim-dominated Pakistan (East and West) and a Hindu-dominated India led to what can only be described as ethnic cleansing as hundreds of thousands of Indians lost their lives to interreligious violence, while an estimated 12.5 million people were uprooted from their homes as Muslims in India traveled east to Pakistan and Sikhs and Hindus went in the opposite directions into India (Metcalf and Metcalf 2006:217–27). The impact of the partition on Indian nationalism was paradoxical. On the one hand, the creation of a Muslim-dominated Pakistan challenged Nehru's secular vision and lent credibility to the communal claims of Hindu religious nationalists (Upadhyaya 1992:830). If Pakistan was for Muslims, the argument went, why wouldn't India naturally be the home for Hindus? As we will see below, some of those arguments were made by delegates during the Constituent Assembly that drafted the Indian Constitution, but this image did not prevail. Instead, the religious violence before and after partition greatly buttressed the argument for secular nationalism. Since religion was a source of disunity, many would argue, it could not be the basis for Indian nationalism. Instead, a broadly shared understanding of India as a multireligious secular democracy would be the key to political unity in the newly independent state of India.

This brief overview of the pre-independence era helps to explain why secular nationalism came to prevail as the official Indian nationalist ideology. India was religiously pluralistic, religion was a powerful force in pre-independence India, and it was a source of deep political contesta-tion. In contrast with Uruguay, where secular nationalism reflected the relative weakness of religious groups and identities, secular national-ism in India developed as a response to the social and political power of religious claims. A nationalism married to a particular religious tradition in India could only undermine the national cause. All of the pre-independence variables argued for secular nationalism, but such a model would nonetheless be contested during the drafting of the Indian Constitution.

RELIGION AND NATIONALISM IN THE CONSTITUENT ASSEMBLY DEBATE

The second factor in the development of a nationalist ideology is the role of religion in state formation. Nothing better epitomizes this process than the drafting of a Constitution which is a regime-defining moment. Over the course of nearly three years, during eleven separate sessions covering 165 days, members of the Constituent Assembly debated nearly every feature of the Indian Constitution. Most of the members of the Assembly were elected by provincial legislatures created by the British, and were intended to be roughly proportional by population and by reli-gious community. Following the withdrawal of the seventy-three Muslim League delegates in 1947, replacements were chosen with an eye toward communal balance (Copland 2010:138). Members of the Congress Party dominated the proceedings. The words "secular" or "secularism" were used hundreds of times, by dozens of delegates, on a variety of issues. It is hard to imagine a group of political elites more rhetorically unified in their commitment to the creation of a secular constitution in India, yet more divided on what exactly they meant by that concept. Implicit in those policy differences were variant ideas among the delegates about the kind of nationalism that they were creating.

Many of the delegates proposed a model of secular nationalism where religion was privatized, religious values and identities had no political purchase, and civic and socialist values would be the glue that held the nation together. Brajeshwar Prasad went so far as to say that he was "quite clear in my own mind that secularism is the negation of all reli-gion" (Constituent Assembly [of India] 1949a). Others were not so dis-missive of religion but wanted to circumscribe its role in national identity. In a debate about separate electorates, Pattabi Sitaramayya urged the delegates to "forget all the antagonisms created in the past. Let us forget the very words – the two names, Congress and League ... Let us drop both these names and have a democratic, republican or socialistic organisation ... based entirely on political grounds. It will eschew all religious predilections" (Constituent Assembly [of India] 1947a). In contrast with Prasad, Sitarmayya was not suggesting that religion could or should disappear. Instead, he wanted to ensure that it not serve as the basis for national integration.

Many of the delegates also used the idea of secular nationalism to contrast India with her regional and ideological rival, Pakistan. H. V. Kamath told his fellow delegates that it "is a historic fact that the Muslim League has demanded and achieved the partition of India on a communal basis, a basis which to my mind is the antithesis of socialism ... let us go forward to build a united, strong, independent, socialist India in a socialist Federation of one free world" (Constituent Assembly [of India] 1947b). Kamath's words are a vivid reminder of the rivalries and divergent concepts of nationhood brought about by the partition. Pakistan might have a religious nationalism based on communal identities, the argument went, but India would define itself as a multireligious secular democracy. For these delegates, India had made a "tryst with destiny," as Nehru famously articulated in his inaugural Independence Day address. India, he said "does not belong to the followers of any particular religion. It is the country of all, of every religion and creed ... our freedom is to be shared equally by every Indian" (Constituent Assembly [of India] 1947c). Secular nationalism thus became both an antidote to the problem of narrow religious identities and a way for Indians proudly to affirm their unique contribution in a region riven with communal cleavages. As we will see later in the chapter, the ideal of secular nationalism is so powerful in India that even Hindu nationalists use the rhetoric of secularism even as they seek to undermine it.

Hindu nationalist groups and their leaders lacked political credibility during the debates. The RSS, under the leadership of Golwalker, had remained out of politics during the independence struggle and refused to cooperate with the Congress (Jaffrelot 2007:16). The assassination of Gandhi about halfway through the sessions by the Hindu nationalist Nathuram Godse further undermined the legitimacy of Hindu nationalist organizations. Nonetheless, some delegates offered a nationalism that cleaved more closely to the values of the Hindu majority. One of those provisions concerned a proposal to protect cows in recognition of the cow's status as a respected creature of God in Hinduism. Shibban Lal Saksena argued "if thirty crores of our population feel that this thing should be incorporated in the laws of the country, I do not think that we as an Assembly representing 35 crores should leave it out merely because it has a religious aspect ... we should not think that because a thing has a religious significance, so it is bad" (Constituent Assembly [of India] 1948a).

More generally, Thirumala Rao contended that the delegates had been "talking too much of a secular State." What he preferred is that the Constitution make clear "that the ancient traditions and culture of this country will be fully protected and developed by the Constitution ... I plead that we should protect our culture, our peculiar national characteristics and traditions" (Constituent Assembly [of India] 1948b). For some of the delegates, "ancient traditions and culture" were code words for Hindu values and practices. Assailing what he called the "specious, oft-repeated and nauseating principle of secularity of the state," P. S. Deshmukh asked if we must "wipe out our own people to prove our secularity ... must [we] wipe out Hindus and Sikhs under the name of secularity, must [we] undermine everything that is sacred and dear to the Indians to prove that we are secular?" Note that it was Hindus and Sikhs, not Muslims and Christians, who were supposedly threatened by a secular state. In his view, "we have seen the formation of Pakistan [established] because the Muslims claimed that they must have a home of their own and a country of their own ... if the Muslims want an exclusive place for themselves called Pakistan, why should not Hindus and Sikhs have India as their home?" (Constituent Assembly [of India] 1949b).

Some of the comments by the delegates foreshadowed arguments that Hindu nationalists would make in the decades ahead. One of the controversial issues that they raised concerned the proposed right to propagate one's faith. Hindu nationalists argued that anticonversion laws were needed to protect "vulnerable" Hindu populations from being exploited by the "foreign" religions of Islam and Christianity. Their concern was that a right to propagate faith would entail a right to convert others. Lokanath Misra saw this provision as a "charter for Hindu enslavement ... that can only mean paving the way for the complete annihilation of Hindu culture." He contended that India would have been a "perfectly secular and homogenous State [if] Islam had not come to impose its will on this land." A secular state, by this reasoning, would not allow public acts of religiosity like conversion. Misra concluded by suggesting that the Constitution was "tabooing religion and yet making propagation of religion a fundamental right" (Constituent Assembly [of India] 1948c). In many ways, Misra predicted the assertion of contemporary Hindu nationalists who claim that the Constitution appeases religious minorities at the expense of the religious majority.

Striking a balance between these opposing nationalist visions was the Gandhian civil religious ideal. A number of delegates rejected what they saw as a western-style secularism that negated any role for religion in the new state (Copland 2010:133). As a powerful force in Indian society, religion was bound to play a part in its nationalism as well. However, they parted company with Hindu nationalists in embracing India's diverse religious traditions and seeing in them a source of potential unity. In a debate on whether or not to include the word "God" in the Preamble to the Constitution, Mahavir Tyagi complained about "some vain politicians who imitate some fashionable slogans of the West [and] have allowed themselves to believe that in a secular State God is taboo." While acknowledging the "many religions in India," Tyagi declared that "the name of God is a common factor among them all," and that it would "help us to unify the state" if the name of God were included in the Preamble (Constituent Assembly [of India] 1948d). Invoking Gandhi's legacy, K. M. Munshi contended that:

if India has anything to give to the world, it is the outlook on life deeply imbued by spirituality, by awareness of God in our midst ... The lever with which Mahatma Gandhi created the present nationalism and won for us a free State was the religious-mindedness of India. This mind will continue to be religious, and the State in India cannot be secular in the sense of being antireligious. (Constituent Assembly [of India] 1948e)

Further complicating the divisions among the delegates was that religion could not be completely taken off the political agenda. Religion powerfully shaped social lives and institutions, and secularism posed a challenge to practices deeply rooted in the country's religious traditions (Jacobsohn 2003:38). Debates on the status of religious law, separate electorates by religion, the status of religious schools, a prohibition on cow slaughter, and the right to propagate one's religion exposed those tensions. Many Muslim delegates wanted the constitution to preserve religious law in areas such as marriage, divorce, and inheritance. Mohamad Ismail, a delegate from the All India Muslim League, maintained that "the right of a group or a community of people to follow and adhere to its own personal law is a fundamental right [and] this secular State which we are trying to create should not do anything to interfere with the way of life and religion of the people" (Constituent Assembly [of India] 1948f; Mohamad Ismail, November 23, 1948). To promote religious rights in this way, however, opened delegates to the charge that they were promoting the much reviled "communalism." Brajeshwar Prasad warned his colleagues that "if we do not take a bold stand at this moment and clearly lay down the principle that the basis of a secular state shall not be allowed to be corrupted by any other consideration, the future of this country is dark" (Constituent Assembly [of India] 1949c). By "any other consideration" Prasad meant religious or caste identities. In a comment dripping with sarcasm Sardar Hukam Singh, a Sikh delegate, countered that "whatever is said and done by the majority in a democratic country or at least in India is pure nationalism and whatever is said by a minority is communalism ... what [we] are afraid of is not the democracy of the majority, but the communalism of the majority" (Constituent Assembly [of India] 1949d). His point was that majority rule did not necessarily imply a nationalism devoid of religion, but might instead reflect Hindu values.

In many respects, the Constitution reflects the secular and socialist political values of Nehru and his many Congress supporters who dominated the proceedings (Hibbard 2010:126). Freedom of religion is guaranteed as a fundamental right, there is no state religion, religious instruction in state schools is banned, and citizens are protected against discrimination on the basis of religion, race, caste, sex, and place of birth. The preamble describes India as a democratic, sovereign Republic and highlights social, economic, and political equality, justice, liberty, and fraternity as goals for the Indian nation. The word "secular" would not be added to the preamble until 1976, but secular political norms were very much institutionalized in the Constitution. Socialist values were also highlighted in the Constitution. Included among the directive principles that were supposed to guide future policy were the right to a living wage, equal pay for men and women, a minimizing in the inequalities of income, and the creation of just and humane work conditions, among others. The commitment to equality was so strong that the Constitution proactively interfered with ostensibly religious practices in the name of the larger value. Under the leadership of the chair of the Drafting Committee, B. R. Ambedkar, who was a distinguished leader of the "untouchable" community, the Constitution forbids untouchability and reserves seats in legislatures for former "untouchables," and with them the equally disadvantaged Scheduled Tribes (Metcalf and Metcalf 2006:232).

Bhargava (2010:26) perceptively notes that the delegates "walked a tightrope" in promoting the twin values of religious liberty and social equality. The former required non-interference with religion, while the latter demanded intervention to overcome religious practices like untouchability that reinforced social and political inequalities. There are several places in the Constitution where secular political values trump religious liberty, a model that Jacobsohn (2003:94) describes as "ameliorative secularism." The idea is that secular political goals led the state to try to improve the conditions of people burdened by inequalities based on religion. For example, in many parts of the country Hindu temples did not allow access to the lowest castes and untouchables, a practice that Gandhi eventually championed in one of his mass-movement campaigns (Lelyveld 2011:269–70). Article 15 of the Constitution ensures equal access to public wells, museums, and temples. Even more explicit is the contrast between the first clause of Article 25 which guarantees people the right "freely to practice their faith," while the second and third clause of the same article affirms that this right does not prevent the State from "making any law for providing social welfare or the throwing open of Hindu religious institutions of a public character to all classes and sections of Hindus."

This is not to suggest that Indian secularism was antireligious. Religious groups retained the right to establish schools, those schools were eligible for public funds, and they could offer religious instruction. Instead of a strict separation of religion from the state, Indian secularism frequently embraced the Gandhian concept of *sarva dharma sambhava* (let all religions prosper). The result was not a French or Turkish style secularism which entailed overt hostility to religion. The idea, instead, was that a secular polity would enable all religions equally to flourish. In various places, the Constitution also provides preferential benefits to members of a lower caste, which in turn reinforces caste identities that are often aligned with religious ones. Madan (1998:312–13) notes that the Constitution simultaneously establishes a secular state while preserving and even encouraging communal or religions divisions. To some extent, however, that was unavoidable. India was a deeply religious society, and while the delegates encouraged the development of a secular constitution and of a secular nationalism, it did not mean that they could simply ignore the place of religion in everyday life.

Some religious issues proved to be so politically contentious, however, that the delegates effectively deferred them to some future date. One section of the Constitution included directive principles of state policy. These were intended to provide guidelines for the framing of future laws, but they were not fundamental rights that were enforceable by the courts (Chiriyankandath 2008:14). Most notably, the goal of a uniform civil code (Article 44) was included as a directive principle but not as a fundamental right. This was done largely in deference to the views of many Muslim delegates. The upshot was that Muslims retained personal law in civil matters, as did Hindus at least in the short term. Like the debate on conversion laws, this provision would become a rallying point for Hindu nationalists who contended that the Constitution favored the rights of religious minorities against the religious majority (Sen 2005:298). Another controversial religious issue was a proposed prohibition on the slaughter of cows. The Constitution granted states the power to legislate the prevention of slaughter and preservation of cows, but instead of mandating this at the national level a prohibition was included as a directive principle. Lerner (2013) suggests that the framers used directive principles as a way to avoid clear-cut decisions on controversial religious issues. The ambiguity inherent in this part of the Constitution might have helped the delegates avoid making some very difficult choices, but it did not solve the dilemma surrounding these religious issues.

The other constitutional provision that angered many Hindu delegates was Article 370 that allowed the only majority Muslim province of India, Jammu and Kashmir, to have a "temporary" special autonomous political status within India. According to this article, except for defense, foreign affairs, finance and communications, Parliament needs the state government's concurrence for applying all other laws. The provision was included in the context of an ongoing war with Pakistan over the region, and concern that this princely state might not join the union at all. From the standpoint of Hindu nationalists, however, Article 370 indicated an unfair preference given to India's Muslim minority (Misra 2000:4).

On one of the last days of the Constituent Assembly, T. J. M. Wilson opined that "the greatest achievement of our Constitution is its secular character ... But the clouds are gathering and they are threatening to darken the secular character of the state and obliterate it. I only pray and trust that the progressive forces of this country ... shall not allow our country to pass once again through destruction and misery" (T. J. M. Wilson, November 23, 1949). Secular nationalism developed in India because religion was socially strong, it posed a potential threat to social unity, and because political elites concluded that democratic and socialist values were more unifying than religious ones. Those secular values were largely replicated in the Constitution that they drafted. The assumptions of the framers about religion were not necessarily wrong, but they failed to take account of the degree to which India remained a communally divided state, and of the capacity and willingness of political leaders to use religion in future years for mobilization purposes. For these and other reasons, India has retained its secular nationalism, but it has been an unstable one that has faced a series of challenges.

POLITICAL CHALLENGES TO SECULAR NATIONALISM

One way to understand the different trajectories for secular nationalism in India and Uruguay is to contrast the role of religion in the lives of the people in the two countries. According to the 2010–14 wave of the World Value Survey (World Values Survey 2011), 67 percent of Indian respondents indicate that religion is a very important part of their life, compared to only 20 percent of Uruguayan respondents. India and Uruguay are both electoral democracies, but there is a much stronger incentive to rally voters along religious lines in India than in Uruguay, and thereby to challenge India's commitment to secular nationalism. One contingent variable that has made India's secular nationalist model an unstable one is the contrast between secularism as a political ideal, on the one hand, and the mobilizing potential of appeals based on religion, on the other.

One of Nehru's most significant policy achievements demonstrated this tension. In a series of bills in the 1950s, Nehru succeeded in passing a uniform civil code for Hindus that signaled a departure from traditional Hindu practices. He did so despite strong opposition from Hindu traditionalists (Chiriyankandath 2008:361). Among other features, the various bills legalized intercaste marriage and divorce, prohibited polygamy, and gave daughters the same inheritance rights as sons. While consistent with the secular thrust of the Constitution, the Hindu Code Bill notably did not apply to members of the Muslim community. Nehru felt that it was morally and politically problematic for the majority Hindu community to impose its will on religious minorities. The difficulty, however, was that this decision exposed the Congress Party, and those who favored secular nationalism, to the pseudosecularism charge of religious nationalists. How could secular nationalists claim the right to intervene in the religious practices of one group to promote social and political rights, they argued, but fail to do so for other religious groups? (Chatterjee 1998:356–61; Copland 2010:137). Over the next half century, Hindu nationalists would point to this apparent constitutional inconsistency to undermine India's secular nationalist model.

Nehru, who served as Prime Minister until his death in 1964, avoided religion-based politics, retained his commitment to secular norms and progressive social values, and largely kept religious nationalists at bay.

Congress party politicians also used Gandhi's assassination by a Hindu nationalist to delegitimize the movement and to promote the idea of India as a unified secular nation (Debs 2013:635–6). The Congress Party dominated Indian politics for nearly four decades, but as Sumantra Bose (2013:12) notes, this institutional prowess was not matched by a similar influence at the societal level. Congress' secular nationalism did not automatically translate to widespread, popular adherence to that model. Instead, increasingly there was a conflict between the secular policies of the Congress political elite and the more religiously inclined views of the masses. Hindu nationalists, and their respective political parties, exploited this opportunity and gradually chipped away at support for the Congress. The RSS helped to organize the first of those nationalist political parties, the Jana Sangh, followed by the multiparty Janata Party, and finally the BJP. In each case, the nationalist party promoted Hindutva as a national ideology, pushed for laws to ban cow slaughter, opposed what it saw as appeasement to religious minorities, and called for a repeal of Article 370 of the Constitution and the complete integration of Jammu and Kashmir into India.

Leaders of the Congress Party continued to give strong rhetorical support to India's secular nationalism in the 1970s. For example, Indira Gandhi incorporated the word "secular" into the preamble to the Constitution, she described the RSS as a "fascist organization [that] preaches an extreme form of Hindu chauvinism" (Gandhi 1984:193), and she frequently affirmed the secular character of India's nationalism. However, Indira Gandhi undermined her commitment to constitutional norms (including secularism) by calling a state of emergency in 1975, arresting scores of political opponents including leaders of the RSS, suspending civil liberties, and establishing a compulsory sterilization campaign. Gandhi's reckless political actions helped to legitimate the Jana Sangh, and its successor BJP party, as a valid political competitor and the standard bearer for antisecular policies (Ganguly 2003:15). She was ousted from power in the first postemergency election by a coalition of parties that included the Jana Singh.

On her return to power, Gandhi more willingly played the so-called "Hindu card" against Muslims in Jammu and Kashmir and Sikhs in Punjab for political advantage. In both cases, she projected the idea that Hindus, who were a minority in these Indian states, faced a threat from separatist movements among the Islamic majority in Jammu and Kashmir and the Sikh majority in Punjab (Alam 2002:100–1). While concerns about separatism were not entirely manufactured, Gandhi nonetheless overdramatized them for her own electoral purposes. Gandhi sent in the army to crush a separatist movement in Punjab which led to the death of several thousand Sikhs. A few months later, Gandhi was assassinated by two of her Sikh bodyguards. The cooptation of religious groups associated with Hindu nationalists not only cost Gandhi her life, but it served to legitimize the issues that religious nationalists had been raising since before independence (Hibbard 2014:123).

Rajiv Gandhi largely followed his mother's example. He described secularism as "the most important component of nation building in India" (Gandhi 1989:298), but at the same time he often tried to coopt rather than to confront religious sensibilities. He intervened in the ethnic/religious politics of Sri Lanka, a decision that would cost him his life. Sri Lanka is an island nation off the southern coast of India that is divided between a Buddhist Sinhalese-speaking majority, and a largely Hindu Tamil minority with close ties to Tamils in India. Violence directed against the Tamil minority by the Sinhalese majority led to a Tamil resistance movement, guerrilla warfare, and even more violence. Fully aware that the Tamil cause had significant support among India's Tamil community, Rajiv gave covert assistance to the rebels. He then agreed to send a "peace keeping" force to the island to disarm the rebels so that elections could be held. Unable to satisfy either side of the conflict, and with mounting casualties among the Indian army, Gandhi ordered a complete withdrawal of the troops in 1990. A year later, Rajiv was killed by a Tamil suicide bomber (Metcalf and Metcalf 2006:263).

An even more dramatic example of his effort to coopt religious votes was his involvement in Shah Bano affair. In 1985, the Indian Supreme Court ruled that a Muslim divorcee, Shah Bano, was entitled to continued financial support from her ex-husband. The court argued that continued support was justified under the country's civil law in order to prevent women from becoming destitute. The court further contended that the decision was consistent with Article 44 which called for the establishment of a uniform civil code. In doing so, the court set aside the Muslim code, which required assistance only for a few months, and in the process challenged the legitimacy and status of Muslim personal law. The decision angered many Indian Muslims who were a vital voting block within the Congress Party. Seeking to capitalize on the controversy that followed and to secure support among Muslim voters, Gandhi passed the Muslim Women's (Protection of Rights in Divorce) Bill, which effectively nullified the Supreme Court's decision and reinstated Muslim personal law. Hindu nationalists in the BJP attacked the bill as another example of pseudosecularism and of appeasement to minority opinion. In the process, they presented themselves as the "true" voices of secularism who were standing up for a uniform civil code that would apply equally, and against "special recognition" for minorities. Hindu nationalists thus used the rhetoric of secularism to defend their implicit religious nationalism (Jacobsohn 2003:147; Hibbard 2010:156–7).

While they never abandoned their rhetorical commitment to secularism, Indira and Rajiv Gandhi nevertheless encouraged political mobilization on religious grounds and thereby helped to legitimate communal politics (Baber 2000:73; Brasted and Khan 2007:440; Hibbard 2010:148–50). They appealed to secularism in order to gain support among religious minorities, while they acknowledged Hindu concerns when it suited their political interests among the majority community. The reason for this electoral mobilization was fairly self-evident. Even at the height of its political power, the Congress Party never won a majority of the nationwide vote. At key moments, electoral competition with the Hindu right for Hindu votes overrode the party's commitment to secularism. The need to appeal to voters on the basis of their religious interests was compelling, but it proved to be difficult for the Congress to defeat the BJP at its own game. The BJP increased the numbers of its seats in the Lok Sabha, the main legislative body, from two in 1984, to eighty-five in 1989, and 161 in 1996. That year's election led to the selection of the country's first BJP Prime Minister, Atal Bihari Vajpayee, though his term in the hung Parliament lasted but sixteen days. Two years later, the BJP won 182 seats, Vajpayee was again selected as Prime Minister, and he served six years.

The political success of the BJP was not simply a function of its nationalist ideology; widespread disenchantment with the Congress Party played an equally important role. Nonetheless, the electoral success of the BJP suggests the instability of India's secular nationalism. The BJP is closely allied with mass-based Hindu nationalist movements like the RSS, which provide essential services to the party. The BJP promotes an ideology of Hindu nationalism, or Hindutva, which equates being Indian with adherence to Hindu culture and tradition and implicitly, and sometimes explicitly, presents religious minorities as outside of the nation (Van der Veer 1994:1; Thapar 2005:198; Hibbard 2010:115). In its 2004 Vision Statement, the BJP called for the enactment of a uniform civil code and the end of personal law, the construction of a Ram temple in Ayodhya (where a mosque had been destroyed in 1992 by Hindu agitators who believed that the mosque was built over the birthplace of the ancient deity Rama), and a ban on conversions through "fraudulent and coercive means." The party also affirmed that "cultural nationalism for which Indianness, Bharatiyata and Hindutva are synonyms – is the basis of our national identity" (Bharatiya Janata Party 2004). That same year, in his presidential speech delivered at the BJP National Executive Committee, L. K. Advani, who was at the time leader of the opposition in the Lok Sabha, warned his audience that "a section of the Congress party, the Communists and some other political forces in this country are conspiring to slowly but systematically erase the Hindu ethos of this country and to obfuscate the basic Hindu identity of our culture and civilization" (Advani 2004). It did not take much imagination on the part of his listeners to conclude that "other political forces" meant religious minorities.

Another factor that has contributed to the instability of India's secular nationalism has been communal violence. If secular nationalism is premised on the idea that religious identities are unimportant in national self-awareness, violence based on religion undermines that model. The Partition violence between Hindus and Muslims marked the beginning of what has become a recurring pattern of communal violence in postindependence India. According to one estimate (Wilkinson 2004:12–13) more than 10,000 persons have been killed in Hindu–Muslim violence since 1950. These have included violence between Muslims and Hindus in Gujarat in 1969 and 2002, the anti-Sikh riots in 1984, and the forced expulsion of Kashmiri Hindus in the early 1990s, among others. According to data collected by the Ministry of Home Affairs, there were an average of 58 incidents of communal violence per month between 2011 and 2015. During that time, the number of incidences of violence and the annual average of deaths from them increased (Dubbudu 2015).

Not only has violence reinforced communal identities and undermined secular loyalties to the nation, but parties and politicians have often benefited from exploiting and encouraging those actions. The destruction of the Babri Mosque in Ayodhya was part of a well-orchestrated campaign by the RSS and the BJP to exploit religious differences for political ends (Jacobsohn 2003:154). According to a study of the 2002 post-violence elections in Gujarat (Dhattiwala and Biggs 2012), the BJP vote increased the most in districts with the worst violence. Narendra Modi, the Chief Minister of Gujarat during that time, was accused of initiating and condoning the violence. A special commission eventually cleared him of the charges, though it concluded that the state government, which he ostensibly ran, had not done enough to prevent the riots. Nearly a decade later, in 2014, the BJP had its best-ever result in the Lok Sabha elections, winning

282 seats and electing Modi as India's fourteenth Prime Minister. Leaders of the BJP have been anything but subtle in demonstrating their fidelity to key Hindu nationalist figures. In the aftermath of the anti-Muslim riots in Gujarat in 2002, L. K. Advani renamed a regional airport after the Hindu nationalist V. D. Savarkar, while Modi described M. S. Golwalker as "a Guru worthy of worship" in his 2008 autobiography (Modi 2014).

A related factor that has helped to destabilize India's secular nationalism has been ongoing disputes with Pakistan. As we noted in several of the country chapters, an external threat can reinforce nationalist sentiment. When that conflict is rooted at least in part on religious differences, or can be presented in that way, religious nationalism is often promoted. Since the Partition, India and Pakistan have gone to war four times and have had numerous border disputes. The main cause for the conflict is the Kashmir issue. The violence has not been restricted to Kashmir. The 2008 Mumbai attacks that killed 164 people were planned and orchestrated by an Islamic terrorist group based in Pakistan. Conflict with Pakistan has allowed the BJP and other Hindu nationalists to reinforce the importance of the Hindu–Muslim divide between the countries and within India (Ruparelia 2006:327; Brasted and Khan 2007). The security concerns are genuine, but the definition of the conflict as one pitting "Muslim" Pakistan against "Hindu" India undermines secular norms and identities as the basis for Indian nationalism.

A final challenge to secular nationalism is both political and pedagogical. The BJP has long sought to rewrite the history of India and of the Indian independence movement. When the party first came to power at the national level in 1998, it established the National Curriculum Framework to change textbook content (Visweswaran et al. 2009). The resulting curriculum extolled the virtues of the Hindu nationalist Veer Savarkar, advanced the idea that Christians and Muslims were foreigners to India, and promoted the cultural sensibilities of the Hindu majority. In one particularly striking example, some of the social science textbooks had deleted all references to Nehru, the architect of the country's secular constitution (Jaffrelot 2016a).

DEMOGRAPHIC CHALLENGES TO SECULAR NATIONALISM

Demographic changes can also be the basis for challenging the inherited nationalism model. In the case of India, it is as much a fear about those changes as any big demographic alteration that has undermined the secularist model. In 1951, 84 percent of the Indian population was

Hindu, followed by Muslim (9.8 percent), Christian (2.3 percent), Sikh (1.9 percent), and all other faiths combined at under 2 percent of the population. Since then there has been a slight decline in the percentage of the Hindu population from 84 percent to just under 80 percent in 2011, and an increase in the percentage of Muslims (from 9.8 to 14.2 percent). The percentages of Christians and Sikhs are largely unchanged (Ghosh and Singh 2015; Sugden 2015). While a decline in the percentage of the Hindu population is not that dramatic, and it has slowed in recent years, Hindu nationalists nonetheless have used this data to argue that Hindu India is under assault. A 2005 Resolution passed by the leadership of the RSS warned that "separatist and terrorist activities have mushroomed in areas where the percentage of Hindu population has declined" (Akhil Bharatiya Pratinidhi Sabha [ABPS]. 2005). One BJP member of Parliament urged Hindu women to have at least four children "in order to protect the Hindu religion" (Ali 2015). Think tanks have produced reports that portend a demographic future where "Indian religions" are a minority by the middle of the century (Johsi, Srivinas, and Bajaj 2003). Not only are such projections based on suspect assumptions, but the use of the pejorative term "Indian religions" suggests that Muslims and Christians, in particular, are foreign and therefore not properly Indian.

Real or imagined, the demographic "threat" has been used by the BJP at the state level to press for the passage of so-called "Freedom of Religion" laws. Ostensibly intended to prevent people from forced conversions, the intent and effect of the law is to limit the ability of Christians to proselytize among the Dalit, or lower-caste Hindu community. While the Constitution guarantees a right to propagate, the Indian Supreme Court has ruled that this does not include a right to convert a person to one's own religion. Over the past decade nearly a dozen states have passed these freedom of religion laws, and in nearly every instance the state government was at the time controlled by the BJP. The harassment directed against religious minorities in these laws is thus a political response to a perceived threat, and an attempt to unify Hindus under a common religious nationalist banner (Huff 2009; Bauman 2016:34–6).

Secular nationalism has also been undermined by the continued salience of religion at the mass level. As we noted above, a sizeable percentage of the Indian population indicate that religion is a "very important" part of their life, and this is largely uniform for Muslims (79 percent), Buddhists (76 percent), Hindus (65 percent), and Christians (57 percent). Remarkably, more than one-third (37 percent) of the admittedly very small number of those who indicated that they had no religion

(0.4 percent) said that religion was a very important part of their life. Less than 10 percent of respondents from each of the religious groups said that religion was not at all or not very important. Not only is religion highly salient, but it seems to have become even more so over the past two decades. The 1989 wave of World Value Survey indicated that 49 percent of Indian respondents affirmed that religion was a very important part of their life, which grew to 56 percent in 1999, and 67 percent in 2010 (World Values Survey 2011). To some extent those figures overlap with the political rise of the BJP.

Developments in India's history have challenged its secular nationalist model. That does not mean, however, that religious nationalism has supplanted it. Instead, the basis for Indian nationalism is contested. Secular nationalism retains a strong ideological hold, and some of the factors that challenge it can also reinforce it. For example, hostility with "Muslim" Pakistan is used by religious nationalists to promote the idea and values of "Hindu" India. However, the "othering" of Pakistan can also take the form of promoting the distinctiveness of India's secular nationalism. In a 1972 speech titled "the Communal Virus," Indira Gandhi spoke about the recent establishment of Bangladesh after its War of Independence with Pakistan. She noted that "the emergence of sovereign secular Bangladesh has conclusively proved that religion cannot be a ground for separate nationhood. This theory has done great harm to our subcontinent" (Gandhi 1975:207). Her not so subtle jab was intended for Pakistan, a country founded on religious grounds. The point is that Gandhi, and many after her, defend secular nationalism as superior to Pakistan's religious nationalism. To the extent that nationalism is about defining one nation in opposition to another, India's secular nationalism often serves that purpose. Communal violence can similarly undermine or reinforce the state's secular identity. Nationalist parties have politically benefited from the violence, as we noted above, but the violence also supports the counterclaim that secular nationalism is the only way to end violence based on religious identities.

The secular nationalist tradition also serves as a constraint on religious nationalism. As Bhargava (2010:255) notes, Hindu nationalists "legitimate their actions in terms of its normative vocabulary." The promotion of cow-protection bills are defended on the grounds that those policies are consistent with the views of the majority. A 2001 resolution on that issue by the RSS leadership thus argued that "in a democratic set up popular sentiments cannot be flouted" (Akhil Bharatiya Pratinidhi Sabha [ABPS] 2001). In a similar way, support for a uniform civil code is presented as true as opposed to "pseudo secularism." A BJP circular on Hindutva contends that "when Hindus realized that pseudo-secularism had reduced them to the role of an innocent bystander in the game of politics, they demanded a true secularism where every religious group would be treated the same and a government that would not take Hindu sentiments for granted" (Bharatiya Janata Party 2009). Finally, Hindu nationalists often assert that India is secular because it is Hindu. In his 2004 presidential speech at the National Executive Committee of the BJP, L. K. Advani argued that "India is secular principally because of its Hindu ethos" (Advani 2004). Bhargava is right to suggest that Hindu nationalists do not take seriously the normative implications of their use of a secular vocabulary. In many respects, they want to undermine the secular basis of the Constitution and of Indian nationalism. That leaders of the BJP feel compelled to use that language nonetheless indicates its continuing linguistic appeal.

PUBLIC OPINION AND NATIONALISM

For the quantitative analysis of abstract nationalism, we used the Indian subsample of the 2013 International Social Survey Programme and focused on roots of differing responses to the question "how close do you feel to India?" Answers ranged from "very close" to "not at all close." We discussed above the historical importance of the partition of South Asia into India and Pakistan, the continued military conflict over control of Kashmir, and the ways in which Indian Muslims' loyalty to the nation can be questioned. Our example of a specific nationalism issue is therefore hostility to Pakistan. We measure such attitudes via the Pakistan-favorability item in the Indian part of the 2010 Spring Pew Global Attitudes survey. Options varied between "very favorable" toward Pakistan to "very unfavorable."

As Table 7.1 shows, Indians are exceedingly nationalistic, but religious identification plays much less of a role than one might suspect. Between Hindus and Muslims, for example, the overall level of attachment to India is very high and virtually identical. Given the deadly partition along this religious cleavage of the subcontinent, a history of religious violence in independent India, and the political mobilization along religious lines, this finding suggests that Indian secular nationalism has successfully pushed national identity above religious affiliation in the minds of ordinary Indian citizens. As we noted, secular nationalism faces

TABLE 7.1. *Nationalism by religious tradition*

Tradition	Mean
Hindu	3.50
Muslim	3.48
Christian	3.41
Other Asian religions	3.99
Other religions	3.85
All respondents	3.51

Source: 2013 International Social Survey Programme, National Identity III, India subsample.

challenges on numerous fronts at the elite and institutional levels, but it seems to prevail in the mass public's symbolic attachment to India. Of the remaining religious groups, Christians feel similarly close to India, while Buddhists, Sikhs, and Jews express the maximum possible level of pro-Indian sentiments.

Table 7.2 explores the determinants of abstract Indian nationalism. As in Table 7.1, being Muslim as opposed to Hindu has no effect. The same is not true, however, for the other religious traditions. After controlling for various socioeconomic factors, belonging to the Christian faith makes one a little less nationalistic. However, devotion to "Other Asian Religions" (e.g., Buddhism or Sikhism) or "Other Religions" greatly boosts national identity. In separate regressions, we estimated the effect of religiosity for each major religious group. The resulting estimates suggested that attendance itself has no effect on nationalism among Hindus, but that it moderately reduces national feeling among Muslims and strongly attenuates Indian identity for Christians. We hypothesize that these outcomes result from the greater exposure to a transnational religious community in mosques and churches. By itself, education tends to weaken nationalism. Our more detailed investigation of data, however, led us to suspect interaction effect with religious attendance. We therefore created the interaction term "Religious Attendance × Education." The very statistically significant result for this variable suggests that greater education has a pronationalist effect when a respondent is especially religious. This finding may help explain why the BJP and other Hindu nationalist parties have focused so much attention on promoting "Hindu values" in education. This result is also consistent with evidence that BJP support is concentrated among the more educated "neo-middle class"

TABLE 7.2. *Religious and other determinants of nationalism*

Variable	Coefficient	Standard error
Muslim	−0.143	0.160
Christian	−0.660*	0.250
Other Asian religions	3.636*	1.601
Other religions	1.938*	0.925
Religious attendance	−0.231*	0.078
Education	−0.556*	0.096
Interaction: religious attendance × education	0.062*	0.017
Income	0.000	0.000
Woman	0.280*	0.111
Age	−0.002	0.004
Urbanicity	0.075	0.049
Hindu proportion by region	−0.010	0.006
Constant 1	−5.861*	0.745
Constant 2	−5.062*	0.739
Constant 3	−3.254*	0.732
N	1509	
Nagelkerke R^2	0.090	

*Denotes an effect that is significantly different from 0 at the 5 percent level for ordered Logit model.
Notes: All regressors are dummy variables except for Religious Attendance (range = 1–8), Education (1–8), Interaction: Religious Attendance × Education (1–56), Income (1,500–150,000), Age (18–90), Urbanicity (1–5), and Hindu Proportion by Region (2.75–95.17).
Source: 2013 International Social Survey Programme, National Identity III, India subsample.

(Jaffrelot and Kumar 2015). We also created a variable for the percentage of a state's population that is Hindu, which varied from 2.8 percent in Mizoram to 95.1 percent in Himachal Pradesh. This variable was not statistically significant, indicating that a state's religious demographics alone did not boost or limit nationalism.

HOSTILITY TO PAKISTAN

Even before gaining its independence, the subcontinent has been riven with conflict over the Muslim/Hindu divide in Kashmir and along the total length of what is today the Indian/Pakistan border. Public hostility

TABLE 7.3. *Hostility to Pakistan by religious tradition*

Tradition	Mean percent
Hindu	3.51
Muslim	3.07
Christian	3.05
Sikh	3.55
All respondents	3.49

Source: 2010 Spring Pew Global Attitudes survey, India subsample.

toward Pakistan thus seems like a reasonable measure of a specific nationalist issue. As Table 7.3 indicates, most Indians have negative views toward Pakistan; in contrast with abstract nationalism, however, this second indicator shows more variation by religious identification. On the one hand, a typical Muslim or Christian has a "somewhat unfavorable" view of India's northern neighbor. Hindus and Sikhs, on the other hand, generally are midway between "somewhat" and "very unfavorable" in their view of Pakistan. This difference should not obscure the primary finding that Indian Muslims, who are often accused of being a kind of Third Column, are not sympathetic to this Islamic country. Thus, even on this particular nationalistic issue, secular nationalism appears to have had some relative success in overcoming the religious divide.

When one controls for such socioeconomic variables as income, education and gender, however, Table 7.4 documents a starker divide by religion. Here, practitioners of the "non-native" religions of Islam and Christianity are a full point less hostile to Pakistan than are adherents of the "indigenous" traditions of Hinduism and Sikhism. In other words, on a four-point scale, a representative respondent would move from "very unfavorable" in his or her view of Pakistan to merely "somewhat unfavorable."

As in Table 7.2, we estimated the effect of an interaction term between education and religious importance (the sample did not include data on Muslims' attendance), but neither religious importance itself nor the interaction achieves statistical significance. Finally, we looked at the effect of religious importance within each religious tradition, but this analysis also failed to produce any significant results. Such findings may suggest that Indians are not being politically mobilized around the Kashmir or Pakistan question the way they appear to be for abstract nationalism.

TABLE 7.4. *Religious and other determinants of hostility to Pakistan*

Variable	Coefficient	Standard error
Muslim	−1.030[*]	0.214
Christian	−1.032[*]	0.354
Sikh	0.135	0.372
Religion importance	0.039	0.065
Education	−0.048	0.043
Income	−0.061[*]	0.023
Woman	−0.128	0.095
Age	0.000	0.004
Constant 1	−4.103[*]	0.394
Constant 2	−2.825[*]	0.383
Constant 3	−1.594[*]	0.379
N	2018	
Nagelkerke R^2	0.025	

[*]Denotes an effect that is significantly different from 0 at the 5 percent level for ordinal Logit model.
Notes: All regressors are dummy variables except for Religion Importance (range = 1–4), Education (1–8), Income (1–16), and Age (18–84).
Source: 2010 Spring Pew Global Attitudes survey, India subsample.

RELIGION AND NATIONALISM IN RELIGIOUS PUBLICATIONS AND PRIME MINISTER SPEECHES

Our public opinion findings partially reinforce our argument about the divisive nature of India's secular nationalism. In order to determine whether schisms also prevail at the elite level, we conducted a content analysis of religious periodicals and official statements for the country's main religious traditions: Hindu nationalist, Moderate Hindu, Muslim, Christian, and Sikh. For each group we identified a representative publication for the tradition as a whole. Hinduism lacks a formalized leadership acceptable to all believers. Consequently, there is no single group that commands universal acceptance. The largest and most politically significant of the various Hindu nationalist organizations, however, is the RSS. The RSS is widely regarded as the parent organization of the BJP and is more moderate than nationalist counterpart organizations like Shiv Sena and the Vishva Hindu Parishad. Identifying a mainstream Hindu organization proved to be problematic. There is no equivalent among moderate Hindus to the RSS. Those organizations that do exist tend to be geographically defined, associated with a particular religious leader, and don't claim to speak for the nation as a whole. In lieu of a strictly religious publication for moderate Hinduism, we selected *The Hindu,* which is one of the largest newspapers in India. We believe that the publications in this newspaper broadly reflect the views of the Hindu community that is not affiliated with the RSS.

For the Indian Muslim community, we identified the *Muslim Mirror* which "highlights problems, issues and viewpoints of the Muslim community" (*Muslim Mirror*). Roman Catholicism is the largest Christian denomination in India. For the representative organization for Catholics we chose publications from the Union of Catholic Asian News India (UCAN) which "provides reliable up-to-date news report and commentary on issues affecting the Church in Asia" (Union of Catholic Asian News). Finally, for the Sikh community we chose publications from Panthic.org, whose goal is "to provide accurate Panthic oriented news and analysis to our worldwide audience" (Panthic.org).

An advantage of the groups and organizations we selected is that each has an online searchable archive of editorials, articles, and commentaries. We located the relevant texts within each webpage using a search for at least the words or phrases "secular" and "secular nation" in all issues for as long a time frame as possible. The searches were done in English or Hindi, based on the language of the relevant documents. The specific time frames were: RSS (2011–16), *The Hindu* (2012–16), *Muslim Mirror* (2013–16), UCAN (2014–16), and Panthic.org (2009–16). We read each of the appropriate documents and coded them on whether they favored secular nationalism, opposed secular nationalism, or were neutral between these opposing perspectives.

Figure 7.1 summarizes the results of our content analysis of the various publications. The results confirm the deeply contested nature of Indian nationalism among different religious groups. The RSS overwhelmingly opposes secular nationalism, while religious minorities (Christian and Muslim) favor it. One RSS document derides "sham secularism" and argues that "anyone who is national in this country, irrespective of ... his creed or mode of worship, is a Hindu" (Rashtriya Swayamsevak Sangh 2012). In this reading, Hinduism is as much a race as a religion, but in any case this document rejects civic nationalism based on secular norms and values. At the other end of the spectrum is a document from the *Muslim Mirror* which quotes a speech delivered by Arshad Madani, the President of one of the leading Islamic organizations in India, the Jamiat Ulema-I-Hind. The article reports that Madani opposes "Muslim political parties" and urges the Islamic community to "join or support secular

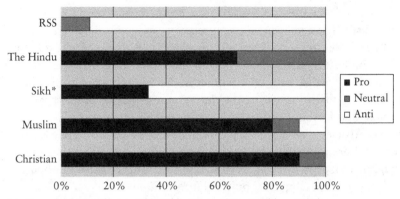

*Anti-secular nationalism in Sikh publications advocate Sikh nationalism rather than Hindu nationalism.

FIGURE 7.1. *Attitudes toward secular nationalism in religious periodicals*

national parties" (*Muslim Mirror* 2016). In a similar way, UCAN quotes a Christian leader urging a "strengthening of secular, constitutional democracy in India" (Union of Catholic Asian News 2016).

Publications in *The Hindu* are somewhat more divided. A 2016 editorial penned by Venkaiah Naidu, a prominent member of the BJP, predictably advocated passage of a uniform civil code as an expression of "true secularism" and as a way to "prevent oppression in the name of religion." At the same time, however, Naidu urged a reasonably moderate approach in suggesting that such a bill should only be implemented "when there is widespread acceptance from all religious communities" (Naidu 2016). But, *The Hindu* also published an opinion piece by the editorial board which rejected a key provision for many on the Hindu right, a new law against conversions. The editorial asserted that "any restriction on religious conversions … will amount to a serious violation of the fundamental right to freedom of religion," and that "what is important is that India survives as a secular nation" (*The Hindu* 2015).

The Sikh publications are unstinting in the criticism of the both the BJP and of the Congress Party. One article describes the BJP as a "fanatical Hindu party [that] wants to suppress all other religions," while it asserts that the Congress Party is "no better than the BJP" (Panthic.org 2006). Many of those documents also affirm secular norms as the basis for Indian nationalism. However, many others promote Sikh independence and, by implication, the idea that the Sikh nation ought to be defined by a shared history and values, including religious values. The same article that firmly rejected both the BJP and the Congress Party presents the Sikh population as a "distinct and indigenous socio-religious and political entity."

In addition to measuring attitudes toward generic nationalism in religious publications, we also assessed what those documents said about the specific nationalist issue of Kashmir. As we noted earlier in the chapter, Hindu nationalists opposed the autonomous political status granted to Jammu and Kashmir under Article 370 of the Constitution. The abrogation of Article 370 is a central part of the party's ideology. While Kashmiri Muslims are at times portrayed as fifth columnist doing Pakistan's bidding, there is very little support among the majority Muslim population in Jammu and Kashmir for political integration into Pakistan. What does garner more support, and is the cause for a good deal of violence, is political independence for Kashmir. In order to measure attitudes toward this nationalist cause, we analyzed each of five publications using the search term "Kashmir" for the same time frame as we utilized in the generic nationalism search. We coded each article as promoting the idea that Kashmir is and always will be part of India (pro-India), as supporting the idea that the status of Kashmir is and should be up for political debate (disputed), or neutral between those opposing positions. As there were more than 200 results in our search of *The Hindu,* we read and coded every ten articles as a representative random sample of the whole.

The results of this analysis confirm the religious divide that we identified on the generic nationalism question (see Figure 7.2). Not surprisingly, each of the articles that referenced the Kashmir dispute on the RSS website promoted the idea that Kashmir is a part of the Indian nation. A 2015 publication, for example, reprinted a 1967 interview with the Hindu nationalist and one-time supreme leader of the RSS, M. S. Golwalker. In that interview, Golwalker argued that "we must keep Kashmir," that "Article 370 must go," and Golwalker asserted that the only goal was the "complete integration" of Kashmir with the rest of India (Rashtriya Swayamsevak Sangh 2015). The current chief of the organization, Mohan Madhukar Bhagawat, reconfirmed this commitment in a 2016 address where he stated: "There should not be any compromise whatsoever on the principle that the whole of Kashmir, including Mirpur, Muzzafarabad, Gilgit and Baltistan, is an inseparable and integral part of Bharat [India]." He also urged the political leaders of the state of Jammu and Kashmir to "act with a nationalistic feeling" (Rashtriya Swayamsevak Sangh 2016).

There is not a sizeable Sikh or Christian population in Jammu and Kashmir, and the articles from those religious traditions show more of

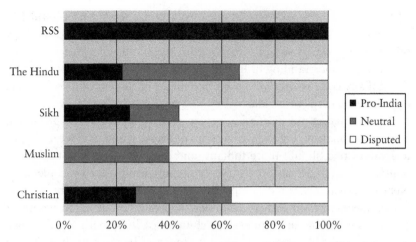

FIGURE 7.2. *Attitudes toward Kashmir in religious periodicals*

a division than in the RSS publications. By and large, however, the Sikh articles interpret the Kashmiri conflict through the lens of their own separatist inclination. One article, as an example, argued for a "right of self-determination" (Panthic.org 2009) for Kashmiris, a position which is consistent with their own views about Sikh autonomy for Punjab. The Muslim publications are more inclined than those of any other religious group to see the Kashmir issue as disputed. However, not a single article that we read promoted the idea that Kashmir, a majority of whose population is Muslim, belongs to Pakistan. Instead, most articles from the *Muslim Mirror* highlight the mistakes made by both Pakistan and India and argue in favor of self-determination for the region. A 2016 editorial noted that it is the Kashmiris who are "at the center of this quagmire" and their only hope is "that a plebiscite will be held one day and they will gain independence on their own" (Mujtaba 2016).

There is no searchable database of prime minister or presidential speeches or official proclamations that would have allowed us to do a search of key terms such as "nation" and "secular" among Indian political leaders. Thus, we chose to do a content analysis of representative speeches by selected prime ministers in India's nearly seventy-year history. Specifically, we looked at the speeches of Nehru (1947–64), Indira Gandhi (1966–77; 1980–4), Rajiv Gandhi (1984–9), Atal Bihari Vajpayee (1998–2004), and Narendra Modi (2014–present). The first three were all members of the Congress Party, Vajpayee was the first member of the

BJP to serve as Prime Minister, and Modi is the second successful BJP candidate for that office. In reading the speeches, we tried to see how they used the term "secular" to describe India and what this suggested about their understanding of Indian nationalism. Second, we also wanted to see if any code words were used that might be understood by listeners through a religious or secular nationalist frame.

As we noted in our discussion earlier in this chapter, Nehru promoted secular nationalism, highlighted a series of socialist and democratic political values that should unite Indians, and rejected all forms of religious politics or of Hindu nationalism as "communalism." In a 1947 message, Nehru warned his listeners not to "encourage communalism or narrowmindedness," but instead to understand that "all of us, to whatever religion we belong, are equally the children of India with equal rights, privileges and obligations" (Nehru 1949:336). In his speeches, Nehru frequently juxtaposed a secular nationalism for India (which was capacious) from a religious one (which was limiting). In a 1948 convocation address delivered at the Muslim University at Aligarh, Nehru asked "do we believe in a national State which includes people of all religions and shades of opinion and is essentially secular as a state, or do we believe in the religious, theocratic conception of a State which considers people of other faiths as something beyond the pale?" (Nehru 1949:337). In a 1961 speech he similarly asserted that "communalism is a badge of a backward nation, not of the modern age ... nationalism cannot exist together with communalism" (Nehru 1964:12). For Nehru, religion was divisive and a sign of the past; religion could never be the basis for national identity. Instead, he promoted social and economic progress, along with secular, democratic political values as the basis for Indian national unity. "Let us be clear about our national objective," he said, "we aim at a strong, free and democratic India where every citizen has an equal place and full opportunity of growth and service, where present-day inequalities in wealth and status have ceased to be" (Nehru 1949:333).

Indira Gandhi largely followed the rhetorical example set by her father in articulating a secular nationalist vision for India. In her inaugural Independence Day speech in 1966, Gandhi asserted the core values of socialism, democracy, and the eradication of poverty as the goals for the Indian nation (Gandhi 1971:13). Three years later in her speech at the same occasion, Gandhi advised the nation to "adhere firmly to our traditional policy of secularism" (Gandhi 1975:121). Gandhi also spoke firmly against communalism, which she described in one speech as a "poisonous weed that takes no time to grow" (Gandhi 1975:205). In particular, she attacked Atal Vajpayee, who was at the time a member of Parliament and would become Prime Minister nearly two decades later, for "launch[ing] an attack on Muslims and on all minorities in general" (Gandhi 1975:200). In her view the majority community had a "special responsibility towards the weaker section," and in most places, "the Hindus are the majority" (Gandhi 1975:202).

As we noted earlier in the chapter, Gandhi called a State of Emergency in 1975 that lasted for nearly 21 months. She used the occasion to amend the preamble to the Constitution, changing the description of India from "sovereign democratic republic" to a "sovereign, socialist secular democratic republic." The addition of the words "socialist" and "secular" were certainly consistent with the nationalist values articulated by Nehru, and her inclusion of those words into the Constitution demonstrated a stylistic commitment on Gandhi's part to those ideals. More importantly, however, the process marked a cynical manipulation of those norms for her own political ends. As many people at the time pointed out, for Gandhi to eliminate press freedoms and arrest her political opponents was not consistent with democratic norms. As a consequence, the meaning and application of both democracy and secularism became contested in a new way by Gandhi's actions. Perhaps in recognition of this fact, Gandhi convened a conference of Educators for Secularism, Socialism, and Democracy in September 1975. In her speech at the start of the conference, Gandhi suggested that secularism "is not just a theory, it is a very practical necessity for the future of this country," that there "can be no socialism or any kind of equality if there is not secularism," and Gandhi rejected what she called "few hard core people who could not reconcile themselves to the policy of secularism" (Gandhi 1975:138–40). What Gandhi meant by the "few hard core people" were members of Hindu nationalist right organizations and political parties, although they were hardly the only groups that opposed Gandhi's unilateral declaration of a state of emergency. Whether she intended to or not, Gandhi politicized the term secularism and equated any group or movement who opposed her actions as guilty of the sin of communalism. She also became more willing with time to adopt the majoritarian discourse of her Hindu right opponents in order to win votes.

The tone does not change much in the speeches given by her son, Rajiv Gandhi during his tenure as Prime Minister from 1984 to 1989. Like his mother and grandfather, Rajiv Gandhi railed against what he described as "religious fanaticism" that would "tear this country apart" (Gandhi 1989:30). On a speech commemorating the fortieth anniversary of India's independence, Gandhi contended that "our secularism must reinforce respect for all communities with the strict separation of religion from politics" (Gandhi 1989:66). In one speech he intoned that "most important is that we must separate religion and politics" (Gandhi 1989:32). He also advanced a list of ideals similar to those of his grandfather when he noted that "the Indian Revolution stands for truth and non-violence, for the purity of means to achieve noble ends; for the dissolution of all barriers which separate human being from human being, all barriers of religion or race, caste, creed or gender" (Gandhi 1989:65). However, like his mother Indira, Rajiv also politicized religion for his own ends. In one speech he asserted that the "recent rise of fundamentalism – Hindu, Muslim, Sikh – remains a challenge to the basic tenets of Indian nationalism" (Gandhi 1989:94), thereby playing the very communal card that he supposedly was trying to overcome. In short, both Indira and Rajiv Gandhi continued to use the term secularism to describe Indian nationalism, but they also politicized the term in a new and destabilizing way.

The tone, if not always the words, changed with the election of BJP Prime Minister Atal Vajpayee (1998–2004). He was no less likely to use the word "secular" to describe Indian nationalism as his Congress predecessors. In his Independence Day Speech in 2000, Vajpayee pointed to India's bright future so long as "we are able to further strengthen our national unity, secularism, social goodwill, and democratic system" (Vajpayee 2002:14). But, Vajpayee redefined secularism as a Hindu religious concept, and in doing so he presented Hinduism as a source of national unity. In a 1988 address to the nation, Vajpayee said "ours is an ancient civilization … It has been built on an active and deep respect for the faiths and practices of all." He then quoted a famous Hindu prayer "just as drops of rain falling on varied places, all gather in streams and flow to the one sea, so all worship leads to the same Deity … In the Indian perspective, this is the only valid meaning of secularism" (Vajpayee 2000:6). The "valid meaning of secularism," in short, was one deeply wedded to a particular reading of the Hindu religious tradition.

Vajpayee also rejected the way that Nehru, Indira, and Rajiv Gandhi presented secular and religious nationalism as opposing ideals. In a 2002 New Year's Eve speech to the nation, the Prime Minister lamented that "secularism is being pitted against Hindutva, under the belief that the two are antithetical to one another. This is incorrect and untenable." It was incorrect, in his view, because "Hinduisms acceptance of the diversity of faiths is the central feature of secularism in India," and because "Hindutva is liberal, liberating and brooks no ill will, hatred or violence among different communities on any ground" (Former Prime Minister of India Speeches a). Implicit in his words was the suggestion that not all faiths were as tolerant as was Hinduism. Vajpayee more explicitly made this point in a speech he delivered shortly after the religious violence in Gujarat that killed 790 Muslims and 254 Hindus. The developments were "condemnable," he intoned, but he asked "who lit the fire? How did the fire spread?" In answer to his own question, Vajpayee suggested that "India was secular even when Muslims hadn't come here and Christians hadn't set foot on this soil. It is not as if India became secular after they came ... No one thought of converting them by force, because this is not practiced in our religion, and in our culture, there is no use for it" (Former Prime Minister Speeches b). India is secular, Vajpayee suggests, because of our Hinduism, not in spite of it. The real threat to that secular tradition is from Islam and Christianity which are not as naturally tolerant and pluralistic as is Hinduism. While the narrative changes are at times subtle, the new emphasis on Hinduism as the basis for India's nationalism is inescapable in Vajpayee's speeches.

Prime Minister Manmohan Singh (2004–14) marked a return to power for the Congress Party, and a renewed emphasis on India as a secular nation. In his 2010 Independence Day speech, Singh (2010) reaffirmed the value of secularism and contended that it would enable all religions in India to flourish:

Secularism is one of the pillars of our democracy. It has been the tradition of our country and society to treat all religions with equal respect. For centuries India has welcomed new religions and all have flourished here.

A few years earlier he made the crucial point that secularism did not mean the negation of religion. In that speech (Singh 2008a) Singh described the country's founders as "truly secular, even as they remained deeply religious," thereby undermining the implicit claim of the BJP that one could not be both secular and religious. Nor was he as he willing as were Indira and Rajiv Gandhi to coopt Hindu political sensibilities for electoral ends. Singh gave a speech in the Lok Sabha shortly after the 2008 attacks on Mumbai by Islamic terrorists that killed 164 people. In an emotionally charged context where he might have defined the attack in religious terms, Singh instead said that "the forces behind these attacks wanted to destabilize our secular polity, create communal discord and undermine our country's economic and social progress" (Singh 2008b). In short, Singh used the attack to reinforce the importance of India's secular polity and nationalism.

As Chief Minister of Gujarat (2001–14), Narendra Modi's early speeches were "peppered with controversial references" that played to Hindu sensibilities (Jaffrelot 2016b). In a 2013 campaign speech (Modi 2013) to become Prime Minister for the BJP, Modi cleverly ridiculed his Congress opposition for their use of the term "secularism":

Friends, it seems that in our nation if you want to get rid of all the sins, crimes, responsibilities and accountability then a few people have found a herb that prevents them from all of it. And that herb is – Secularism … ! Just start talking on secularism and all your sins are taken away … !

In those few words he called attention to the fact that some leaders of the Congress Party had used the term "secularism" for political ends, and he undermined the very idea that secular nationalism was the basis of Indian national identity. Later in the speech he posed a challenge to his opponents: "Instead of weighing everything on the scale of secularism, accept my challenge if they can. Friends, what is our thinking? Our mantra is, that the government has no religion but one – India first, nation first" (Modi 2013). In a clever turn of phrase, in short, Modi presented secular nationalism as divisive, rather than unifying, and India first (whatever that meant) as the point of unity.

When he became Prime Minister (2014–present), however, Modi's speeches focused primarily on issues of good governance and economic development. Nonetheless, Modi has been willing to use discourse that promotes Hindu religious nationalism. His 2016 Independence Day speech, for example, notes that "India is an ancient nation. We have a history and cultural heritage of thousands of years" (Modi 2016). This relatively benign affirmation of national distinctiveness takes on a slightly different meaning when Modi offers some examples for India's unique cultural heritage: "From Vedas to Vivekananda, from Upanishads to satellites, from Lord Krishna to Mahatma Gandhi, and from Bhima of Mahabharata to Bhim Rao; we have a long historic journey and heritage" (Modi 2016). In short, Modi defines India's cultural distinctiveness by referring to Hindu scriptures (Vedas), a Hindu deity (Lord Krishna), a Hindu monk (Vivekananda), Hindu philosophy (Upanishads), a Hindu epic tale (Bhima of Mahabharata), and a Hindu reformer (Gandhi). In a speech he delivered later that year on Dussera, a Hindu festival, Modi opened and closed his address with the words (repeated five times at the end) "Jai Sri Ram" (Hail Lord Ram). The slogan was coined by BJP leaders at the time of the campaign for the construction of a Ram temple at the site of the Babri mosque in Ayodha. It was hard not to read Modi's use of the term as an attempt to mobilize on religious grounds by asserting a form of Hindu nationalism (Munshi 2016). Finally, Modi's appointment of Yogi Adityanath, a Hindu nationalist hardliner, as the Chief Minister of the country's most populous state, Uttar Pradesh, suggests that India's Prime Minister is even more openly embracing Hindu nationalism (Bal 2017).

CONCLUSION

Indian nationalism stands at a crossroads. The founders of the country, particularly from the dominant Congress Party, wrote a largely secular Constitution and they sought to identify a set of civic values that would unite Indians across religious traditions. The Partition of Pakistan on religious grounds and the subsequent communal violence solidified their concerns about the destabilizing effects of a religiously based nationalism. But this secular nationalism was always unstable. The model was more or less imposed from above on an Indian population that was and remains deeply religious. While the Constitution was largely secular, there were various provisions dealing with religion that were unresolved, and this kept religious issues at the forefront of politics. The subsequent failure of the Nehru–Gandhi political dynasty to deliver on their electoral promises and their own playing of the communal card in electoral politics undermined the appeal of secular nationalism and opened a space for a more overt political mobilization along religious lines. The BJP is the latest and most successful of the Hindu nationalist parties to have questioned the validity of India's secular nationalism as Nehru and other founders of the Indian state understood it. The party explicitly appeals to the Hindu majority on such issues as the construction of Hindu temples on Islamic holy sites, anticonversion laws, cow protection, the content of the country's history, and the singing of *Vande Mataram*. Finally, periodic conflict with Pakistan acts to reinforce the significance of the religious divide in India, solidifying an insider/outsider dichotomy that implicitly questions the patriotic bona fides of religious minorities. Secular nationalism is hardly dead in India, but it clearly is on the decline.

The rise of religiously based political movements that has been threatening India's secular-nationalist model is almost entirely absent in Uruguay. The Uruguayan population is much less religiously practicing, there is little electoral motivation for mobilizing along religious lines, and no external threat reinforces the nation's religious identity. Lacking those variables which are all-too-prevalent in India, Uruguay has enjoyed almost two centuries of stable secular or near-secular nationalism.

8

Pitfalls and Opportunities on the Religious
Path to Nationalism

A key finding in our book is that there are multiple religious-nationalist models; what matters crucially in the emergence of religious nationalism, secular nationalism, and civil-religious nationalism are the combination of variables unique to each case. In our view the main factors in this process are a country's religious demographics, whether religious groups support or oppose the nationalist frame emerging at the point of state formation, and the institutional links created between religion and the state in the country's Basic Law or Constitution.

Founding stories and institutions matter a lot in this process. As Rogers Smith (2003) has argued, political groups need narratives of meaning, stories that give shape and direction to the collective yearnings of a country and its people. Nationalism is one of the most important tales that people tell about themselves. For many countries, those founding narratives involve some role for religious groups. American school children learn that the pursuit of religious freedom compelled the Pilgrims to come to our shores, every Indian school child knows that Gandhi was a deeply religious Hindu who had the honorific religious title of Mahatma, and children in Greece learn that Orthodox priests fought and died for the cause of independence from the Ottoman Empire. Of course, the founding stories of these countries are more complex than told, they often involve a long of train of abuses against various groups, and they tend to ignore some of the more painful aspects of that process. But the point is that those stories are told, taught, and retold in a way that reinforces their power and truth. Short of a political revolution, there is no way to relive a country's founding, and so it creates a powerful process shaping a nation's official narrative going forward. Jesus might have commanded Nicodemus to be born again, but there is no second birth for nations.

Founding institutions are also vitally important for religious nationalism, secular nationalism, and civil-religious nationalism. While many have tried, it is hard to make a religious nationalist case in the United States because the First Amendment guarantees religious free exercise rights for all, while the ban on an established religion places constraints on how far the state can go to benefit a particular religion. Christian religious nationalists have consistently arisen in American history, but their tortured interpretations of the Constitution have simply not prevailed. Israel is a more complex case as its de facto Basic Law promotes the idea of Israel as simultaneously a Jewish and a democratic state. Not surprisingly, therefore, the debate on the role of religion in its nationalism often comes down to which of the founding values is most important to national self-identity.

The same important role for institutions matters in places as diverse as Greece and Malaysia, both of which fit our model of religious nationalism. In each case, the Constitution explicitly recognizes a religious tradition and accords it benefits not automatically guaranteed to other faith traditions. In Greece, this has meant that orthodox religious leaders can and have made the argument that they should control the content of religious education, while in Malaysia it has led religious and political leaders to press the claim that an officially Islamic state should advance Islamic religious values. Absent those provisions of their respective constitutions, it would be harder to make that case. The secular constitutions of Uruguay and India, by contrast, place limits on how far religious groups can claim particular privileges from the state. Of course, religious and political leaders in India have done just that, but they have had to do so within the parameters of a rhetorical commitment to secular nationalism. While it might not seem much of a constraint for the Bharatiya Janata Party to use the language of secularism to try to undermine it, they are at least compelled by the logic of the Indian Constitution to debate on the terms of secularism itself. Founding stories and institutions, while not determinative of future outcomes, nonetheless provide guardrails that shape politics.

As important as founding stories and institutions are in the creation and sustenance of a nationalist model, they are not entirely predictive for how a country's nationalism will develop in the future. If the underlying conditions change enough, a country can come to adopt a different model. The instability of India's secular nationalism has much to do with the contrast between a secular narrative and a deeply religious population at the time of the country's founding. Challenges to that model over time, including periodic conflict with Muslim-majority Pakistan and the political appeal of mobilization along religious lines have further threatened the original model. It is possible to imagine a scenario in which India will develop a fully formed religious nationalism. America's civil-religious nationalism is largely stable in our view, but it is not inherently so. The essential demographics in the United States are changing. The secular percentage of the population is growing, particularly among younger Americans, and as we saw in the country chapter, nonreligious respondents are less likely to embrace a religious foundation for American governance. Moreover, the increasing polarization of the two major parties by religiosity is historically unique. While parties have always been divided by religious tradition, they have both included substantial numbers of religious believers, and in that context both could affirm the country's civil-religion. That may not be true in the future.

We also conclude that none of the three models is inherently stable or unstable. Instead, we find that there are stable and unstable forms of religious nationalism, secular nationalism, and civil-religious nationalism. These twin results suggest that it is misguided to presume that a model that works or well in one country would necessarily function in the same way in a very different context. There is often a presumption that secular nationalism is morally and politically preferable because it separates religious and national identity, thus both privatizing and depoliticizing religion. But this model only works if the underlying conditions support it. Secular nationalism is stable in Uruguay largely because religion was relatively weak at the founding and was therefore not a source of national identity. That model has remained stable over time as Uruguay has become both more secular and more religiously pluralistic, conditions that have reinforced the original model. But it is naïve and potentially dangerous to presume that the Uruguayan model applies in very different contexts, where civil peace is less likely to be won by ignoring religion than by openly recognizing its significance. India is a cautionary reminder that the attempt to impose secular nationalism (even one that promoted religious freedom for all) on a highly religious population is unlikely to succeed in the long run, at both a normative and a political level. Far from depoliticizing religion, the attempt to decouple religion from national identity in India has ironically encouraged political mobilization along religious lines.

It stands to reason that religion will be a source of these national political narratives in countries that are highly religious. While it might be fashionable in some circles to roll one's eyes at the "God talk" inherent in civil-religious or religious nationalism, such discourse is not inherently destabilizing. In fact, under the right conditions it can be quite the opposite – unifying. At its best, American civil-religion can learn to adapt to religious traditions that it might initially have shunned. Those religious newcomers thus can define themselves into that civic religious tradition. The same can also be true in a country with religious nationalism as part of its narrative frame. Greece affirms religious and democratic values in its constitution and in its nationalism, a marriage that can create a unifying discourse for the vast majority of the Greek population who embrace those twin values.

By the same token, we are well aware that each of the three models is susceptible to challenges unique to each case. The obvious danger of religious nationalism is that it implicitly questions the place and status of persons outside of the religious majority. These countries are marked by a Constitution or Basic Law that accords a special status, and often a set of privileges, to the recognized religion. These provisions often lead religious elites to advance their particularistic claims to the state using the provisions of the Constitution, while political elites mobilize voters along religious lines for electoral ends. Greece represents our model stable religious nationalism, but that stability is threatened when Orthodox leaders suggest that the religious rights of Muslims and other religious minorities should not be recognized. That challenge will become paramount as Greece becomes more secular and more religiously pluralistic.

Secular nationalism poses an entirely different set of potential problems. In certain contexts, an aggressive form of secular nationalism serves as an ersatz religion, which in turn muffles all competitors, and in particular religious groups and claims. For some, a French style *laïcité* demands the removal of religion from all public spheres, which in turn denies fundamental rights to deeply religious persons. Yet the elimination of religion from public life is not compatible with democratic values, and it ignores the reality that religious people will seek a nationalist language that comports with their spiritual worldview. Even a softer form of secular nationalism, like that in India, can be seen as advancing the claim that religion has no role to play in shaping the country's national identity. There is much to commend in an Indian-style secularism which seeks to enable all religions to prosper, but even it runs the danger of negating a religious idiom that speaks to the aspirations of the Indian people.

Civil-religious nationalism, finally, always faces the challenge of how to enfold new religious groups into the national narrative. The demonization of Muslims by President Trump is the latest in a series of examples in which a political leader has narrowly construed the groups that properly belong in the American narrative. His divisive rhetoric threatens to undermine the unifying potential of American civil-religion in favor of a particularistic brand of Judeo–Christian religious nationalism. Civil-religion in Israel has similarly found it difficult to embrace the disparate groups that have been and are part of the Zionist project (Haredi Leumi, Reformed, National Religious, Secular), not to mention the growing percentage of the population of Israel that is not Jewish (Muslim and Christian).

What seems to be a constant in each model is that the greatest threat to stability comes from an electoral, partisan mobilization along religious lines. Civil-religious and religious nationalist regimes are undermined when religious leaders of a given tradition preach that support for a particular party violates the tenets of that religion or represents disloyalty to the nation. When it suits their purposes, political leaders are very willing to advance the same divisive narrative. So too, secular nationalism runs the risk of instability when party leaders assert that religious considerations have no place in public discourse or in public policy, or that loyalty to the nation supersedes fidelity to one's faith.

Religion remains enormously influential in the formation of communal identities throughout most of the world, and nationalist ideologies will likely continue to draw on religious symbols and ideas for moral and political legitimacy. Perhaps the more achievable goal is for political and spiritual leaders to seek the most humane or generous interpretation of their particular religious traditions instead of emphasizing narrow, ethnocentric interpretations of their faith. As Nandy perceptively notes (1989:292) "the opposite of religious and ethnic intolerance is not secularism, but religious and ethnic tolerance." Fortunately, the world's major religious traditions have rich histories, multiple interpretations of how believers should interact with the nation, and a reservoir of resources that can be accessed for such a purpose. Modi and Gandhi count as believing Hindus, but religious minorities in India would hope that the latter's view of Hinduism prevails in public policy and in the definition of Indian nationalism. Franklin Graham and Martin Luther King, Jr. are both recognized as Christians, but King's vision provides a more stable foundation for America's civil-religion. Osama bin Laden and Badshah Khan, Gandhi's close Muslim ally in the struggle against the British Empire, read the same Quran but came to radically different conclusions about the morality of political violence. In each case, the former offers a narrow religious perspective while the latter provides a more all-encompassing one.

With the exception of Uruguay, each of the countries of our study has experienced the rise of a significant political movement, party, or populist leader that allies itself with a religious majority. We have noted how this can be destabilizing for a country's nationalist narrative and how it harms religious minorities. What is equally true, but less noted, is how this mobilization damages religion in general, including the dominant tradition. As Tocqueville (1945[1830]: chapter 17) noted nearly two centuries ago, "the church cannot share the temporal power of the state without being the object of a portion of that animosity which the latter excites." Not only does the conjoining of temporal and religious power alienate people from religion, but it also threatens to pervert the religion. Political leaders might cynically speak the language of Christian, Muslim, Hindu, Jewish, or Buddhist values but have little or no regard for the true meaning of the faith they claim to represent.

The inevitable consequence of this commingling is the decline of faith. In just over two decades, the percentage of Americans who have rejected any religious identity has more than doubled (from 12 to 26 percent between 1996 and 2016). This trend is particularly pronounced among millennials, 35 percent of whom have abandoned all religious affiliation. A principal cause of this dramatic shift appears to have been the conclusion among young people that the American church is synonymous with a retrograde form of intolerant politics.

Religious groups are better served to recapture the prenationalist narratives that launched their traditions. Each faith contains a prophetic heritage which calls into question the actions of rulers, even when those leaders speak in the name of the faith. The seductions of the political world and the marrying of religion and nationalism are real enough even for spiritual authorities to sacrifice the long-term interest of their faith community for the short-term pleasures of political influence. Religion is at its prophetic best when it nurtures a respectful, but healthy skepticism about earthly concerns, including nationalism.

Bibliography

Abulof, Uriel. 2014. "The Roles of Religion in National Legitimation: Judaism and Zionism's Elusive Quest for Legitimacy." *Journal for the Scientific Study of Religion* 53(3):515–33.

Acevedo, Pablo Blanco. 1936. *El gobierno colonial en el Uruguay y los orígenes de la nacionalidad*, 2nd edn, Vol. I. Montevideo: no publisher listed.

Acts of Convention of the Episcopal Church. 2003. "Urge Church Members to Study Just War Theory and Criteria." www.episcopalarchives.org/cgibin/acts/acts_resolution.pl?resolution=2003-A033 (accessed October 15, 2014).

2006. "Oppose the War in Iraq and Support Nonviolent Means to Ending Conflict." www.episcopalarchives.org/cgibin/acts/acts_search.pl (accessed October 14, 2014).

Adams, John. 1856. The Works of John Adams, Second President of the United States: With a Life of the Author, Notes and Illustrations, by his Grandson Charles Francis Adams. Boston: Little, Brown and Co. 10 volumes. Vol. 9. Chapter: To Benjamin Rush. http://oll.libertyfund.org/title/2107/161463 on 2014-02-19 (accessed June 12, 2016).

1799. "Proclamation – Recommending a National Day of Humiliation, Fasting, and Prayer." March 6. www.presidency. ucsb.edu/ws/index.php?pid=65675 &st= god&st1=nation (accessed February 18, 2015).

Administración Nacional de Educación Pública. 2016. "25 de agosto de 1825: Declaratoria de la Independencia." *Montevideo: Uruguay Educa.* www .uruguayeduca.edu.uy/Userfiles/P0001/File/LEYES_DE_INDEPENDENCIA .pdf (accessed August 23, 2016).

Advani, L. K. 2004. "Presidential Speech by Shri L. K. Advani." www.bjp.org/en/media-resources/speeches/presidential-speech-by-shri-l-k-advani1 (accessed August 26, 2016).

Afzal, M. Rafique. 2013. *A History of the All-India Muslim League, 1906–1947.* Karachi: Oxford University Press.

Agiesta, Jennifer. 2015. "Misperceptions Persist about Obama's Faith, But aren't so Widespread." www.cnn.com/2015/09/13/politics/barack-obama-religion-christian-misperceptions/index.html (accessed January 3, 2018).

Akhil Bharatiya Pratinidhi Sabha (ABPS). 2001. "Cow Protection." www.archivesofrss
.org/Resolutions.aspx (accessed September 6, 2016).

2005. "Declining Hindu Population – Call to Religious and Social Leaders."
www.archivesofrss.org/Resolutions.aspx (accessed September 6, 2016).

Alam, Anwar. 2002. "Secularism in India: A Critique of Current Discourse."
Pp. 85–117 in Brass, Paul R. and Achin Vanaik, eds., *Competing Nationalisms
in Asia: Essays for Asghar Ali Engineer*. New Delhi: Orient Longman.

Albarran Puente, Glicerio. 1953. *El Pensamiento de José Enrique Rodó*. Madrid:
Ediciones Cultura Hispana.

Ali, Mohammad. 2015. "Produce 4 Kids to Protect Hinduism: Sakshi Maharaj." *The
Hindu*, January 7. www.thehindu.com/news/national/sakshi-stokes-another-
controversy-asks-hindus-to-have-4-kids/article6763837.ece (accessed August
26, 2016).

Alisky, Marvin. 1969. *Uruguay: A Contemporary Survey*. New York: Praeger.

Altunaş, Nezahat. 2010. "Religious Nationalism in a New Era: A Perspective
from Political Islam. *African and Asian Studies* 9:418–35.

Alvariza Allende, Rafael, and Jonatán Cruz Ángeles. 2014. "Secularización, laicismo y reformas liberals en Uruguay." *Revista de Estudios Jurídicos* 14
(second period):1–16.

American Jewish Historical Society. Executive Committee. 1906. *The Two
Hundred and Fiftieth Anniversary of the Settlement of the Jews in the United
States: Addresses Delivered at Carnegie Hall, New York on Thanksgiving
Day 1905, Together with other Selected Addresses and Proceedings*. New
York: New York Cooperative Society.

Amnesty International. 2017. "Malaysia: Continued Persecution of Anwar Ibrahim
Symbolizes Crackdown on Human Rights." Press release, February 10. www
.amnesty.org/en/latest/ news/2017/02/malaysia-continued-persecution-of-anwar
-ibrahim-symbolizes-crackdown-on-human-rights/ (accessed August 3, 2017).

Anbinder, Tyler. 1992. *Nativism and Slavery: The Northern Know Nothings and
the Politics of the 1850s*. Oxford: Oxford University Press.

Andaya, Barbara Watson, and Leonard Y. Andaya. 2001. *A History of Malaysia*,
2nd edn. Honolulu: University of Hawai'i Press.

2017. *A History of Malaysia*, 3rd edn. New York: Palgrave Macmillan.

Anderson, Benedict. 1983. *Imagined Communities: Reflections on the Origin and
Spread of Nationalism*. London: Verso.

Annavarapu, Sneha. 2015. "Religious Nationalism in a Global Age: The Case of
Hindu Nationalism." *Journal of Developing Societies* 31(1):125–46.

Annuar, Amalina. 2016. "An Enlightment for Syed Saddiq." Portal Islam&Melayu,
July 1. www.ismaweb.net/2016/07/enlightment-syed-saddiq/ (accessed September
20, 2017).

Antuña, Hugo. 1948. *La Palabra de Hugo Antuña: Conferencias y Discursos*.
Juan Vicente Chiarino and Numa Mangado, eds. Montevideo: A Barreiro y
Ramos.

Ardao, Arturo. 1970. *Rodó: Su Americanismo*. Montevideo: Biblioteca de Marcha.

Arena, Domingo. 1939. *Batlle y los problemas sociales en el Uruguay*. Montevideo:
Claudio García.

Arias, Cecilia. 2007. "Laicidad: estado actual de un debate." *Cuadernos de Historia de las Ideas* 8(May):133–50.

Armet, Stephen Louis. 2014. "Education Policy as a Means for Secularization in a Catholic Majority Country: The Case of Uruguay (1877–1932)." PhD dissertation, Sociology. South Bend, IN: Notre Dame University.

Arad, Uzi and Gal Alon. 2006. *Patriotism and Israel's National Security: Herzliya Patriotism Survey 2006.* Herzliya: Institute for Policy and Strategy.

Artigas, José Gervasio. 1813a. "Instrucciones del Año XIII." www.bicentenario .gub.uy/wp-content/uploads/2013/03/Instrucciones-del-a%C3%B1o-XIII-folleto.pdf (accessed March 22, 2016).

      1813b. "Oración inaugural (leída el 5 de abril)." Montevideo: La Biblioteca Artiguista. www.artigas.org.uy/fichas/artigas/artigas_instrucciones_02.html (accessed March 22, 2016).

Arye, Netanel. 2013. "Upon Thy Walls, O Jerusalem." August 11. www.tzohar .org.il/?page_id=15 (accessed August 8, 2016).

Asamblea General [Constituyente Legislativa, 1828–1830]. 1870. *Discusión de la Constitución del Estado Oriental del Uruguay.* Montevideo: Cámara de Representantes.

Asiaín, Carmen. 2014. "Algunas reflexiones sobre la libertad religiosa en el Uruguay." Article, Consorcio Latinoamericano de Libertad Religiosa. www .libertadreligiosa.org/articulos/Libertad_ Religiosa_Uruguay.pdf (accessed February 8, 2016).

Association of Religion Data Archives. 2015. "Religion and State Project." www .thearda. com/ras/ (accessed July 23, 2015).

Av, Menachem. 2009. "A Response to the Expulsion of Jews." June 6. www .mercazharav.org/index.html (accessed August 8, 2016).

Ayoob, Mohammed. 2008. *The Many Faces of Political Islam: Religion and Politics in the Muslim World.* Ann Arbor: The University of Michigan Press.

Baber, Zaheer. 2000. "Religious Nationalism, Violence, and the Hindutva Movement in India." *Dialectical Anthropology* 25:61–76.

Bajpai, Rochana. 2002. "The Conceptual Vocabularies of Secularism and Minority Rights in India." *Journal of Political Ideologies* 7(2):179–97.

Bal, Hartosh Singh. 2017. "India's New Face." *The New York Times,* April 24. www .nytimes.com/2017/04/24/opinion/indias-new-face.html (accessed May 1, 2017).

Banfi-Vique, Analia, Oscar A. Cabrera, Fanny Gómez-Lugo, and Martín Hevia. 2011. "The Politics of Reproductive Health Rights in Uruguay: Why the Presidential Veto to the Right to Abortion is Illegitimate." *Revista de Direito Sanitário [São Paolo]* 12(2):178–205.

Barr, Michael D., and Anantha Raman Govindasamy. 2009. "Hegemony without Conversion: Religious Nationalism in Modern Malaysia." *OCIS, Global Change, Peace and Security* 21(1):1–34.

      2010. "The Islamisation of Malaysia: Religious Nationalism in the Service of Ethnonationalism." *Australian Journal of International Affairs* 64(3):293–311.

Barrionuevo, Alexei. 2009. "Leftist Wins Uruguay Presidential Vote." *The New York Times,* October 29, p. A8. www.nytimes.com/2009/11/30/world/ americas/30uruguay.html (accessed August 25, 2017).

Basdekis, Athanasios. 1977. "Between Partnership and Separation: Relations between Church and State in Greece under the Constitution of 9 June 1975." *Ecumenical Review* 29:52–61.

Baskan, Birol. 2014. "State Secularization and Religious Resurgence: Diverging Fates of Secularism in Turkey and Iran." *Politics and Religion* 27:28–50.

Bauman, Chad M. 2016. "Faith and Foreign Policy in India: Legal Ambiguity, Selective Xenophobia, and Anti-Minority Violence." *The Review of Faith and International Affairs* 14(2):31–9.

Begin, Menachem. 1979. "Highlights of Statement by Prime Minister Begin to Herut Convention, 3 June 1979." http://mfa.gov.il/MFA/ForeignPolicy/MFADocuments/Yearbook4/Pages/18%20Highlights%20of%20statement%20by%20Prime%20Minister%20Begin.aspx (accessed January 23, 2017).

    1982. "Address by Prime Minister Begin on Independence Day." http://mfa.gov.il/MFA/ForeignPolicy/MFADocuments/Yearbook5/Pages/121%20Address%20by%20Prime%20Minister%20Begin%20on%20Independenc.aspx (accessed January 25, 2017).

Bellah, Robert N. 1967. "Civil Religion in America." *Daedalus* 96(Winter):1–21.

    1975. *The Broken Covenant: American Civil Religion in Time of Trial.* New York: The Seabury Press.

Benedetti, Mario. 1966. *Genio y figura de José Enrique Rodó.* Buenos Aires: Editorial Universitaria de Buenos Aires.

Ben-Gurion, David. 1954. *Rebirth and Destiny of Israel,* translated by Mordekhai Nurock. New York: Philosophical Library.

    1987. *Zikhronot [Memoirs],* 6 volumes. Tel Aviv: 'Am 'oved.

Bewes, Wyndham A. 1920. "The Constitution of Uruguay." *Journal of Comparative Legislation and International Law,* 3rd series. 2:60–3.

Bharatiya Janata Party. 2004. "Vision Statement 2004." www.bjp.org/en/documents/vision-document?u=vision-document-2004 (accessed August 26, 2016).

    2009. "Hindutva: The Great Nationalist Ideology." www.bjp.org/index.php?option=com_content&view=article&id=369:hindutva-the-great-nationalist-ideology&Itemid=501 (accessed September 6, 2016).

Bhargava, Rajeev. 2010. *The Promise of India's Secular Democracy.* Oxford: Oxford University Press.

BHMA. 2016. "PM Tsipras and Archbishop Ieronymos visit Agios Efstratios on Friday." October 26th. www.tovima.gr/en/article/?aid=D839615 (accessed August 2, 2017).

Bien, Peter. 2005. "Inventing Greece." *Journal of Modern Greek Studies* 23(2):217–34.

BINA. 2016. "About Bina." www.bina.org.il/en/about-bina/ (accessed August 8, 2016).

Blackstone, Bethany, Hetsuya Matsubayashi, and Elizabeth A. Oldmixon. 2014. "Israeli Attitudes on Synagogue and State." *Religion and Politics* 7(2):122–47.

Bladna. 2016. "Former Defense Minister Moshe Arens: 'The Golan Druze are Abandoning Syrian Identity.'" March 29. www.bladna.co.il/?mod=articles&ID=12659 (accessed August 8, 2016).

Blakkarly, Jami. 2016. "Malaysia's former PM Mahathir Mohamad Unites with Enemy Anwar Ibrahim in bid to oust Najib Razak." *ABC News,* September 9.

www.abc.net.au/news/2016-09-09/mahathir-mohamad-meets-with-enemy-anwar-ibrahim-in-malaysia/7827558 (accessed August 3, 2017).

Blaustein de Kasztan, Edith. 1988. "Centro de Etudios Judaicos: un informe sobre los orígenes, objectivos, investigaciones y organización de nuestro Centro." *Contextos: Revista al tema judío* 1(1):14–19.

Blum, Edward J. 2016. "Slavery and Religion in (Not Just) a Christian Nation." Pp. 25–42 in Sutton, Matthew Avery and Darren Dochuk, eds., *Faith in the New Millennium: The Future of Religion and American Politics*. New York: Oxford University Press.

Bose, Sumantra. 2013. *Challenges to the World's Largest Democracy*. Cambridge: Harvard University Press.

Brading, D. A. 1998. *Marmoreal Olympus: José Enrique Rodó and South American Nationalism*. Working paper no. 47. Cambridge: Centre of Latin American Studies, University of Cambridge.

Brasted, Howard, and Adell Khan. 2007. "Pakistan, the BJP, and the Politics of Identity." Pp. 430–48 in McGuire, John and Ian Copland, eds., *Hindu Nationalism and Governance*. New York: Oxford University Press.

Brena, Valentina. 2011. *Hacia una Plan Nacional contra el Racismo y la Discriminación, Informe Final: Informo Diagnóstico, Mecanismos de Discriminación sobre Religion*. Montevideo: Ministerio de Educación y Cultura, Dirección de Derechos Humanos.

Brownson, Orestes. 1852. *Essays and Reviews Chiefly on Theology, Politics, and Socialism*. New York: D. & J. Sadlier & Company.

Brubaker, Rogers. 2012. "Religion and Nationalism: Four Approaches." *Nations and Nationalism* 18(1):2–20.

Bruce, Steve. 2002. *Politics and Religion*. Cambridge: Cambridge University Press.

Bunge, Frederica M., and Nena Vreeland, eds. 1984. *Malaysia: A Country Study*, 4th edn. Washington, DC: Secretary of the Army.

Byrne, Patricia. 1995. "American Ultramontanism." *Theological Studies* 56(2):301–26.

Byrnes, Timothy A. 2002. "The Challenge of Pluralism: The Catholic Church in Democratic Poland." Pp. 27–44 in Jelen, Ted Gerard and Clyde Wilcox, eds., *Religion and Politics in Comparative Perspective: The One, the Few, the Many*. Cambridge: Cambridge University Press.

Caetano, Gerardo. 2013a. "Laicidad, ciudadanía y política en el Uruguay contemporáneo: matrices y revisiones de una cultura laicista." *Cultura y Religión* 7(1):116–39.

ed. 2013b. *El "Uruguay Laico": Matrices y revisiones (1859–1934)*. Montevideo: Taurus.

Caetano, Gerardo, and Roger Geymonat. 1997. *La secularización uruguaya (1859–1919)*. Montevideo: Taurus.

Capozzola, Christopher. 2008. *Uncle Sam Wants You: World War I and the Making of the Modern American Citizen*. New York: Oxford University Press.

Carlson, John D. 2017. "Losing Our Civil Religion." *Religion and Politics*, September 26. religionandpolitics.org/2017/09/26/losing-our-civil-religion/ (accessed September 28, 2017).

Carey, Patrick W. 2010. *Avery Cardinal Dulles, S.J.: A Model Theologian, 1918–2008.* New York: Paulist Press.

Carreras de Bastos, Laura. 1909. *Acción social de la mujer ante el divorcio absoluto.* Montevideo: La Buena Prensa.

Carrere, Ricardo. 2005. *Pulp Mills: From Monocultures to Industrial Pollution.* Montevideo: World Rainforest Movement.

Carrillo, Héctor. 2013. "How Latin Culture Got More Gay." *New York Times,* May 17, p. A21. www.nytimes.com/2013/05/17/opinion/how-latin-culture-got-more-gay.html (accessed August 25, 2017).

Castellanos, Alfredo R. 1955. *Juan Antonio Lavalleja, libertador del pueblo oriental: ensayo biográfico.* Montevideo: Medina.

Catholic Telegraph. 1835, March 27. "Are Catholics Friends to Civil and Religious Liberty?" p. 4.

  1842, January 12. "A Word in Defense of the Catholics," p. 12.

Cavanaugh, William T. 2011. *Migrations of the Holy: God, State, and the Political Meaning of the Church.* Grand Rapids, MI: William B. Eerdmans Publishing Company.

Cayota, Mario. 2010. "El inicuo destierro de un ilustre ciudadano: José Benito Monterroso." *Cuadernos Franciscanos del Sur,* Serie "Raíces," no. 8. Montevideo: Centro Franciscano de Documentación Histórica. www.issuu.com/centrofranciscano/docs/jos__benito_monterroso?e=2303106/2656670 (accessed April 5, 2016).

  2011. *José Benito Monterroso: El inicuo destierro de un ilustre ciudadano.* Montevideo: Dedos.

Central Board of Jewish Communities in Greece. 2015, October 22. "International Conference 'Centers & Diasporas' in Athens between Judaism and Christian Orthodox Church." https://kis.gr/en/index.php?option=com_content&view=article&id=600:international-conference-centers-a-diasporas-in-athens-between-judaism-and-chrisitian-orthodox-church-&catid=12:2009&Itemid=41 (accessed July 31, 2017).

  2016, July 20. "Announcement on the Pew Survey on European Fears Relevant to Refugee Influx – Greece's Score." https://kis.gr/en/index.php?option=com_content&view=article&id=653:announcement-for-the-pew-survey-on-european-fears-relevant-to-refugee-influx-greeces-scores&catid=9:deltiatypoy&Itemid=32 (accessed July 31, 2017).

  2017, May 3. "KIS Announcement for the Statement of the Metropolitan of Pireaus." https://kis.gr/en/index.php?option=com_content&view=article&id=710:kis-announcement-for-the-statement-of-the-metropolitan-of-piraeus&catid=12:2009&Itemid=41 (accessed July 31, 2017).

Central Intelligence Agency. 1976. "The Outlook for Malaysia." *OPI 122 (National Intelligence Council), Job 91R00884R, Box 5,* National Intelligence Estimate 54-1-76, *Folder 17.* www. history.state.gov/historicaldocuments/frus1969-76ve12/d302 (accessed August 1, 2017).

Cha, Seong Hwan. 2000. "Korean Civil Religion and Modernity." *Social Compass* 47(4):467–85.

Chand, R. B. Lal. 1938. *Self-Abnegation in Politics.* Lahore: The Central Hindu Yuvak Sabha.

Chapp, Christopher B. 2012. *Religious Rhetoric and American Politics: The Endurance of Civil Religion in Electoral Campaigns*. Ithaca, NY: Cornell University Press.

Chatterjee, Partha. 1998. "Secularism and Tolerance." Pp. 344–79 in Bhargava, Rajeev, ed., *Secularism and Its Critics*. New York: Oxford University Press.

Cheah, Book Kheng. 2009. "The Communist Insurgency in Malaysia, 1948–1990: Contesting the Nation-State and Social Change." *New Zealand Journal of Asian Studies* 11(1):132–52.

Chin Peng. 2003. *Alias Chin Peng: My Side of History*. Singapore: Media Masters.

Chiriyankandath, James. 2008. "Creating a Secular State in a Religious Country: The Debate in the Indian Constituent Assembly." *Commonwealth and Comparative Politics* 38(2):1–24.

Christodolous, Archbishop of Athens and All Greece. 2006. "Europe is Losing Its Identity." www.ecclesias.gr/englishnews/print_it.asp?id=461 (accessed July 19, 2017).

Chrysoloras, Nikos. 2004. "Why Orthodoxy? Religion and Nationalism in Greek Political Culture." *Studies in Ethnicity and Nationalism* 4(2):217–34.

Clarín. 2006. "Papeleras: la asamblea resolvió suspender el corte en Gualeguaychú." March 20. www.edant.clarin.com/diario/2006/03/20/um/m-01161943.htm (accessed February 2, 2016).

Clogg, Richard. 2013. *A Concise History of Greece*, 3rd edn. Cambridge: Cambridge University Press.

Código Vida. 2016. www.facebook.com/PeriodicoCodigoVida (accessed September 14, 2016).

Cohen, Naomi W. 2008. *What the Rabbi Said: The Public Discourse of 19th Century American Rabbis*. New York: New York University Press.

Cohen, Asher and Bernard Susser. 1996. "From Accommodation to Decision: Transformations in Israel's Religio-Political Life." *Journal of Church and State* 38(4):817–939.

Cohen, Asher and Jonathan Rynold. 2005. "Social Covenants: The Solution to the Crisis of Religion and State in Israel?" *Journal of Church and State* 47 (3):725–45.

CommonLII. 2017. "Constitution of Malaysia 1957." www.commonlii.org/my/legis/const/ 1957/1.html (accessed July 21, 2017).

Conferencia Episcopal del Uruguay. 2016. "La laicidad como signo de identidad de la cultura uruguaya; Primer foro del Atrio de los Gentiles Montevideo." Iglesiacatolica.org.uy/noticeu/la-laicidad-como-signo-de-identidad-de-la-cultura-uruguaya (accessed September 7, 2016).

Conforti, Yitzhak. 2010. "East and West in Jewish Nationalism: Conflicting Types in the Zionist Vision?" *Nations and Nationalism* 16(2):201–19.

Constituent Assembly [of India]. 1947a. *Debates (Proceedings)*, July 17, vol. 4. http://164.100.47.132/LssNew/cadebatefiles/C17071947.html (accessed July 22, 2016).

　1947b. *Debates (Proceedings)*, July 16, vol. 4. http://164.100.47.132/LssNew/cadebatefiles/C16071947.html (accessed July 12, 2016).

　1947c. *Debates (Proceedings)*, August 14, vol. 5. http://164.100.47.132/LssNew/cadebatefiles/C14081947.html (accessed July 12, 2016).

1948a. *Debates (Proceedings)*, November 24, vol. 7. http://164.100.47.132/ LssNew/cadebatefiles/C24111948.html (accessed July 10, 2016).

1948b. *Debates (Proceedings)*, November 9, vol. 7. http://164.100.47.132/ LssNew/cadebatefiles/C09111948.html (accessed July 10, 2016).

1948c. *Debates (Proceedings)*, December 3, vol. 7. http://164.100.47.132/LssNew/ cadebatefiles/C03121948.html (accessed July 14, 2016).

1948d. *Debates (Proceedings)*, December 27, vol. 7. http://164.100.47.132/ LssNew/cadebatefiles/C27121948.html (accessed July 15, 2016).

1948e. *Debates (Proceedings)*, December 27, vol. 7. http://164.100.47.132/ LssNew/cadebatefiles/C27121948.html (accessed July 15, 2016).

1948f. *Debates (Proceedings)*, November 23, vol. 7. http://164.100.47.132/ LssNew/cadebatefiles/C23111948.html (accessed July 16, 2016).

1949a. *Debates (Proceedings)*, August 26, 1949, vol. IX. http://164.100.47.132/ LssNew/cadebatefiles/C26081949.html (accessed July 21, 2016).

1949b. *Debates (Proceedings)*, August 11, vol. IX. http://164.100.47.132/ LssNew/cadebatefiles/C11081949.html (accessed July 14, 2016).

1949c. *Debates (Proceedings)*, October 14, vol. X. http://164.100.47.132/ LssNew/cadebatefiles/C14101949.html (accessed July 10, 2016).

1949d. *Debates (Proceedings)*, September 14, vol. IX. http://164.100.47.132/ LssNew/cadebatefiles/C14091949.html (accessed July 12, 2016).

1949e. *Debates (Proceedings)*, November 23, vol. XI. http://164.100.47.132/ LssNew/cadebatefiles/C23111949.html (accessed July 15, 2016).

Convención Constituyente [de la República Oriental del Uruguay]. 1918. *Actas de la Comisión de Constitución (1916–1917)*. Montevideo: Imprenta Nacional.

Cooper, Samuel. [1780]1998. "A Sermon Preached on the Day of the Commencement of the Constitution." In *Political Sermons at the American Founding Era, 1730– 1805*, Volume 1, 2nd edn., ed. Ellis Sandoz. Indianapolis, IN: Liberty Fund.

Copland, Ian. 2010. "What's in a Name? India's Tryst with Secularism." *Commonwealth and Comparative Politics* 48(2):123–47.

Corbo, Tomás Sansón. 2011. "La iglesia y el proceso de secularización en el Uruguay moderno (1859–1919)." *Hispania Sacra* 63(127):283–303.

Corti, Anibal. 2011. "La fe no es un asunto público." July 15. www.cclu.org.uy/ news_detail. php?title=La-fe-no-es-un-asunto-publico (accessed September 14, 2016).

Cristi, Marcela, and Lorne L. Dawson. 1996. "Civil Religion in Comparative Perspective: Chile under Pinochet (1973–1989)." *Social Compass* 43(3): 319–338.

Da Costa, Néstor. 2009. "La laicidad uruguaya." *Archives des sciences sociales des religions* 146:137–55.

Da Silveira, Pablo, and Susana Monreal. 2003. *Liberalismo y Jacobismo en el Uruguay Batllista: La polémico entre José E. Rodó y Pedro Díaz*. Montevideo: Taurus.

Dabezies Antía, Pablo. 2009. *No se amolden al tiempo presente: Las relaciones Iglesia-sociedad en los documentos de la Conferencia Eposcopal del Uruguay (1965–1985)*. Montevideo: Observatorio del Sur and Facultad de Teología del Uruguay Mons. Mariano Soler.

Dabilis, Andy. 2012. September 21. "Greece's Muslim Leaders Says Samaras Racist." *Greek Reporter*, www.greece.greekreporter.com/2012/09/21/greeces-muslim-leader-says-samaras-racist/ (accessed July 22, 2017).

Davie, Grace. 1994. *Religion in Britain since 1945: Believing without Belonging.* Oxford: Blackwell.

De Aréchaga, Justino J., ed. 1894. *Código Civil de la República Oriental del Uruguay.* Montevideo: A. Barreiro y Ramos.

Debs, Mira. 2013. "Using Cultural Trauma: Gandhi's Assassination, Pakistan and Secular Nationalism in Post-Independence India." *Nations and Nationalism* 19(4):635–53.

Deccan Chronicle. 2016. "Chant Bharat Mata ki Jai or leave India, Fadnavis' Alleged Remark Sparks Row." www.deccanchronicle.com/nation/current-affairs/030416/maharashtra-cm-faces-heat-for-alleged-bharat-mata-ki-jai-remark.html (accessed July 5, 2016).

DeForrest, Mark Edward. 2003. "An Overview and Evaluation of State Blaine Amendments: Origins, Scope, and First Amendment Concerns." *Harvard Journal of Law & Public Policy* 26(2):551–626.

Democracy Fund Voter Study Group. 2017. "Race, Religion, and Immigration in 2016: How the Debate over American Identity Shaped the Election and What It Means for a Trump Presidency." www.voterstudygroup.org/reports/2016-elections/race-religion-immigration-2016 (accessed August 11, 2017).

Democratic Action Party. 2017. "Our Objectives." www.dapmalaysia.org/en/about-us/vision-mission/our-objectives/ (accessed August 3, 2017).

Department of Statistics Malaysia. 2011. *Population Distribution and Basic Demographic Characteristics 2010.* Kuala Lumpur: Population and Housing Census of Malaysia.

Dhattiwala, Raheel and Michael Biggs. 2012. "The Political Logic of Ethnic Violence: The Anti-Muslim Pogrom in Gujarat, 2002." *Politics and Society* 40(4):483–516.

Dingley, James. 2011. "Sacred Communities: Religion and National Identities." *National Identities* 13(4):389–402.

Dkoor, Jameel. 2000. "Confiscating Lands and Settlements: Concerning Israel's so-called Legal Policy." www.adalah.org/uploads/oldfiles/Public/file/sefer%20katom-zeva.pdf (accessed August 8, 2016).

Doane, William Croswell. 1894. "The Roman Catholic Church and the School Fund." *The North American Review* 158(446):30–44.

Don-Yehiya, Eliezer. 1998. "Zionism in Retro-perspective." *Modern Judaism* 18 (3):267–76.

Douglass, Frederick. 1852. "What to the Slave is the Fourth of July?" http://teachingamericanhistory.org/library/document/what-to-the-slave-is-the-fourth-of-july/ (accessed September 5, 2017).

Dow, Leon Wiener. 2016. "U.S. Jews, You've Given Up on Israel's Liberal Values but Still Proud to Fight for America's?" July 22. www.bina.org.il/en/u-s-jews-youve-given-israels-liberal-values-still-proud-fight-americas/ (accessed August 24, 2016).

Dubbudu, Rakesh. 2015. "India had 58 Communal Incidents per Month in the Last 5 Years & 85% of these Incidents Occurred in Just 8 States." *Factly*, December 1.

https://factly.in/communal-incidents-in-india-statistics-57-communal-incidents-per-month-last-4-years-85-these-incidents-happen-in-8-states/ (accessed August 26, 2016).

Duffield, George. [1784]1998. "A Sermon Preached on a Day of Thanksgiving." In *Political Sermons at the American Founding Era, 1730–1805*, Volume 1, 2nd ed., ed. Ellis Sandoz. Indianapolis, IN: Liberty Fund.

Durkheim, Emile. [1912]2001. *The Elementary Forms of Religious Life, a Study in Religious Sociology*. Oxford: Oxford University Press.

Eastwood, Jonathan and Nikolas Prevalakis. 2010. "Nationalism, Religion, and Secularization: An Opportune Moment for Research." *Review of Religious Literature* 52(1):90–111.

Edmonds, Amy. 2013. "Moral Authority and Authoritarianism: The Catholic Church and the Military Regime in Uruguay." *Journal of Church and State* 56(4):644–69.

El País. 2014. "Uruguay, el país más agnóstico de la región; casi igualan a católicos." April 17. www.elpais.com.uy/informacion/uruguay-pais-mas-agnostico-region.html (accessed February 5, 2016).

Elazar, Daniel J. 1990. "Constitution-Making: The Pre-Eminently Political Act." Pp. 3–27 in Elazar, Daniel J., ed., *Constitutionalism: The Israeli and American Experiences*. Lanham, MD: University Press of America.

Elbaum, Dov. 2015. "Israeli Talmud – Tractate of Independence." April 23. www.bina.org.i./news/articles/talmud-israeli (accessed August 6, 2016).

Ely, Ezra Stiles. [1827]1946. "A Christian Party in Politics." In *American Philosophic Addresses, 1700–1999*, ed., Joseph L. Blau. New York: Columbia University Press.

England, Reverend John. 1837. "Substance of a Discourse." https://babel.hathitrust.org/cgi/pt?id=hvd.ah4eij;view=1up;seq=183 (accessed March 1, 2015).

Espinosa, J. Manuel. 1940. "The Rôle of Catholic Culture in Uruguay." *Catholic Historical Review* 26(1):1–15.

Esponera Cerdán, Alfonso. 1992. *Los Dominicos y la evangelización del Uruguay*. Salamanca: Editorial San Esteban.

Evans, Hiram W. 1924. *The Public School Problem in America: Outlining Fully the Policies and the Program of the Knights of Ku Klux Klan toward the Public School System*. [United States]: K.K.K.

Farmers' Cabinet. 1853, May 26. "Romanism in the United States." Farmers' Cabinet. 51(42):6.

Farooq, Umar. 2016, November 12. "As Greece's Government takes on Orthodox Church over Mosque Construction, Minority Muslims Stand to Benefit." *Los Angeles Times*. www.latimes.com/world/europe/la-fg-greece-muslims-20161112-story.html (accessed July 19, 2017).

Favaro, Edmundo. 1950. *Damaso Antonio Larrañaga: Su vida y su época*. Montevideo: Rex.

Feldman, Miguel. 1989. "La noche de cristal en el Uruguay." *Contextos: Revista al tema judío* 1(4):20–2.

Fernando, Joseph M. 2006. "The Position of Islam in the Constitution of Malaysia." *Journal of Southeast Asian Studies* 37(2):249–66.

Ferrari, Lisa L. 2006. "The Vatican as a Transnational Actor." Pp. 33–50 in Paul Christopher Manuel, Lawrence C. Reardon, and Clyde Wilcox, eds., *The Catholic Church and the Nation-State: Comparative Perspectives.* Washington, DC: Georgetown University Press.

Fetzer, Joel S., and J. Christopher Soper. 2005. *Muslims and the State in Britain, France, and Germany.* Cambridge: Cambridge University Press.

2013. *Confucianism, Democracy, and Human Rights in Taiwan.* Lanham, MD: Lexington Books.

Finke, Roger, and Rodney Stark. 1989. "How the Upstart Sects Won America: 1776–1850." *Journal for the Scientific Study of Religion* 28(1):27–44.

2005. *The Churching of America, 1776–2005: Winners and Losers in Our Religious Economy.* Rutgers, NJ: Rutgers University Press.

Fitzgibbon, Russell H. 1953. "The Political Impact on Religious Development in Uruguay." *Church History* 22(1):21–32.

Flores Mora, Manuel. 1951. "Los secretarios de Artigas." Pp. 237–51 in Edmundo M. Narancio, ed. *Artigas: Estudios publicados en "El Pais" como homenaje al jefe de los Orientales en el centenario de su muerte 1850–1950.* Montevideo: Colombino.

Fokas, Effie. 2009. "Religion in the Greek Public Sphere: Nuancing the Account." *Journal of Modern Greek Studies* 27(2):349–74.

Ford, Gerald R. 1975. "Remarks at the National Prayer Breakfast." www.presidency .ucsb.edu/ws/index.php?pid=5249&st=god&st1=nation (accessed February 18, 2015).

Former Prime Minister of India Speeches. 2002a. "Prime Minister Shri Atal Bihari Vajpayee's musings from Gao: Let us Celebrate – and Strengthen – Our Indianess," December 31, 2002. http://archivepmo.nic.in/abv/speech-details .php?nodeid=9133 (accessed January 5, 2017).

2002b "English text of the speech, delivered in Hindi, by Prime Minister Shir Atal Vajpayee at a public meeting in Gao," April 12, 2002. http://archivepmo .nic.in/abv/speech-details.php?nodeid=9017 (accessed January 5, 2017).

Fox, Jonathan. 2008. *A World Survey of Religion and the State.* New York: Cambridge University Press.

Fox, Jonathan, and Jonathan Rynhold. 2008. "A Jewish and a Democratic State? Comparing Government Involvement in Religion in Israel and other Democracies." *Totalitarian Movements and Political Regimes* 9(4):507–31.

Frazee, Charles A. 1969. *The Orthodox Church and Independent Greece, 1821– 1852.* Cambridge: Cambridge University Press.

Friedland, Roger. 2001. "Religious Nationalism and the Problem of Collective Representation." *Annual Review of Sociology* 27: 125–52.

Galanter, Marc, and Jayanth Krishnan. 2000. "Personal Law and Human Rights in India and Israel." *Israel Law Review* 34(1):101–33.

Gandhi, Indira. 1971. *Selected Speeches of Indira Gandhi,* Volume 1. New Delhi: Publications Division Government of India.

1975. *The Years of Endeavor: Selected Speeches of Indira Gandhi, August 1969–August 1972.* New Delhi: Publications Division Government of India.

1976. *Democracy and Discipline: Speeches of Shrimati Indira Gandhi* [electronic resource]. New Delhi: Ministry of I & B, Government of India.

1984. *Selected Speeches and Writings of Indira Gandhi*, Volume 3. New Delhi: Publications Division Government of India.

Gandhi, Mahatma. 1939. *The Unseen Power* [electronic resource], ed. Jag Parvesh. Chander Lahore: Free India Publications.

1958. *All Men are Brothers: Life and Thoughts of Mahatma Gandhi as told in his Own Words*. Paris: UNESCO.

Gandhi, Rajiv. 1989. *Rajiv Gandhi: Selected Speeches and Writings*, Volume 3. New Delhi: Publications Division Government of India.

Ganguly, Sumit. 2003. "The Crisis of Indian Secularism." *Journal of Democracy* 14(4):11–25.

Garibaldi, Giuseppe. 1888. *Memorie autobiografiche*. Florence: G. Barbèra.

Gaudiano, Pedro. 2002. *Artigas Católico*. Montevideo: Universidad Católica.

Gaustad, Edwin S., ed. 1982. *A Documentary History of Religion to the Civil War*. Grand Rapids, MI: Eerdmans Publishing Company.

Gaustad, Edwin S., and Leigh Schmidt. 2002. *The Religious History of America*. New York: Harper Collins Publishers.

Gellner, Ernest. 1983. *Nations and Nationalism*. Oxford: Basic Blackwell.

Ghosh, Abantika, and Vijaita Singh. 2015. "Census: Hindu Share Dips below 80%, Muslim Share Grows but Slower." *The Indian Express*, January 24. http://indianexpress.com/article/india/india-others/census-hindu-share-dips-below-80-muslim-share-grows-but-slower/ (accessed August 26, 2016).

Goñi, Uki. 2016. "Uruguay's Quiet Democratic Miracle." *New York Times*, February 9. www.nytimes.com/2016/02/10/opinion/uruguays-quiet-democratic-miracle.html?_r=0 (accessed March 12, 2016).

González Demuro, Wilson, and Cecilia Robilotti. 2005. "Iglesia y crisis monárquica en el Río de la Plata al finalizar la época colonial. Un caso: Montevideo y su cura vicario, Juan José Ortiz (1783–1815)." *Anuario de Estudios Americanos* 62(1):161–80.

González Laurino, Carolina. 2001. *La construcción de la identidad uruguaya*. Montevideo: Universidad Católica and taurus.

Gorski, Philip S., 2000. "The Mosaic Moment: An Early Modernist Critique of Modernist Theories of Nationalism." *American Journal of Sociology* 105(5): 1428–68.

2017. *American Covenant*. 2017. Princeton, NJ: Princeton University Press.

Gorski, Philip S. and Gülay Türkmen-Dervişoğlu. 2013a. "Religion, Nationalism, and International Security: Creation Myths and Social Mechanisms." Pp. 136–147 in Chris Seiple, Dennis R. Hoover, and Pauletta Otis, eds., *The Routledge Handbook of Religion and Security*. London: Routledge Press.

2013b. "Religion, Nationalism, and Violence: An Integrated Approach." *Annual Review of Sociology* 39:193–210.

Grant, Melville Rosyn. 1921. *Americanism vs. Roman Catholicism*, 2nd ed. Gulfport, MS: Truth Publishing Company.

Green, John, and E. J. Dionne, Jr. 2008. "Religion and American Politics: More Secular, More Evangelical, or Both?" Pp. 194–224 in Ruy Teixeira, ed., *Red, Blue, and Purple America: The Future of Election Demographics*. Washington, DC: Brookings Institution Press.

Grigoriadis, Ionnis N. 2011. "Rethinking the Nation: Shifting Boundaries of the 'other' in Greece and Turkey." *Middle Eastern Studies* 47(1):167–82.

Grompone, Antonio M. 1967. *La ideología de Batlle*, 3rd edn. Montevideo: ARCA.

Guardian. 2016. "Thousands Call for Malaysian Prime Minister Najib Razak to Quit." November 19. www.theguardian.com/world/2016/nov/19/thousands-call-for-malaysian-prime-minister-najib-razak-to-quit (accessed August 3, 2017).

Guigou, L. Nicolás. 2008. "La religión como saber: Procesos de subjetivación de las religions afro-brasileñas en el Uruguay." *Debates do NER [Porto Alegre]* 9(13): 145–4.

Gumbleton, Bishop Thomas J. 2002. "The Peace Pulpit: Homilies by Bishop Thomas J. Gumbleton." www.ncronline.org/blogs/peace-pulpit (accessed September 22, 2014).

Gusfield, Joseph R. 1963. *Symbolic Crusade: Status Politics and the American Temperance Movement.* Urbana, IL: University of Illinois Press.

Halabi, Osama Rafeeq. 2000. "Israeli Confiscation of Palestinian Land: Law and Policy on Settlements." Haifa: Adalah/The Legal Center for Arab Minority Rights in Israel. www.adalah.org/uploads/oldfiles/Public/file/sefer%20katom-zeva.pdf (accessed August 8, 2016).

Hale, Christopher. 2013. *Massacre in Malaya: Exposing Britain's My Lai.* Gloucestershire: History Press.

Halikiopoulou, Daphne. 2008. "The Changing Dynamics of Religion and National Identity: Greece and the Republic of Ireland in a Comparative Perspective." *Journal of Religion in Europe* 1:302–28.

Halikiopoulou, Daphne and Sofia Vasilopoulou. 2013. "Political Instability and the Persistence of Religion in Greece: The Policy Implications of the Cultural Defense Paradigm." RECODE Working Paper no. 18. www.recode.info

Halkin, Hillel. 2014. *Jabotinsky: A Life.* New Haven, CT: Yale University Press.

2016a. "What Ahad Asam Saw and Hertzl Missed – and Vice Versa." *Mosaic Magazine*, October 5. https://mosaicmagazine.com/essay/2016/10/what-ahad-haam-saw-and-herzl-missed-and-vice-versa/ (accessed it on January 17, 2017).

2016b. "Why Ahad Ha'Am Still Matters." *Mosaic Magazine*, November 3.

Hannigan, Joni B. 2004. "Soldiers Need U.S. Support … And Faith in God." www.sbclife.net/Articles/2004/09/sla7 (accessed September 25, 2014).

Hastings, Adrian. 1997. *The Construction of Nationhood: Ethnicity, Religion, and Nationalism.* Cambridge: Cambridge University Press.

Hatch, Nathan O. 1989. *The Democratization of American Christianity.* New Haven, CT: Yale University Press.

Healy, A. M. 1982. *Tunku Abdul Rahman.* St. Lucia: University of Queensland Press.

Heclo, Hugh. 2007. *Christianity and American Democracy.* Cambridge, MA: Harvard University Press.

Heller (Rabbi), James G. 1917. *Crises.* Philadelphia: [s.n.]. https://babel.hathitrust.org/cgi/pt?id=uc2.ark:/13960/t0oz7296v;view=1up;seq=3 (accessed March 12, 2016).

Hertzl, Theodor. 1896. *Der Judenstaat: Versuch einer modernen Lösung der Judenfrage.* Leipzig and Vienna: M. Breitenstein.

Hibbard, Scott W. 2010. *Religious Politics and Secular States: Egypt, India, and the United States.* Baltimore, MD: Johns Hopkins University Press.

2014. "Religion and State in India: Ambiguity, Chauvinism, and Tolerance." Pp. 121–40 in Tamadonfar, Mehran and Ted G. Jelen, eds., *Religion and Regimes: Support, Separation, and Oppositions*. Lanham, MD: Lexington Books.

Higham, John. 1988. *Strangers in the Land: Patterns of American Nativism, 1860–1925*. New Brunswick, NJ: Rutgers University Press.

Hindu Malaysia Sangam. 2015. "Basic Principles of Hinduism and Practices a Hindu Should Observe." mhsns.org/pages.php?id=65 (accessed September 20, 2017).

Hirsch, Rabbi Meir. 2014. "Exclusive Interview with Rabbi Meier Hirsch." July 23. http://the-levant.com/exclusive-interview-rabbi-meir-hrisch-neturei-karta/ (accessed August 8, 2016).

Hitam, Musa. 1984. *Threat to Muslim Unity and National Security*. White paper. Kuala Lumpur: Ministry of Home Affairs.

Hobsbawm, Eric. 1990. *Nations and Nationalism since 1780*. Cambridge: Cambridge University Press.

Hoffstaedter, Gerhard. 2011. *Modern Muslim Identities: Negotiating Religion and Ethnicity in Malaysia*. Copenhagen: NIAS [Nordic Institute of Asian Studies] Press.

Holsti, Ole R. 1994. *Public Opinion and American Foreign Policy*. Ann Arbor: University of Michigan Press.

Holy Synod of the Church of Greece. 2006. "Greek Independence Day Anniversary Celebrated throughout the Country." http://ecclesia.gr/englishnews/default.asp (accessed May 4, 2017).

2008. "Archbishop Ieronymos Enthroned." www.ecclesia.gr/englishnews/print_it.asp?id=3477 (accessed May 1, 2017).

2011. "Letter to The President of the European Commission, Mr José Manuel Durão Barroso Esq." www.ecclesia.gr/English/holysynod/press_releases/13_10_2011.html (accessed July 20, 2017).

2014. "A Reply to the Unhistorical Views Regarding the Part of the Orthodox Church in the 1821 Greek War of Independence." www.ecclesia.gr/English/holysynod/committees/identity/1821_comm_2014.pdf (accessed February 17, 2017).

Horowitz, Donald L. 2001. *The Deadly Ethnic Riot*. Berkeley and Los Angeles: University of California Press.

Hudson, Rex A., and Sandra W. Meditz, eds. 1992. *Uruguay: A Country Study*, 2nd edn. Washington, DC: Federal Research Division, Library of Congress.

Huff, James Andrew. 2009. "Religious Freedom in India and Analysis of the Constitutionality of Anti-Conversion Laws." *Rutgers Journal of Law and Religion* 10(2):1–36.

Hutchinson, John, and Anthony D. Smith. 1994. *Nationalism: A Reader*. Oxford: Oxford University Press.

Hvithamar, Annika, Margit Warburg, and Brian Arly Jacobsen, eds. 2009. *Holy Nations and Global Identities: Civil Religion, Nationalism, and Globalisation*. Leiden: Brill.

Ibrahim, Ahmad. 1978. "The Position of Islam in the Constitution of Malaysia." Pp. 41–68 in Tun Mohamed Suffian, H. P. Lee, and F. A. Trindade, eds. *The Constitution of Malaysia: Its Development: 1957–1977*. Kuala Lumpur: Oxford University Press.

1979. "The Position of Islam in the Constitution of Malaysia." Pp. 41–68 in Tun Mohamed Suffian, H. P. Lee, and F. A. Trindade, eds. *The Constitution of Malaysia: Its Development 1957–1977.* Kuala Lumpur: Oxford University Press.

Ibrahim, Anwar. 2006. "Universal Values and Muslim Democracy." *Journal of Democracy* 17(3):5–12.

2014. "Islam and Democracy: Malaysia in Comparative Perspective." Speech at Stanford University on November 20. www.anwaribrahimblog.com/2014/11/24/islam-and-democracy-malaysia-in-comparative-perspective/ (accessed September 25, 2017).

Ibrahim, Rozita, Nazri Muslim, and Ahmad Hidayat Buang. 2011. "Multiculturalism and Higher Education in Malaysia." *Procedia Social and Behavioral Sciences* 15:1003–9.

Ieronymos II, Archbishop of Athens and All Greece. 2012. "Social Interventions by His Beatitude Ieronymos II, Archbishop of Athenbs and All Greece." www.ecclesia.gr/englishnews/id=4572 (accessed May 2, 2017).

2016. "Interview of the Archbishop of Athens and All Greece, Ieronymos II (Alexis Papchelas). *Stories on Sky Channel.* www.tovima.gr/files/1/2016/11/01/ier.pdf (accessed June 29, 2017).

Ignasi Saranyana, Josep, ed. 2002. *Teología en América Latina: El siglo de las teologías latinoamericanistas.* Volume III. Madrid: Iberoamericana/Vervuert.

Infobae. 2010. "José 'Pepe' Mujica y el acuerdo con la Argentina: 'No es un día histórico, es un día de historieta'." July 29. www.infobae.com/2010/07/29/528682-jo-se-pepe-mujica-y-el-acuerdo-la-argentina-no-es-un-dia-historico-es-un-dia-historieta (accessed February 3, 2016).

Inglis, Tom. 1998. *Moral Monopoly: The Rise and Fall of the Catholic Church in Modern Ireland.* Dublin: University College Dublin Press.

International Court of Justice. 2010. "Pulp Mills on the River Uruguay (Argentina v. Uruguay)." Judgement. I.C.J. Reports, p. 14.

Iqbal, Muhammad Sir. 1954. *The Reconstruction of Religious thought in Islam.* Lahore: M. Ashraf

1977. *Speeches, Writings, and Statements of Iqbal [electronic resource],* compiled and edited by Latif Ahmed Sherwani. Lahore: Iqbal Academy.

Ireland, John. 1905. *The Church and Modern Society: Lectures and Addresses.* St. Paul, MN: The Pioneer Press.

Isasa, Ricardo. 1909. "Nota del Excmo. Sr. Administrador Apostólico de la Arquidiócesis." P. 5 in Laura Carreras de Bastos, ed. *Acción social de la mujer ante el divorcio absoluto.* Montevideo: La Buena Prensa.

Ismail, Ibrahim. 2002. *Pemikiran Dr. Mahathir Tentang Islam.* Kuala Lumpur: Utusan.

Ismaweb. 2016. "China akan bina bangunan di pulau kecil di Laut China Selatan [China will build structures on a small island in the South China Sea]." *Portal Islam&Melayu,* August 25. www.ismaweb.net/2016/04/china-akan-bina-bangunan-di-pulau-kecil-di-laut-china-selatan/ (accessed September 21, 2017).

Ives, Mike. 2016. "Convicted of Sodomy, Malaysian Opposition Leader Loses Bid for Freedom." *New York Times,* December 14. www.nytimes.com/2016/12/14/world/asia/malaysia-anwar-ibrahim-sodomy-court.html (accessed August 3, 2017).

Jacobsohn, Gary Jeffrey. 2003. *The Wheel of Law: India's Secularism in Comparative Constitutional Context*. Princeton, NJ: Princeton University Press.

Jacobson, Rabbi Moses Perez. 1913. *"Is this a Christian Country?"* Shreveport: M.L. Bath Company.

Jaffrelot, Christophe, and Sunjay Kumar. 2015. "The Impact of Urbanization on the Electoral Results of the 2014 Indian Elections: With Special Reference to the BJP Vote." *Studies in Indian Politics* 3(1):39–49.

Jaffrelot, Christophe. 2007. *Hindu Nationalism: A Reader*. Princeton, NJ: Princeton University Press.

2016a. "Why the BJP Rewrites History: The Party's Aversion to Nehru Draws from its Notion of India and Indian Citizenship." *The Indian Express*, November 7.

2016b. "Narendra Modi between Hindutva and Subnationalism: The Gujurat Asmita of a Hindu Hriday Samrat." *India Review* 15(2):196–217.

Jamal, Amal. 2004. "The Ambiguities of Minority Patriotism: Love for Homeland versus State Among Palestinian Citizens of Israel." *Nationalism and Ethnic Politics* 10(3):433–71.

Jenkins, Jack. 2017. "Faith Groups Across the Country Condemn Trump's Ban on Refugees and Immigrants from Muslim Countries." January 26, *Think Progress*. https://thinkprogress.org/faith-groups-country-immigrants-muslim-b22798233c90/ (accessed September 26, 2017).

Jerusalem Patriarchate. 2016, March 31. "The Greek President, Mr. Prokopis Pavlopouls, at the Patriarchate." www.jp-newsgate.net/en/2016/03/31/22079 (accessed August 2, 2017).

Jinnah, Mahomed Ali. 1942. *Some Recent Speeches and Writings of Mr. Jinnah*. Collected and edited by Jamil-ud-Dim Ahmad. Lahore: Muhammad Ashraf.

Johnson, Jenna. 2015. "Trump Calls for 'Total and Complete Shutdown of Muslims Entering the United States'." *Washington Post*, December 7. www.washingtonpost.com/news/post-politics/wp/2015/12/07/donald-trump-calls-for-total-and-complete-shutdown-of-muslims-entering-the-united-states/?utm_term=.6bffca24a13d (accessed September 26, 2017).

Joshi, A. P., M. D. Srivnivas, and J. K. Bajaj. 2003. *Religious Demography of India*. Chennai, India: Centre for Policy Studies.

Jones, Robert P., and Daniel Cox. 2016. *America's Changing Religious Identity: Findings from the 2016 American Values Atlas*. Washington, DC: Public Religion Research Institute. www.prri.org/wp-content/uploads/2017/09/PRRI-Religion-Report.pdf (accessed September 28, 2017).

Joppke, Christian. 2015. *The Secular State Under Siege: Religion and Politics in Europe and America*. Cambridge: Polity Press.

Juergensmeyer, Mark. 1994. *The New Cold War: Religious Nationalism Confronts the Secular State*. Berkeley: University of California Press.

2008. *Global Rebellion: Religious Challenges to the Secular State, from Christian Militants to Al Qaeda*. Berkeley: University of California Press.

2010. "The Global Rise of Religion." *Australian Journal of International Affairs* 64(3):262–73.

Junta Nacional de Vida y Misión. 2007. *Cuando el árbol nos impide ver el bosque: Una opinión de la Iglesia Metodista del Uruguay sobre el litigio que enfrentan Uruguay y Argentina*. Montevideo: Comisión de Comunicaciones.

Kabala, James S. 2013. *Church–State Relations in the Early American Republic, 1787–1846*. London: Pickering and Chatto Publishers.

Katzenstein, Peter J., and Timothy, A. Byrnes. 2006. "Transnational Religion in an Expanded Europe." *Perspectives on Politics* 4(4) (December):679–94.

Kent, Alexandra. 2007. *Divinity and Diversity: A Hindu Revitalization Movement in Malaysia*. Singapore: Institute of Southeast Asian Studies.

Kinsman, F. Joseph. 1924. *Americanism and Catholicism*. New York: Longmans, Green.

Kitromilides, Paschalis M. 1989. "Imagined Communities and the Origins of the National Question in the Balkans." *European History Quarterly* 19:149–194.
2006. "From Republican Patriotism to National Sentiment: A Reading of Hellenic Nomarchy." *European Journal of Political Theory* 5(1):50–60.

Kleppner, Paul. 1970. *The Cross of Culture: A Social Analysis of Midwestern Politics 1850–1900*. New York: The Free Press.

Kolatt, Israel. 2008. *Tsiyonut ve-Yiśra'el bi-re'i ha-hisṭoryon: asupat ma'amarim [The Historiography of Zionism and Israel: Collected Essays]*. Jerusalem: Yad Yitsḥaḳ Ben-Tsevi.

Kolluoğlu, Biray. 2013. "Excesses of Nationalism: Greco-Turkish Population Exchange." *Nations and Nationalism* 19(3):532–50.

Kook, Rabbi Chaim Shteiner. 2008. "Issues on the Status of the Land of Israel." May 21. www.mercazharav.org/index.html (accessed August 8, 2016).

Kook, Rav Tzvi Yehuda. 1967. "On the Nineteenth Anniversary of Israel's Independence." http://israel613.com/books/ERETZ_ANNIVERSARY_KOOK.pdf (accessed January 24, 2017).

Koumandaraki, Anna. 2002. "The Evolution of Greek National Identity." *Studies in Ethnicity and Nationalism* 2(2):39–53.

Kramer, Lloyd. 1997. "Historical Narratives and the Meaning of Nationalism." *Journal of the History of Ideas* 53(3):525–45.

Kruse, Kevin M. 2015. *One Nation Under God: How Corporate America Invented Christian America*. New York: Basic Books

Küçükcan, Talip. 1999. "Re-claiming Identity: Ethnicity, Religion and Politics among Turkish-Muslims in Bulgaria and Greece." *Journal of Muslim Minority Affairs* 19(1):49–68.

Kuppusamy, Baradan. 2010. "Can Christians Say 'Allah'? In Malaysia, Muslims Say No." *Time*, January 8. www.content.time.com/time/printout/0,8816,1952497,00.html (accessed August 2, 2017).

Kurth, James. 2007. "Religion and National Identity in America and Europe." *Sociology* 44:120–5.

Kuru, Ahmet T. 2009. *Secularism and State Policies toward Integration: The United States, France, and Turkey*. Cambridge: Cambridge University Press.

La Gaceta. 2011. "El video en el que Tabaré Vázquez habló sobre una guerra por las pasteras: El ex mandatario uruguayo confesó que consideró esa hipótesis en pleno conflicto con la Argentina." October 12. www.lagaceta.com.ar/nota/459748/Politica/video-Tabare-Vazquez-hablo-sobre-guerra-pasteras-.html (accessed February 3, 2016).

Lago, Julio. 1973. *El Verdadero Rodó: Estudios Críticos*. Montevideo: Comunidad del Sur.

Lapidus, Ira M. 1988. *A History of Islamic Societies*. Cambridge: Cambridge University Press.

Larson, Edward J., and Michael P. Winship. 2005. *The Constitutional Convention: A Narrative History from the Notes of James Madison*. New York: The Modern Library.

Lathrop, John. 1799. *Patriotism and Religion: A Sermon, Preached on the 25th of April, 1799, the Day Recommended by the President of the United States, to be Observed as a National Fast*. Boston, MA: John Russell.

Lathrop, Joseph. 1787. "A Sermon on the Day Appointed for Publick Thanksgiving." In *Political Sermons at the American Founding Era, 1730–1805*, Volume 1, 2nd edn, ed. Ellis Sandoz. Indianapolis, IN: Liberty Fund.

Latinobarómetro. 2015. "Latinobarómetro Análisis de datos." Online database. www. Latinobarometro.org/latOnline.jsp (accessed August 30, 2016).

Lee Kam Hing. 2007. "A Key Man Behind the Alliance." *The Star Online*, July 30. www.thestar.com.my/opinion/letters/2007/07/30/a-key-man-behind-the-alliance/ (accessed August 17, 2017).

Lee, Raymond L. M. 1988. "Patterns of Religious Tension in Malaysia." *Asian Survey* 28(4):400–418.

——— 1990. "The State, Religious Nationalism, and Ethnic Rationalization in Malaysia." *Ethnic and Racial Studies* 13(4):482–502.

Leege, David C., and Lyman A. Kellstedt. 1993. *Rediscovering the Religious Factor in American Politics*. Armonk, NY: M.E. Sharpe.

Lelyveld, Joseph. 2011. *Great Soul: Mahatma Gandhi and His Struggle with India*. New York: Alfred A. Knopf.

Leong, Susan. 2016. "Is 'Allah Just for Muslims'? Religion, Indigenization and Boundaries in Malaysia." Pp. 119–141 in Catherine Gomes, ed. *The Asia-Pacific in the Age of Transnational Mobility: The Search for Community and Identity on and through Social Media*. London: Anthem Press.

Leow, Julian Beng Kim. 2015. "Merdeka and Malaysia Day Message from Archbishop of Kuala Lumpur Julian Leow Beng Kim." *Herald Malaysia Online*, August 31. www. heraldmalaysia.com/news/merdeka-and-malaysia-day-message-from-archbishop-of-kuala-lumpur-julian-leow-beng-kim/24891/5 (accessed September 20, 2017).

Lerner, Hannah. 2009. "Entrenching the Status Quo: Religion and State in Israel's Constitutional Proposals." *Constellations* 16(3):445–61.

——— 2013. "Permissive Constitutions, Democracy, and Religious Freedom in India, Indonesia, Israel, and Turkey." *World Politics* 65(4):609–55.

Levinson, Chaim, and Yair Ettinger. 2012. "Rabbi Kook's Followers Are Still Debating His Legacy." *Haaretz*, March 11. https://www.haaretz.com/1.5204045 (accessed December 14, 2016).

Liagkis, Marios Koukounaras. 2014. "Religious Education in Greece: A New Curriculum, an Old Issue." *British Journal of Religious Education* 37(2):153–169.

Liebman, Charles S., and Bernard Susser. 1997. "The Forgotten Center: Traditional Jewishness in Israel." *Modern Judaism* 17(3):211–20.

Liebman, Charles S., and Eliezer Don-Yehiya. 1983. *Civil Religion in Israel: Traditional Judaism and Political Culture in the Jewish State*. Berkeley: University of California Press.

Lilly, John. 2007. "Our Man in Rome." *National Catholic Register.* www.ncregister
.com/site/article/our_man_in_rome/ (accessed February 17, 2015).

Lim Sue Goan. 2013. "Pakatan Lost, but Not Defeated." *Malaysia Today*, May 9.
web.archive.org/web/20130510213028/http://malaysia-today.net/mtcolumns/
guest-columnists/56609-pakatan-lost-but-not-defeated (accessed August 2, 2017).

Liow, Joseph Chinyong. 2004. "Political Islam in Malaysia: Problematising
Discourse and Practice in the UMNO–PAS 'Islamisation race'." *Commonwealth
& Comparative Politics* 42(2):184–205.

2009. *Piety and Politics: Islamism in Contemporary Malaysia.* Kuala Lumpur:
Oxford University Press.

2016. *Religion and Nationalism in Southeast Asia.* Cambridge: Cambridge
University Press.

Loizides, Neophytes. 2009. "Religious Nationalism and Adaptation in Southeast
Europe." *Nationality Papers* 37(2):203–27.

Lorch, Netanel, ed. 1993. *Major Knesset Debates, 1948–1981.* Lanham, MD:
University Press of America and the Jerusalem Center for Public Affairs.
http://jcpa.org/article/major-knesset-debates-1948-1981.

Lowrance, Sherry. 2005. "Being Palestinian in Israel: Identity, Protest, and Political
Exclusion." *Comparative Studies of South Asia, Africa, and the Middle East*
25(2):487–99.

Loza, Jorgelina. 2011. "Las naciones Rioplatenses: la construcción de percepciones
contemporáneas sobre la nación en militantes uruguayos y argentinos." *RECSO:
Revista de ciencias sociales de la Universidad Católica del Uruguay* 2:105–28.

Ludden, David, ed. 1996. *Contesting the Nation: Religion, Community, and the
Politics of Democracy in India.* Philadelphia: University of Pennsylvania Press.

Luker, Kristin. 1984. *Abortion and the Politics of Motherhood.* Berkeley:
University of California Press.

Malaysian Buddhist Association [馬來西亞佛教總會]. 2009a. "1974 年 [The Year
1974]." August 7. www.malaysianbuddhistassociation.org/index.php/2009
-04-26-15-07-25/2009-04-26-15-28-12/433-1974.html (accessed September
20, 2017).

2009b. "1984 年 [The Year 1984]." June 4. www.malaysianbuddhistassociation
.org/index.php/2009-04-26-15-07-25/2009-04-26-15-30-10/277-1984.html
(accessed September 22, 2017).

Mabry, Tristan James. 1998. "Modernization, Nationalism and Islam: An
Examination of Ernest Gellner's Writings on Muslim Society with Reference
to Indonesia and Malaysia." *Ethnic and Racial Studies* 21(1):64–88.

Madan, T. N. 1998. "Secularism in Its Place." Pp. 297–320 in Rajeev Bhargava,
ed., *Secularism and its Critics.* New York: Oxford University Press.

Mahathir, Mohamad. 2002. "The Role of Islam in the Modern State." Speech in New
York on February 3. Kuala Lumpur: Prime Minister's Office. www.pmo.gov.my/
ucapan/?m=p&p=mahathir&id=1564 (accessed September 25, 2017).

2003. "Muslim Unity in the Face of Challenges and Threats." Speech at
Al-Azhar University, Cairo, Egypt, on January 21. Kuala Lumpur: Prime
Minister's Office. www.pmo.gov.my/ucapan/?m=p&p=mahathir&id=576
(accessed September 25, 2017).

Makris, A. 2015. January 6. "Greek PM and Opposition Leader Attend Epiphany
Celebration." *Greek Reporter*, http://greece.greekreporter.com/2015/01/06

/greek-pm-and-opposition-leader-attend-epiphany-celebration/ (accessed July 21, 2017).

Marsh, Christopher. 2007. "Religion and Nationalism." Pp. 99–110 in *Nations and Nationalism in Global Perspective: An Encyclopedia of Origins, Development, and Contemporary Transitions*, vol. 1, Guntram Herb and David Kalplan, eds. Santa Barbara, Calfornia: ABC-CLIO, inc.

Marty, Martin E. 1976. *A Nation of Behavers*. Chicago, IL: University of Chicago Press.

Marx, Anthony. 2003. *Faith in Nation: Exclusionary Origins of Nationalism*. New York: Oxford University Press.

Matchen, Leanne L., and Maggie Carnahan. 2016. "*Malaysia: Law and Religion Framework Overview*." Provo, UT: International Center for Law and Religion Studies, Brigham Young University. www.religlaw.org/common/document.view.php?docId=7194 (accessed August 17, 2017).

Mauzy, Diane K. 2006. "The Challenge to Democracy: Singapore's and Malaysia's Resilient Hybrid Regimes." *Taiwan Journal of Democracy* 2(2):47–68.

Mavrogordatos, George Th. 2003. "Orthodoxy and Nationalism in the Greek Case." Pp. 117–36 in Madeley, John and Zsolt Enyedi, eds., *Church and State in Contemporary Europe: The Chimera of Neutrality*. London: Frank Cass.

McClintock, Samuel [1784]1998. "A Sermon on Occasion of the Commencement of the New Hampshire Constitution." In *Political Sermons at the American Founding Era, 1730–1805*, Volume 1, 2nd edn, ed. Ellis Sandoz. Indianapolis, IN: Liberty Fund.

McGreevy, John T. 2003. *Catholicism and American Freedom*. New York: W.W. Norton.

McLeod, John. 2002. *The History of India*. Westport, CT: Greenwood Press.

Menthol Ferré, Alberto. 1969. "El proceso de separación entre Iglesia y Estado." Special issue on "Las Corrientes Religiosas." *nuestra tierra* 35:40–53.

Metcalf, Barbara D., and Thomas R. Metcalf. 2006. *A Concise History of Modern India*, 2nd edn. Cambridge: Cambridge University Press.

Michael, Michális Stavrou. 2009. *Resolving the Cyprus Conflict: Negotiating History*. New York: Palgrave Macmillan.

Milne, R. S., and Diane K. Mauzy. 1999. *Malaysian Politics under Mahathir*. London: Routledge.

Mirsky, Yehudah. 2014. *Rav Kook: Mystic in a Time of Revolution*. New Haven, CT: Yale University Press.

Misra, Amalendu. 2000. "Hindu Nationalism and Muslim Minority Rights in India." *International Journal of Minority and Group Rights* 7:1–18.

Modi, Narendra. 2013. "Full Text of Shri Modi's speech at Lalkaar Rally, Jammu." www.narendramodi.in/full-text-of-shri-modis-speech-at-lalkaar-rally-jammu-2806 (accessed September 21, 2017).

———. 2014. "Narendra Modi On MS Golwalkar, Translated By Aakar Patel – Part 1." *The Caravan: A Journal of Politics and Culture*, May 31. www.caravan-magazine.in/vantage/modi-golwalkar-part-1 (accessed September 1, 2016).

———. 2016. "Independence Day Speech." http://indianexpress.com/article/india/india news-india/pm-narendra-modis-speech-on-independence-day-2016-here-is-the-full-text/ (accessed March 17, 2017).

Mohamad, Mahnaz. 2002. "From Nationalism to Post-Developmentalism: The Intersection of Gender, Race and Religion in Malaysia." *Macalester International* 12(12 [Malaysia: Crossroads of Diversity in Southeast Asia]):80–102.

Moloktos-Liederman, Lina. 2007. "The Greek ID Card Controversy: A Case Study of Religion and National Identity in a Changing European Union." *Journal of Contemporary Religion* 22(2):187–203.

Monsma, Stephen V. 2012. *Pluralism and Freedom: Faith-Based Organizations in a Democratic Society*. Lanham, MD: Rowman and Littlefield.

Montevideo Archdiocese. 1918. *Estatutos de la Arquidiócesis de Montevideo y Diócesis Sufragáneas de Salto y Melo*. Montevideo: Talleres Gráficos Don Bosco.

Morris, Benny. 2014. "The New Historiography: Israel Confronts Its Past." Pp. 11–28 in Morris, Benny, ed., *Making Israel*. Ann Arbor: University of Michigan Press.

Mueller, John. 1994. *Policy and Opinion in the Gulf War*. Chicago, IL: University of Chicago Press.

Mujtaba, Syed Ali. 2016. "Conspiracy of Hope and Kashmir Issue." *The Muslim Mirror*, August 13. http://muslimmirror.com/eng/conspiracy-of-hope-and-kashmir-issue/ (accessed November 18, 2016).

Müller-Fahrenholz, Geiko. 2007. *America's Battle for God: A European Christian Looks at Civil Religion*. Grand Rapids, MI: Eerdmans Press.

Munshi, Suhas. 2016. "Jai Shri Ram: Why Modi's Dussehra Speech was Just Dog-Whistle Hindutva." *Catch News*, October 12. www.catchnews.com/politics-news/jai-shri-ram-why-modi-s-dussehra-speech-was-just-dog-whistle-hindutva-1476290909.html (accessed March 15, 2017).

Murphy, Andrew R. 2009. *Moral Decline and Divine Punishment from New England to 9/11*. Oxford: Oxford University Press.

Murray, John Courtney, S.J. 1960. *We Hold These Truths: Catholic Reflections on the American Proposition*. New York: Sheed and Ward.

Muslim Mirror. 2012. "About Us." http://muslimmirror.com/eng/about/ (accessed August 27, 2016).

———. 2016. "AIUDF of Moulana Badruddin Ajmal has Strengthened BJP: Arshad Madani." http://muslimmirror.com/eng/aiudf-of-moulana-badruddin-ajmal-has-strengthened-bjp-arshad-madani/ (accessed August 17, 2016).

Mylonas, Harris. 2013. *The Politics of Nation-Building: Making Co-Nationals, Refugees, and Minorities*. Cambridge: Cambridge University Press.

Nación, La. 2006. "Volvieron a cortar la ruta hacia Uruguay." April 5. www.lanacion.com.ar/794842-volvieron-a-cortar-la-ruta-hacia-uruguay (accessed February 2, 2016).

Naidu, M. Venkaiah. 2016. "Why not a Common Civil Code for all?" *The Hindu*, July 16. www.thehindu.com/opinion/lead/union-minister-venkaiah-naidu-on-uniform-civil-code-why-not-a-common-civil-code-for-all/article8855995.ece (accessed June 25, 2016).

Naim, Smadar Dekel. 2013. "To be a Free Nation also in Marriage." April 3. www.ynet.co.il/articles/0,7340,L-4363226,00.html (accessed August 8, 2016).

Najib Razak. 2010. "Don't Let Racial Issues Destroy What Has Been Painstakingly Built – PM." News article, August 30. Kuala Lumpur: Prime Minister's Office. www.pmo.gov.my/home.php?menu=newslist&news_id=4579&news_cat=13

&cl=1&page=1731&sort_year=2010&sort_month (accessed September 25, 2017).

2016. "Talking Points Yab. Dato' Sri Mohd Najib Bin Tun Abd. Razak, Prime Minister of Malaysia, Special Commemorative Seminar on Tun Aabdul Razak (Father of Malaysia's Development) Dan Pelancaran Buku Tulisan Tun Ahmad Sarji." Speech at the Royale Chulan, Kuala Lumpur, on January 14. Kuala Lumpur: Prime Minister's Office. www.pmo.gov.my/home.php?menu=speech&page=1908&news_id=789&speech_cat=2 (accessed September 25, 2017).

2017. "JKMPKA, A Mechanism to Boost National Understanding and Harmony – PM." News article, February 24. Kuala Lumpur: Prime Minister's Office. www.pmo.gov.my/home.php?menu=newslist&page=1731&news_id=17025&news_cat=13 (accessed September 25, 2017).

Nandy, Ashis. 1998. "The Twilight of Certitudes: Secularism, Hindu Nationalism and other Masks of Deculturation." *Postcolonial Studies* 1(3):283–98.

National Catholic Reporter. 2003. "Iraq is a Stop on Bush 'unipolarist' Track." April 4. www.natcath.org/NCR_Online/archives2/2003b/040403/040403s .htm (accessed August 17, 2014).

National Herald. 2017, July 21. "Archbishop Warns Tsipras Over Church–State Separation, Religion." www.thenationalherald.com/137579/archbishop-warns-tsipras-church-state-separation-religion-classes/ (accessed July 20, 2017).

Nehru, Jawaharlal. 1949. *Jawaharlal Nehru's Speeches*, Volume 1. New Delhi: Publications Division Government of India.

1964. *Jawaharlal Nehru's Speeches*, Volume 4. New Delhi: Publications Division Government of India.

1979. *Selected Works of Jawaharlal Nehru*, Volume 12. New Delhi: Orient Longman.

1981. *Selected Works of Jawaharlal Nehru*, Volume 14. New Delhi: Orient Longman.

Neo, Jaclyn Ling-chien. 2006. "Malay Nationalism, Islamic Supremacy and the Constitutional Bargain in the Multi-ethnic Composition of Malaysia." *International Journal on Minority and Group Rights* 13:95–118.

Netanyahu, Benjamin. 2013. "PM Netanyahu's Remarks at the Israel towards 2020 Conference at the Begin–Sadat Center for Strategic Studies." www .pmo.gov.il/English/MediaCenter/Speeches/Pages/speechbegin061013.aspx (accessed January 27, 2017).

2014. "Address by Prime Minister Benjamin Netanyahu at the Ceremony Marking the 47th Anniversary of the Unification of Jerusalem." www .pmo.gov.il/English/MediaCenter/Speeches/Pages/speechjerday280514.aspx (accessed January 4, 2015).

2015. "PM Netanyahu's Speech at the 37th Zionist Congress." www.pmo .gov.il/English/MediaCenter/Speeches/Pages/speechcongress201015.aspx (accessed January 27, 2017).

Neuhaus, Richard John. 1984. *The Naked Public Square*. Grand Rapids, MI: Eerdmans Press.

New Englander and Yale Review. 1844. "Romanists and the Roman Catholic Controversy." *New Englander and Yale Review* 2(2):233–55.

Ng Kam Weng. 2010. "All or Tuhan in the Rukun Negara? – A Separate Issue from Allah in the Alkitab." Press release, National Evangelical Christian Fellowship Malaysia. www.necf.org.my/newsmaster.cfm?&menuid=43& action=view&retrieveid=1193 (accessed September 20, 2017).

Ng Sze-Chieh. 2011. *"Silenced Revolutionaries: Challenging the Received View of Malaya's Revolutionary Past."* MA thesis. Phoenix: Arizona State University.

Njoku, Chukwenenye Clifford, and Hamidin Abd. Hamid. 2014. "Religion in a Secular State and State Religion in Practice: Assessing Religious Influence, Tolerance, and National Stability in Nigeria and Malaysia." *Journal for the Study of Religions and Ideologies* 13:203–35.

Noll, Mark A. 1992. *A History of Christianity in the United States and Canada.* Grand Rapids, MI: William B. Eerdmans Publishing Company.

2002. *America's God: From Jonathan Edwards to Abraham Lincoln.* Oxford: Oxford University Press.

Noonan, John T. Jr. 2005. *A Church That Can and Cannot Change: The Development of Catholic Moral Teaching.* Notre Dame, IN: University of Notre Dame Press.

Northwest Ordinance. 1787. www.ourdocuments.gov/doc.php?flash=true&doc =8&page=transcript (accessed November 14, 2013).

Nurhidayah, Ismail. 2016. "An Afternoon with the Liberals." *Portal Islam&Melayu,* September 28. www.ismaweb.net/2016/09/an-afternoon-with-the-liberals/ (accessed September 20, 2017).

O'Brien, Connor Cruise. 1988. *God Land: Reflections on Religion and Nationalism.* Cambridge: Cambridge University Press.

Oddone, Juan. 2003. *Vecinos en Discordia: Argentina, Uruguay y la política hemisférica de los Estados Unidos. Selección de documentos. 1945–1955.* Montevideo: Universidad de la República.

Oded, Haklai. 2011. *Palestinian Ethnonationalism in Israel.* Philadelphia: The University of Pennsylvania Press.

Odell, Luis E. 1975. "Reflections on the Total Withdrawal of Missionaries in the Methodist Church of Uruguay." *International Review of Mission* 64(254):198–199.

Oldmixon, Elizabeth A., and Rebekah Samaniego. 2014. "Israel as a Jewish and Democratic State." Pp. 73–95 in Mehran Tamadonfar and Ted G. Jelen, eds., *Religion and Regimes: Support, Separation, and Opposition.* Lanham, MD: Lexington Books.

Olivera, Ademar. 2009. *Forjando caminos de liberación: la Iglesia Metodista en tiempo de dictadura.* Montevideo: Trilce.

Omer, Atalia, and Jason A. Springs. 2013. *Religious Nationalism: A Reference Handbook.* Santa Barbara, CA: ABC-CLIO.

Oneto y Viana, Carlos. 1910. *Divorcio: Ley Sancionada por el Poder Legislativo el 26 de Octubre de 1907, Reformada el 6 de Julio de 1910.* Montevideo: N. Tommasi.

Orbach, Uri. 2013. "Jerusalem: Unique in its Unification." July 2. www.tzohar .org.il/?p=2229 (accessed August 8, 2016).

Özdalga, Elisabeth. 2009. "Islamism and Nationalism as Sister Ideologies: Reflections on the Politicization of Islam in a Longue Durée Perspective." *Middle East Journal* 45(3):407–23.

Palermo, Vicente, and Carlos Reboratti, eds. 2007. *Del otro lado del río: Ambientalismo y política entre uruguayos y argentinos*. Buenos Aires: edhasa.

Panthic.org. 2006. "157 Years of Colonialism and Subjugation of the Sikh Nation." www.panthic.org/articles/2692 (accessed August 17, 2016).

Panthic.org. 2009. "Sikh and Kashmiris Mark August 15th as a Black Day for their Communities." www.panthic.org/articles/5139 (accessed November 18, 2016).

Panthic.org. 2016. "About Panthic.org." http://panthic.org/about.php (accessed September 6, 2016).

Papastathis, Charalambos. 2005. "State and Church in Greece." Pp. 115–38 in Robbers, Gerhard, ed., *State and Church in the European Union* (Baden-Baden: Nomos).

2012. "From Mobilization to a Controlled Compromise: The Shift of Ecclesiastical Strategy under Archbishop Hieronymus." Pp. 207–28 in Willert, Trine Stauning and Lina Molokotos-Lierderman, eds., *Innovation in the Orthodox Christian Tradition? The Question of Change in Greek Orthodox Thought and Practice*. Burlington, VT: Ashgate Publishing Company.

2015. "Greece: A Faithful Orthodox Christian State." Pp. 339–75 in Martinez-Torron, Javier and W. Cole Durham, Jr. eds., *Religion and the Secular State: National Reports*. Madrid: Serviciode Publicianes de la Facultad de Derecho de la Unversidad Compulense de Madrid.

Parlamento del Uruguay. 2016a. "Constitución de la República." parlamento .gub.uy/documentosyleyes/constitución (accessed December 28, 2016).

2016b. "Discursos de Presidentes de la República." Montevideo: Parlamento de la República Oriental del Uruguay. parlamento.gub.uy/documentosyleyes/ discursos/presidentes-rou (accessed August 25, 2017).

Peleg, Ilan. 1998. "Israel's Constitutional Order and the Kulturkampf: The Role of Ben-Gurion." *Israel Studies* 3(1):230–50.

Pendle, George. 1963. *Uruguay*, 3rd edn. Oxford: Oxford University Press.

Penfold, S. Vouler. 1926. *Why a Roman Catholic Cannot be President of the United States*. New York: American Protestant Historical Society.

Pérez Antón, Romeo. 1987. *Los Cristianos y la política en el Uruguay*. Montevideo: Ediciones del Nuevo Mundo.

Peterson, Lars Edward. 2014. "In the Shadow of Battle: Workers, States, Officials, and the Creation of the Welfare State in Uruguay, 1900–1916." PhD dissertation. Pittsburgh: University of Pittsburgh.

Pew Research Center. 2016. "Europeans Fear Wave of Refugees Will Mean More Terrorism, Fewer Jobs." www.pewglobal.org/2016/07/11/europeans-fear-wave-of-refugees-will-mean-more-terrorism-fewer-jobs/ (accessed July 31, 2017).

Pew Research Center. 2017a. "Religious Belief and National Belonging in Central and Eastern Europe." www.pewforum.org/2017/05/10/religious -belief-and-national-belonging-in-central-and-eastern-europe/ (accessed June 2, 2017).

2017b. "U.S. Muslims Concerned about their Place in Society, but Continue to Believe in the American Dream." www.pewforum.org/2017/07/26/findings-from-pew-research-centers-2017-survey-of-us-muslims/ (accessed October 4, 2017).

Pintos, Martín. 2010. *La ruptura: Historias secretas del conflict con Argentina.* Montevideo: Fin de Siglo.

Pittsburgh Platform. 1885. www.jewishvirtuallibrary.org/jsource/Judaism/pittsburgh_program.html (accessed February 11, 2014).

Ponce de León, Vicente. 1905. *El Divorcio: Discurso pronunciado en la Cámera de Representantes al discutirse el proyecto sobre divorcio absoluto.* Montevideo: Unión Católica del Uruguay.

Porritt, Vernon L. 2004. *The Rise and Fall of Communism in Sarawak, 1940–1990.* Victoria: Monash University Press.

Porzecanski, Teresa. 2009. "Private Life and Identity Construction: Memories of Immigrant Jews in Uruguay." *Latin American and Caribbean Ethnic Studies* 4(1):73–91.

Pou Ferrari, Ricardo, and Fernando Mañé Garzón, 2005. *Luis Pedro Lenguas (1862–1932): maestro de cirujanos y precursor de la doctrina social católica en Uruguay.* Montevideo: El Toboso.

Powers, Gerard F. 2009. "The U.S. Bishops and War since the Peace Pastoral." *U.S. Catholic Historian* 27(2):73–98.

Presbyterian Synod of the U.S.A. Synod of the Carolinas. 1790. *"A Pastoral Letter."* Fayetteville, NC: Sibley and Howard.

Press Project. 2015, January 13. "PM vows that Religious Icons will remain in Public Buildings." www.thepressproject.gr/article/71330/PM-vows-that-religious-icons-will-remain-in-public-areas (accessed August 2, 2017).

Preston, Thomas Scott. 1870. *The Catholic View of the Public School Movement.* New York: Robert Coddington Publisher.

Provisorische Verfassung Griechenlands. www.verfassungen.eu/griech/verf22-index .htm (accessed June 5, 2017).

Putnam, Robert D., and David E. Campbell. 2010. *American Grace: How Religion Unites and Divides Us.* New York: Simon and Schuster.

Rashid, Syerleena Abdul. 2015. "It's Time We Decide the Country We Want." *Herald Malaysia Online*, January 23. www.heraldmalaysia.com/news/its-time-we-decide-the-country-we-want/22353/9 (accessed September 20, 2017).

Ram, Uri. 2008. "Why Secularism Fails? Secular Nationalism and Religious Revival in Israel." *International Journal of Politics, Culture, and Society* 21 (1):57–73.

Rashtriya Swayamsevak Sangh. 2012. "What is Hindu Rashtra?" www.rss.org// Encyc/2012/10/22/Why-Hindu-Rashtra—.aspx?lang=1 (accessed August 30, 2016).

2015. "Article 370 must go – excerpts from Shri Guruji's interviews." www.rss .org//Encyc/2013/12/4/Article-370-must-go—excerpts-from-Shri-Guruji-s -interviews.aspx?lang=1 (accessed November 18, 2016).

Rashtriya Swayamsevak Sangh. 2016. "Summary of the Address of Sarsanghchalak Dr. Mohanji Bhagwat on the Occasion of Vijayadashami – Tuesday 11th October 2016." www.rss.org//Encyc/2016/10/11/vijayadashami2016eng .aspx?lang=1 (accessed November 18, 2016).

Rautenbach, Christa. 2006. "Phenomenon of Personal Laws in India: Some Lessons for South Africa." *The Comparative and International Law Journal of Southern Africa* 39(2):241–64.

Ravid, Barak, Jonathan Lis, and Jack Khoury. 2014. "Netanyahu Pushing Basic Law Defining Israel as Jewish State." *Haaretz*. May 1, 2014. www.haaretz .com/news/national/1.588478 (accessed June 5, 2014).

Real de Azúa, Carlos. 1997. *Historia y politica en el Uruguay*. Montevideo: Cal y Canto.

Rehfeldt, Jonathan. 2011. "*Church Planting in an Urban City in Uruguay, South America*." Paper presented for the course "Church Planting." Watertown, WI: Maranatha Baptist Bible College.

Reid Commission. 1957. *Report of the Federation of Malaya Constitutional Commission, 1957*. London: Her Majesty's Stationery Office.

Reyes Abadie, Washington. 2001. "El 25 de Agosto de 1825." Montevideo: Centro de Capacitación y Perfeccionamiento Docente Juan Pivel Devoto. ipes.anep.edu.uy/documentos/articulos_2004/Documentos_art/pdf/25%20 de%20agosto.pdf (accessed January 29, 2016).

Rieffer, Barbara-Ann J. 2003. "Religion and Nationalism: Understanding the Consequences of a Complex Relationship." *Ethnicities* 3(2):215–41.

Roberts, Tom. 2003. "Inside NCR." natcath.org/NCR_Online/archives/032803 /032803b.htm (accessed September 4, 2014).

Rocha Imaz, Ricardo. 1984. *Nacionalismo, socialism y el Uruguay moderno*. Montevideo: ediciones blancas.

Rodó, José Enrique. [1900]2009. *Ariel*. Edición de Belén Castro, 5th edn. Madrid: Cátedra.

Rodríguez Araya, Agustín. 1955. *Génesis constitucional de la República Oriental del Uruguay*. Montevideo: S. A. Cisa.

Roff, William R. 1994. *The Origins of Malay Nationalism*, 2nd edn. Kuala Lumpur: Oxford University Press.

Romero, Simon. 2013. "Uruguay Acts to Legalize Marijuana." *New York Times*, December 11, p. A8. www.nytimes.com/2013/12/11/world/americas/uruguay -acts-to-legalize-marijuana.html (accessed August 25, 2017).

Roshwald, Aviel. 2006. *The Endurance of Nationalism: Ancient Roots and Modern Dilemmas*. Cambridge: Cambridge University Press.

Rubin, Aviad. 2013. "The Status of Religion in Emergent Political Regimes: Lessons from Turkey and Israel." *Nations and Nationalism* 19(3): 493–512.

Rubin, Lawrence. 2015. *Why Israel outlawed the Northern Branch of the Islamic Movement*. Washington, DC: The Brookings Institution. www.brookings .edu/2015/12/07/why-israel-outlawed-the-northern-branch-of-the-islamic -movement/ (accessed August 8, 2016).

Ruparelia, Sanjay. 2006. "Rethinking Institutional Theories of Political Moderation: The Case of Hindu Nationalism in India, 1996–2004." *Comparative Politics* 38(1):125–46.

Ruppin, Arthur. 1913. *The Jews of Today*. London: G. Bell and Sons.

Saari, M. Yusof, Erik Dietzenbacher, and Bart Los. 2014. "Income Distribution across Ethnic Groups in Malaysia: Results from a New Social Accounting Matrix." *Asian Economic Journal* 28(3):259–78.

Sachar, Howard M. 1996. *A History of Israel: From the Rise of Zionism to our Time*. New York: Alfred A. Knopf.

Salim, Agoes. 1983. "The Role of the Rukunegara in Nation Building: A Retrospective View." *Negara* 2(1):26–30.

Salinas, Cecilia G. 2010. *Añorada esperanza: Respuestas locales a las políticas neoliberals Uruguay y la industria de la celulosa*. Oslo: UiO:Leve.

Sansón, Tomás. 1998. *El Catolocismo popular en Uruguay: Una aproximación histórica*. Montevideo: Asociación de Escritores de Cerro Largo.

Sansón Corbo, Tomás. 2011. "La iglesia y el proceso de secularización en el Uruguay modern (1859–1919)." *Hispania Sacra* 63(127):283–303.

Santiago, Jose. 2009. "From Civil Religion to Nationalism as the Religion of Modern Times: Rethinking a Complex Relationship." *Journal for the Scientific Study of Religion* 48(2):394–401.

Savarkar, Vinayak Damodar. 1923. *Essentials of Hindutva*. www.savarkar.org/content/pdfs/en/essentials_of_hindutva.v001. pdf (accessed July 15, 2016).

Secco Illa, Joaquín. 1916. *La Iglesia y el Estado*. Montevideo: La Buena Prensa.
1946. *Historia de la Unión Civica*. Montevideo: Zorrilla de San Martín.

Sen, Amartya. 2005. *The Argumentative Indian: Writings on Indian History, Culture and Identity*. New York: Farrar, Strauss and Giroux.

Shafie, Ghazali. 1985. *Rukunegara: A Testament of Hope*. Kuala Lumpur: Creative Enterprises.

Shah, Dian. 2015. "The 'Allah' Case: Implications for Religious Practice and Expression in Malaysia." *Oxford Journal of Law and Religion* 4(1):141–46.

Shamir, Yitzhak. 1993. *For the Sake of Zion: Vision and Faith. Addresses and Speeches of Yitzhak Shamir*. Tel-Aviv: A. Stern Publishing House.

Shapira, Anita. 2014. *Ben-Gurion: Father of Modern Israel*. New Haven, CT: Yale University Press.

Shapira, Rabbi Avraham. 2009. "On the Halachic Ruling Regarding Refusing an Order." June 23. www.mercazharav.org/index.html (accessed August 24, 2016).

Shea, Mark. 2011. "Patriotism and Family." www.ncregister.com/blog/mark-shea/patriotism-and-family (accessed February 17, 2015).

Shelef, Nadav G. 2010. *Evolving Nationalism, Identity, and Religion in Israel, 1925–2005*. Ithaca, NY: Cornell University Press.

Shelton, Jason E. 2010. "E Pluribus Unum? How Racial, Ethnic, and Religious Group Memberships Impact Beliefs about American National Identity." *Nationalism and Ethnic Politics* 16(1):67–91.

Shindler, Colin. 2008. *A History of Modern Israel*. Cambridge: Cambridge University Press.

Simon, Scott. 2002. "Even Pacifists Must Support this War." www.sbclife.net/Articles/2002/01/sla7 (accessed October 1, 2014).

Singh, Manmohan. 2008a. "PM delivers Bhimsen Sachar Memorial Lecture." http://archivepmo.nic.in/drmanmohansingh/speech-details.php?nodeid=745 (accessed September 21, 2017).
2008b. "Excerpts of PM's Intervention in Lok Sabha during discussion on the Recent Terrorist Attacks in Mumbai." http://archivepmo.nic.in/drmanmohansingh/speech-details.php?nodeid=739 (accessed September 21, 2017).
2010. "Prime Minister's Independence Day Speech, 2010." http://archivepmo.nic.in/drmanmohansingh/speech-details.php?nodeid=917 (accessed May 7, 2017).

Short, Anthony. 1975. *The Communist Insurrection in Malaya, 1948–1960*. London: Frederick Muller Ltd.

Schwab, Issac. 1878. *Can Jews be Patriots? An Historical Study*. New York: Industrial School of the Hebrew Orphan Asylum.

Sikkenga, Jeffrey. 2010. "Rational Theology: Thomas Jefferson and the Foundation of America's Civil Religion." Pp. 207–35 in Weed, Ronald and John von Heyking, eds., *Civil Religion in Political Thought: Its Perennial Questions and Enduring Relevance in North America*. Washington, DC: Catholic University Press.

Smith, Anthony D. 1986. *The Ethnic Origins of Nations*. Oxford: Blackwell Publishers.

1999a. *Myths and Memories of the Nation*. Oxford: Oxford University Press.

1999b. "Ethnic Election and National Identity: Some Religious Origins of Nationalist Ideals." *Nations and Nationalism* 5(3):331–55.

2000. "The 'Sacred' Dimension of Nationalism." *Millennium: Journal of International Studies* 29(3):791–814.

2003. *Chosen Peoples: Sacred Sources of National Identity*. Oxford: Oxford University Press.

Smith, Goldwin. 1891. "New Light on the Jewish Question." *The North American Review* 153(417):129–43.

Smith, Rogers M. 1997. *Civic Ideals: Competing Visions of Citizenship in U.S. History*. New Haven, CT: Yale University Press.

2003. *Stories of Peoplehood: The Politics and Morals of Political Membership*. New York: Cambridge University Press.

Smith, William. [1784]1998. "A Sermon Preached Before a Convention of the Episcopal Church." In *Political Sermons at the American Founding Era, 1730–1805*, Volume 1, 2nd edn, ed. Ellis Sandoz. Indianapolis, IN: Liberty Fund.

Soh, Byungkuk. 2010. "Dato Onn bin Jaafar's and Tunku Abdul Rahman's Visions: Ideology and Nation-Building in Malaya, 1948–1957." *International Area Review* 13(3):3–30.

Sorek, Tamir and Alin, M. Ceobanu. 2009. "Religiosity, National Identity and Legitimacy: Israel as an Extreme Case." *Sociology* 43(3):477–96.

Sotiropoulos, Evagelos. 2017, June 3. "Holy Pentecost: The Holy and Great Council Commences." *The Huffington Post*, www.huffingtonpost.com/entry/holy-pentecost-the-holy-and-great-council-commences_us_59329f-b7e4b00573ab57a3a7 (accessed August 2, 2017).

South China Morning Post. 2017. "Malaysian Prime Minister Najib Razak woos Islamic Heartland, Mixing Religion and Politics to Survive." August 26. www.scmp.com/news/asia/southeast- asia/article/2108402/malaysian-prime-minister-najib-razak-woos-islamic-heartland (accessed October 6, 2017).

Southern Baptist Convention. 2002. "On the War on Terrorism." www.sbc.net/resolutions/1115/on-the-war-on-terrorism (accessed October 21, 2014).

2003. "On the Liberation of Iraq." www.sbc.net/resolutions/1126 (accessed October 15, 2014).

2006. "On Prayer for the President and the Military." www.sbc.net/resolutions/1164 (accessed October 21, 2014).

Spohn, Willfried 2003. "Multiple Modernity, Nationalism, and Religion: A Global Perspective." *Current Sociology* 51(3/4):265–86.

Staerkle, Christian, Jim Sidanius, Eva G.T. Green, and Ludwin E. Molina. 2010. "Ethnic Minority–Majority Asymmetry in National Attitudes around the World: A Multilevel Analysis." *Political Psychology* 31(4):491–519.

Stan, Lavinia and Lucian Turcescu. 2011. *Church, State, and Democracy in Expanding Europe*. Oxford: Oxford University Press.

Statistical Abstract of Israel. 2016. www.cbs.gov.il/www/hodaot2016n/11_16_134e .pdf (accessed January 24, 2017).

Status Quo Letter. http://strangeside.com/israels-status-quo-agreement/ (accessed July 6, 2014).

Stavrakakis, Yannis. 2002. "Religious Populism and Political Culture: The Greek Case." *South European Society and Politics* 7(3):29–52.

2003. "Politics and Religion: On the Politicization of Greek Church Discourse." *Journal of Modern Greek Studies* 21(2):153–81.

Sternhell, Zeev. 1997. *The Founding Myth of Israel: Nationalism, Socialism, and the Making of the Jewish State*. Princeton, NJ: Princeton University Press.

Street, John. 1959. *Artigas and the Emancipation of Uruguay*. Cambridge: Cambridge University Press.

Strong, Josiah. 1885. *Our Country: Its Possible Future and its Present Crisis*. New York: The American Home Missionary Society.

Sugden, Joanna. 2015. "Where Are India's 2011 Census Figures on Religion?" *The Wall Street Journal*, January 9. http://blogs.wsj.com/indiarealtime/2015/01/09/ where-are-indias-census-figures-on-religion/ (accessed August 26, 2016).

Tan Sri Tan Chee Khoon. 1984. "Constitutional Provisions for Religious Freedom in Malaysia." Pp. 27–44 in Tunku Abdul Rahman Putra et al., eds., *Contemporary Issues in Malaysian Religions*. Kuala Lumpur: Percetakan.

Tejani, Shabnum. 2013. "Defining Secularism in the Particular: Caste and Citizenship in India, 1909–1950." *Politics and Religion* 6:703–29.

Thapar, Romila. 2005. "Politics and the Revisiting of History in India." *Critical Quarterly* 47(1–2):195–203.

"The Future Vision of the Palestinian Arabs in Israel." 2006. Nazareth: The National Committee for the Heads of the Arab Local Authorities in Israel.

The Hindu. 2015. "Debating Religious Conversions." March 25. www.thehindu .com/opinion/editorial/debating-religious-conversions/article7028789.ece (accessed June 25, 2016).

Theopholis III. 2013. "His Beatitude Address at the Holiday Reception Hosted by the President of Israel." Jerusalem: Jerusalem Patriarchate. www.jp-newsgate .net/en/2013/12/30/3719 (accessed August 8, 2016).

2015. "His Beatitude Address at the Annual New Year Reception for the Municipality of Jerusalem." Jerusalem: Jerusalem Patriarchate. www .jp-newsgate.net/en/2015/01/28/11818 (accessed August 8, 2016).

Tocqueville, Alexis de. [1830]1945. *Democracy in America*, Volume I. Translated by Henry Reeve. New York: Knopf.

[1830]1969. *Democracy in America*, Volume I. Translated by George Lawrence. Garden City, NY: Anchor Books.

Toft, Monica Duffy, Daniel Philpott, and Timothy Samuel Shah. 2011. *God's Century: Resurgent Religion and Global Politics*. New York: W.W. Norton.

Toller, Verónica. 2009. *Daños colaterales: Papeleras, contaminación y resistencia en el río Uruguay*. Buenos Aires: Marea Editorial.

Triandayfllidou, Anna, and Rudy Gropas. 2009. "Constructing Difference: The Mosque Debates in Greece." *Journal of Ethnic and Migration Studies* 35(6):957–75.

Trump, Donald J. 2017. "Remarks at the Family Research Council's Values Voter Summit," October 13. www.presidency.ucsb.edu/ws/index.php?pid=128418&st=value+voters+summit&st1= (accessed January 4, 2018).

Tunku, Abdul Rahman Putra. 1957. "Proclamation of Independence, Merdeka Stadium, Kuala Lumpur, 31 August 1956." www.harimalaysia.com/tunku-speech.html (accessed September 25, 2017).

——— 1960. "Ucapan perdana mentiri dalam persidangan perhimpunan Agung UMNO di Rumah UMNO, Kuala Lumpur pada 16 April, 1960 [The inaugural speech at the UMNO General Assembly conference at UMNO House, Kuala Lumpur, on April 16, 1960]." Kuala Lumpur: Arkib Negara Malaysia [Malaysian National Archive]. www.arkib.my /documents/10157/e43704a2-0b4a-4f22-a83d-2208f2c86a2e (accessed September 25, 2017).

——— 1963. "Tunku Abdul Rahman's Malaysia Day Speech Sept 16, 1963." *Malay Mail Online*, September 16, 2013. www.themalaymailonline.com/what-you-think/article/tunku-abdul-rahmans-malaysia-day-speech-sept-16-1963#lz2sTvsHcUgWE8fb.97 (accessed September 25, 2017).

——— 1983. *Lest We Forget: Further Candid Reminiscences*. Singapore: Eastern Universities Press.

——— 1984. "Role of Religion in Nation Building." Pp. 17–25 in Tunku Abdul Rahman Putra et al., eds. *Contemporary Issues in Malaysian Religions*. Kuala Lumpur: Percetakan.

Turnbull, C. M. 2009. *A History of Modern Singapore*. Singapore: NUS Press.

Tzohar. 2016. "About Us." www.tzohar.org.il/English/about/ (accessed August 8, 2016).

Union of Catholic Asian News. "About UCAN India." www.ucanindia.in/page/about-us/1/ (accessed August 30, 2016).

Union of Catholic Asian News. 2016. "Christian Leaders Reject Hindu Group's Overtures." www.ucanindia.in/news/christian-leaders-reject-hindu-groups-overtures/31458/daily (accessed August 17, 2016).

United States Conference of Catholic Bishops. 2002. "Letter to President Bush on Iraq." www.usccb.org/issues-and-action/human-life-and-dignity/global-issues/middle-east/iraq/letter-to-president-bush-from-bishop-gregory-on-iraq-2002-09-13.cfm (accessed September 28, 2014).

——— 2003. "Statement on the War in Iraq." www.usccb.org/issues-and-action/human-life-and-dignity/global-issues/middle-east/iraq/statement-on-iraq-2002-11-13.cfm (accessed September 28, 2014).

United States Department of State. 2014. "International Religious Freedom Report." www.state.gov/j/drl/rls/irf/religiousfreedom/index.htm#wrapper (accessed July 23, 2015).

Upadhyaya, Prakash. 1992. "The Politics of Indian Secularism." *Modern Asian Studies* 26(4):815–53.

Urofsky, Melvin I. 2009. *Louis D. Brandeis: A Life.* New York: Pantheon Books.

Vajpayee, Atal Bihari. 2000. *Prime Minister Atal Bihari Vajpayee Selected Speeches,* Volume 1. New Delhi: Publications Division Government of India.

2002. *Prime Minister Atal Bihari Vajpayee Selected Speeches,* Volume 3. New Delhi: Publications Division Government of India.

Van der Veer, Peter. 1994. *Religious Nationalism: Hindus and Muslims in India.* Berkeley: University of California Press.

Vanger, Milton I. 2010. *Uruguay's José Batlle y Ordóñez: The Determined Visionary, 1915–1917.* Boulder, CO: Lynne Rienner.

Vigil, Mercedes. 2003. *Matilde, la mujer de Batlle.* Buenos Aires: Planeta.

Visweswaran, Kamala, Michael Witzel, Nandini Manjrenkar, Dipta Bhog, and Uma Chakravarti. 2009. "The Hindutva View of History: Rewriting Textbooks in India and the United States." *Georgetown Journal of International Affairs* 10(1):101–12.

von Vorys, Karl. 1975. *Democracy without Consensus: Communalism and Political Stability in Malaysia.* Princeton, NJ: Princeton University Press.

Wald, Kenneth D. 2002. "The Religious Dimension of Israeli Political Life." Pp. 99–124 in Jelen, Ted Gerard and Clyde Wilcox, eds., *Religion and Politics in Comparative Perspective: The One, the Few, and the Many.* Cambridge: Cambridge University Press.

Wald, Kenneth D., and Allison Calhoun-Brown. 2007. *Religion and Politics in the United States,* 5th edn. Lanham, MD: Rowman and Littlefield Press.

Wales, Samuel. [1785]1998. "The Dangers of our National Prosperity; and the Way to Avoid Them." In *Political Sermons at the American Founding Era, 1730–1805,* Volume 1, 2nd edn, ed. Ellis Sandoz. Indianapolis, IN: Liberty Fund.

Walker, Jack C. 1992. "Modernization and Secularization in Uruguay 1880–1930." MA thesis. Abilene, TX: Abilene Christian University.

Walzer, Michael. 2015. *The Paradox of Liberation: Secular Revolutions and Religious Counterrevolutions.* New Haven, CT: Yale University Press.

Washington, George. 1796. "Farewell Address." http://avalon.law.yale.edu/18th_century/washing.asp

Watson, Thomas E. 1912. *The Roman Catholic Hierarchy: The Deadliest Menace to American Liberties and Christian Civilization.* Thomson, GA: Jefferson Publishing Company.

Weinstein, Martin. 1988. *Uruguay: Democracy at the Crossroads.* Boulder, CO: Westview Press.

Whitaker, Arthur P. 1964. "Nationalism and Religion in Argentina and Uruguay." Pp. 75–90 in William V. D'Antonio and Fredrick B Pike, eds., *Religion, Revolution, and Reform: New Forces for Change in Latin America.* New York: Praeger.

Wilkinson, Steven I. 2004. *Votes and Violence: Electoral Competition and Ethnic Riots in India.* Cambridge: Cambridge University Press.

Willert, Trine Stauning. 2012. "A New Role for Religion in Greece? Theologians Challenging the Ethno-Religious Understanding of Orthodoxy and Greekness." Pp. 183–204 in Willert, Trine Stauning and Lina Molokotos-Lierderman, eds., *Innovation in the Orthodox Christian Tradition? The Question of Change in Greek Orthodox Thought and Practice*. Burlington, VT: Ashgate Publishing Company.

Willford, Andrew C. 2005. "The Modernist Vision from Below: Malaysian Hinduism and the 'Way of Prayers'." Pp. 45–68 in Andrew C. Willford and Kenneth M. George, eds., *Spirited Politics: Religion and Public Life in Contemporary Southeast Asia*. Ithaca, NY: Southeast Asia Program Publications, Cornell University.

Williams, Rhys H. and Todd Nicholas Fuist. 2014. "Civil Religion and National Politics in a Neoliberal Era." *Sociology Compass* 8(7):929–38.

Witherspoon, John. [1776]1998. "The Dominion of Providence over the Passions of Men." In *Political Sermons at the American Founding Era, 1730–1805*, Volume 1, 2nd edn, ed. Ellis Sandoz. Indianapolis, IN: Liberty Fund.

Witte, John, Jr., and Joel A. Nichols. 2011. *Religion and the American Constitutional Experiment*, 3rd edn. Boulder, CO: Westview Press.

Wolf, Herbert. 2010. *Pope and Devil: The Vatican's Archives and the Third Reich*. Translated by Kenneth Kronenberg. Cambridge, MA: Belknap Press of Harvard University Press.

World Values Survey. 2011. www.worldvaluessurvey.org/wvs.jsp (accessed June 28, 2016).

Wright, Matthew, and Jack Citrin. 2009. "God and Country: Religion, Religiosity, and National Identity in American Public Opinion." Paper prepared for delivery for the 2009 Annual Meeting of the American Political Science Association, September 3–6, Toronto, Canada.

Wuthnow, Robert. 1988. *The Restructuring of American Religion: Society and Faith Since World War II*. Princeton, NJ: Princeton University Press.

Yakobson, Alexander. 2008. "Jewish Peoplehood and the Jewish State, How Unique? A Comparative Survey." *Israel Studies* 13(2):1–27.

Yanai, Nathan. 1996. "The Citizen as Pioneer: Ben-Gurion's Concept of Citizenship." *Israel Studies* 1(1):127–43.

Yu Lingbo [于凌波]. 2009. "當代馬來西亞佛 [Contemporary Malaysian Buddhism]." August 5. www.malaysianbuddhistassociation.org/index.php/2009-04-27-01-48-19/431-2009-08-05-07-34-01.html (accessed September 22, 2017).

Zubillaga, Carlos, and Mario Cayota. 1982a. *Cristianos y cambio social*. Vol. I, no. 26. Montevideo: centro latinoamericano de economía humana (C.L.A.E.H.).

1982b. *Cristianos y cambio social*. Vol. II, no. 27. Montevideo: centro latino-americano de economía humana (C.L.A.E.H.).

1982c. *Cristianos y cambio social*. Vol. III, no. 28. Montevideo: centro latino-americano de economía humana (C.L.A.E.H.).

Zubrzycki, Geneviève. 2006. *The Crosses of Auschwitz: Nationalism and Religion in Post-Communist Poland*. Chicago, IL: The University of Chicago Press.

Index